Travels and Identities

Life Writing Series

In its Life Writing Series, Wilfrid Laurier University Press publishes life writing, and new life-writing criticism and theory, in order to promote autobiographical accounts, diaries, letters, memoirs, and testimonials written and/or told by women and men whose political, literary, or philosophical purposes are central to their lives. The Series features accounts written in English, or translated into English from French or the languages of the First Nations, or any of the languages of immigration to Canada.

The audience for the Series includes scholars, youth, and avid general readers, both in Canada and abroad. Wilfrid Laurier University Press hopes to continue its work as a leading publisher of life writing of all kinds through this imprint, aiming at scholarly excellence and striving to represent lived experience as a tool for both historical and autobiographical research.

We publish original life writing representing the widest range of experiences of lives lived with integrity. The Series also publishes original theoretical investigations about life writing, as long as they are not limited to one author or text.

Series Editor
Marlene Kadar
Humanities, York University

Travels and Identities

Elizabeth and Adam Shortt in Europe, 1911

Edited with commentary by
Peter E. Paul Dembski

WLU PRESS

WILFRID LAURIER
UNIVERSITY PRESS

LAURIER
Inspiring Lives.

Wilfrid Laurier University Press acknowledges the support of the Canada Council for the Arts for our publishing program. We acknowledge the financial support of the Government of Canada through the Canada Book Fund for our publishing activities. This work was supported by the Research Support Fund.

Canada

ONTARIO ARTS COUNCIL
CONSEIL DES ARTS DE L'ONTARIO
an Ontario government agency
un organisme du gouvernement de l'Ontario

Canada Council   Conseil des Arts
for the Arts   du Canada

Library and Archives Canada Cataloguing in Publication

Travels and identities : Elizabeth and Adam Shortt in Europe, 1911 / Peter E. Paul Dembski, editor.

(Life writing series)
Includes bibliographical references.
Issued in print and electronic formats.
ISBN 978-1-77112-225-2 (paperback).—ISBN 978-1-77112-226-9
(pdf).—ISBN 978-1-77112-227-6 (epub)

1. Smith, Elizabeth, 1859–1949—Travel—Europe. 2. Shortt, Adam, 1859–1931—Travel—Europe. 3. Smith, Elizabeth, 1859–1949—Diaries. 4. Shortt, Adam, 1859–1931—Diaries. 5. Canadians—Travel—Europe. 6. Europe—Description and travel. I. Dembski, Peter E. Paul, 1938–, editor II. Smith, Elizabeth, 1859–1949. Diaries. Selections. III. Shortt, Adam, 1859–1931. Diaries. Selections. IV. Title: Elizabeth and Adam Shortt in Europe, 1911. V. Series: Life writing series

D921.T73 2016   914.04ʹ88   C2016-904838-1
                                                        C2016-904839-X

Cover design by Blakeley Words+Pictures. Front-cover photo of Elizabeth and Adam Shortt, 1914, courtesy University of Waterloo Library, Elizabeth Smith Shortt fonds; image no. WA10_2303-1. Front-cover photo of the *Royal George* courtesy of the Norway Heritage Collection, www.norway heritage.com. Source: www.heritage-ships.com. Text design by Sandra Friesen.

For the great loves of my life,
Julie, Chad, and Bryn

Contents

List of Illustrations

Preface

The book that follows originated with my reading of *A Woman with a Purpose: The Diaries of Elizabeth Smith 1872–1884*, ably edited and introduced by Veronica Strong-Boag. This acquainted me with Elizabeth Smith (Shortt) and eventually led to an article on her mentor Jenny Trout, a project that was further assisted by consulting the Elizabeth Smith Shortt Papers in the Doris Lewis Room of the University of Waterloo's Dana Porter Library. Once the Trout essay was completed, I returned to the Smith Shortt collection, hoping to pursue new topics contained in this treasure chest of primary materials.

Later I discovered Margaret Addison's book, *Diary of a European Tour, 1900*, skilfully edited by Jean O'Grady. Soon afterward, I began to peruse four diaries, penned by Mrs. Shortt during a 1911 trip to Europe, for comparative purposes. In the process, my next academic enterprise was launched. Then, from the Queen's University Archives, I obtained Mr. Shortt's less extensive, but valuable, diaries on the same visit to the Old World. These writings of Elizabeth and Adam, along with some of the couple's related letters, supplied the foundation for the present volume.

After investigating the documents, I realized that they furnished numerous insights into a wide variety of historical subjects. I further recognized that I shared Adam's penchant for finding and analyzing such primary sources. For example, Elizabeth's diaries and letters are filled with interesting and controversial opinions, where the meaning is seldom in doubt. They are perceptive, engaging, and often amusing—in brief, simply a delight to read.

There is relatively little written about the Shortts and virtually nothing dealing with them as a couple. Thus, I began this book with a comprehensive definition of their identity as a couple down to 1911. Further, I sought to provide an account of what Elizabeth and Adam saw and experienced in Europe. It soon became apparent that this was closely linked to the national identities perceived by the Shortts in the five countries they visited.

Here, Beth's incisive criticisms were especially revealing. For example, she was displeased with the improperly trained British nurses, a manipulative Catholic church in Austria, and an intense militarism in pre–World War I Germany. Her thinking extended to international as well as national issues, a theme not generally enunciated in published works on Mrs. Shortt. There were, of course, positive as well as negative images that enraptured Mrs. Shortt in the Old World. For instance, she was delighted with the venerable parliamentary buildings in London, as well as the stunning scenery and culture in Switzerland. While she had misgivings about Catholic hegemony in Austria, Beth was overwhelmed by the beauty of St. Stephen's Church in Vienna.

Historians have paid a greater degree of attention to Adam Shortt, but here, too, the documents in this volume add much to our understanding of his past importance. For example, while in Great Britain, Principal Daniel M. Gordon of Queen's University and Shortt were given the power to appoint English applicants to that university's faculty without any further consultation with the administration or teachers back home in Kingston. Adam Shortt remained a significant force in determining his alma mater's development, even after he had left that institution to become one of two commissioners overseeing the federal civil service. The primary materials in this book also reveal much about Adam's preferences that cannot be found elsewhere. His love of good meals followed by lively discussions, and his athletic prowess, which caused a fifty-one-year senior bureaucrat to climb a mountain in Switzerland, bring to the reader's attention a number of traits not examined in existing publications. Here, the material discloses important aspects of Mr. Shortt's personal identity.

These revelations—and there are many more in the pages to follow—present on a micro level individual reactions, which complement and extend the macro accounts of English Canadian visitors to Europe, such as the recently published "A Happy Holiday": English Canadians and Transatlantic Tourism, 1870–1930, by Cecilia Morgan. Both approaches must be included in a comprehensive history of English Canadian tourism on the world stage. I can only hope that the material that follows contributes modestly to this worthy purpose. If it does, I owe a great debt to Veronica

Strong-Boag, Jean O'Grady, and the supportive librarians at the University of Waterloo and Queen's University.

Wherever possible, the Shortts' writings have been analyzed in the prefaces to each relevant chapter; thus, their views on the national identities of Switzerland, Austria, Germany, and the Netherlands have been assessed in the prefaces to chapters 4, 5, and 6. However, their discourse on the British identity extended over four chapters, and could be discussed coherently only in the conclusion. One other subject, which ranged over two chapters, was reserved for consideration in the final section: Elizabeth's evaluation of visual art in Austria, Germany, and the Netherlands. This topic furnishes an enlightening commentary on how a well-educated, influential Canadian woman evaluated Europe's artistic identity in the early twentieth century. Their definitions of the British identity and European art in 1911 show that the Shortts' diaries and letters deal with multiple identity questions, which make them valuable references for understanding both Canada and the Old World during an era of great change.

Thus, it seems appropriate to title this work *Travels and Identities*. Finally, I have placed Elizabeth's name first in recognition of the fact that her writings supplied the cornerstone for this undertaking. Adam's diaries and letters were significant, but also secondary. Now that the stage has been set, it is time to present the two main actors in our introduction after a few more preliminary comments.

Acknowledgements

Many people helped to make this book viable, but here I will mention only the most evident. At Wilfrid Laurier University Press, Jacqueline Larson fostered my early work on the project, while Lisa Quinn, Mike Bechthold, Clare Hitchens, Siobhan McMenemy, Rob Kohlmeier, and contract copy editor Edwin Janzen guided it to completion. It has been a rewarding experience to work with this highly proficient and congenial publisher. Meanwhile, Professors Cynthia Comacchio and Suzanne Zeller of the Department of History at Wilfrid Laurier University offered opinions and encouragement that were vital to a favourable outcome.

Three libraries also made this volume possible. At the University of Waterloo's Special Collections and Archives, all the staff—including Susan Mavor, Jane Britton, Susan Seabrook, Nick Richbell, Jessica Blackwell, Martha Lauzon, Susan Plouffe, and Danielle Robichaud—facilitated the slow movement of the materials from the research stage to the point of conclusion. It would be difficult to find a more amiable, cooperative, and efficient research centre anywhere else. John McCallum, Diane Wilkins, Deborah Wills, and others at the WLU Library were also on hand to promote the enterprise in a number of significant ways. Finally, useful documents, as well as personal support, were forthcoming from the librarians at the Queen's University Archives.

Two historians whom I greatly admire—A. Margaret Evans and Oscar Cole-Arnal—read early versions of this potential book and provided constructive ideas on revisions. The same can be said of the anonymous readers furnished by WLU Press, who made necessary suggestions for improving what now seems like a very rough draft. Sara Benediktson, a computer wizard, rendered an essential service by translating my final editing revisions into the electronic copy. Last, but certainly not least, was the constant inspiration and practical assistance rendered by my wife, Julie, without whose collaboration this volume would not have been possible. Thanks to all for their help, which in no way diminishes my full responsibility for any errors that will be found in the ensuing pages.

Abbreviations

A. *or* Ad. — Adam
A.D.C. — aide-de-camp
acc. — according
Alta. — Alberta
amt. — amount
anx. — anxiety
assoc. — association
blds. — buildings
blk. — black
Br. — British
C. Northern — Canadian Northern
  Railway
C.S. — civil service
Can. Com. — Canadian High
  Commission
Chas. — Charles
Col. — colonel
Coll. — college
com. — committee
comp. — composition
depart. *or* dept. — department
diff. — different *or* difference
do. — dollar(s)
Ed. — Edward
Eng. — England *or* English
eno. — enough

evg. *or* even. — evening
ft. — feet
G.T.R. — Grand Trunk Railway
Geo. — George
Gov.-Gen. — governor general
H.C. *or* H. Com. — high
  commissioner
hrs. — hours
immig. — immigration
Inst. — institute
L. — Lake
Lt. Gov. — lieutenant governor
Lon. — London
M.P.P. — member of provincial
  parliament
med. — medicine
min. — minister *or* minute
Min-ta. — Minnesota
mt. *and* mts. — mountain *and*
  mountains
no. — number
P.O. *or* P. Office — Post Office
Post-M. Gen. — postmaster general
Prin. — principal
prob. — probably
pub. — public

R.C. — Roman Catholic
R.M.C. — Royal Military College
rec. — receive, received, *or* receiving
rep's — representatives
Ry. *or* Rl'y — railway
S. — south
S.D. — special delivery
scabs. — scabbards
sec. or secty. — secretary
sq. — square
st. — street
sups. — supplementals

Switz. — Switzerland
temp. — temperature
tho. — though
thro. — through
transp. — transportation
Vien. — Vienna
w or ⍵ — with
wgt. — weight
wh. — which
wk. *or* wks. — week *or* weeks
yr. — year

Frequently Mentioned Names

Adam and Elizabeth's Children

Muriel, 22, graduated from Queen's University in 1909, and during 1911 resided at the Shortts' family home in Ottawa. Like her mother, she participated in numerous clubs and associations, as well as performing household chores. In the summer of 1911, Muriel looked after the Shortts' abode at 5 Marlborough Avenue.

George, 17, was a recent graduate of Trinity College School in Port Hope, Ontario. During the summer of 1911, he was preparing to take supplemental examinations to enter Queen's University in the fall. A remarkably active person, George also worked at the Dominion Archives in Ottawa and pursued outdoor interests, even while relying on wooden legs after losing his natural limbs in an accident at age 10.

Lorraine, 13/14, was a public school student in the Ottawa area. She was fond of travelling and during the summer of 1911 would visit a close friend in Kingston, and then an uncle and aunt in Winona, before returning to her home in Ottawa.

Elizabeth's Family

Damaris Isabella Smith (née McGee) was Elizabeth's mother. She worked strenuously on the family farm near Vinemount, Ontario, until 1886, when she retired to live with her daughter, Gertrude, in Hamilton.

Gertrude was Elizabeth's younger sister, who never married. She resided with her mother in a house that "Gertie" had personally designed. She also continued the family history begun by Mrs. Smith after the latter's death in 1913.

Ernest D'Israeli Smith was Elizabeth's elder brother. He founded the E. D. Smith Company, which processed and distributed fruit, jam, and related products throughout Canada, making its proprietor a very wealthy man. He had represented the riding of South Wentworth as a Conservative Member of Parliament from 1900 to 1910. In 1911, Ernest and his wife, **Christina**, resided on a large estate in Winona, Ontario.

Mauritana, commonly called Martha or Myrtie, was the elder sister of Elizabeth. Mauritana lived with her husband, Hervey A. Coon, and their three children on a farm in Norwich, Ontario.

The eldest daughter of Hervey and Mauritana Coon was **Alice Coon**, who received a B.A. from the University of Toronto in 1910, and the following year used it to secure a position as a public school teacher in Saskatchewan.

Cecil was Elizabeth's younger brother. By 1911, he had become a leading electrical engineer in the province who had helped to establish the Ontario Hydro-Electric Commission, where he subsequently served as one of three commissioners. In 1911, Cecil was assisting a power company in Portland, Oregon, to build a similar system for that city.

Arthur, 16, and Harold, 13, were the two sons of Cecil Smith. In the summer of 1911, they worked at the same engineering firm as their father in Portland.

Violet was Elizabeth's youngest sister, who at the time of the latter's trip to England and Europe lived in Edmonton, Alberta, and taught public school.

Other Characters

Captain and Mrs. Desborough often entertained Adam and Elizabeth in the British capital, introducing them to other prominent Londoners, as the Shortts' diaries make clear. Captain Desborough was a retired army officer who had served in India, while "Mrs. D.," as Elizabeth often referred to her, showed the highly receptive Mrs. Shortt around some of the city's finest shops.

Arthur George Doughty was the Dominion's first archivist when he was appointed in 1904, and three years later collaborated with Adam Shortt on the publication of constitutional documents relating to Canada. After the death of his first wife, Doughty married Kathleen Browne in 1911. On their honeymoon, the Doughtys travelled to England with their close friends, the Shortts.

Mrs. Jessie Ewart and her daughter, **Gladys**, travelled with Mr. and Mrs. Shortt on their voyage to England aboard the *Royal George*. **John S. Ewart** joined his family, along with Adam and Elizabeth, on the return trip to Canada. Mr. Ewart was a friend of the Shortts in Ottawa, where he had become a prominent constitutional lawyer who often argued cases before the judicial committee of the British Privy Council in London.

Principal Daniel M. Gordon of Queen's University was an ordained minister of the Church of Scotland. He had taught systematic theology at the Presbyterian College in Halifax until his appointment as Queen's principal in 1903. He was a close friend of the Shortts, and continued to rely on Adam's advice regarding a number of questions relating to the Kingston school even after the latter's relocation in Ottawa.

William Lawson Grant was the son of George Monro Grant, principal of Queen's University from 1877 to 1902. In 1910, William became a professor of colonial history at Queen's after lecturing on the same topic at Oxford for six years. On 1 June 1911, he married **Maude Erskine Parkin**, a daughter of the prominent Canadian imperialist George Robert Parkin, who by that date was the organizing secretary of the Rhodes Scholarship Trust in London, the imperial capital.

Edward Peacock was a partner in the esteemed Baring Brothers financial firm in London. He was generally considered one of Adam Shortt's most outstanding students at Queen's University, and later became the first Canadian-born director of the Bank of England.

Earl Alan Ian Percy was the surviving son and heir of the 7th Duke of Northumberland. Lord Percy was returning to England from Canada, where he had been aide-de-camp to Earl Grey, the governor general. During the summer of 1911, Percy was to wed Lady Helen Gordon-Lennox, the daughter of the Duke of Richmond.

Introduction

In 1859, Elizabeth Smith and Adam Shortt were born in Upper Canada, which eight years later became the influential province of Ontario within the new and auspicious British Dominion of Canada. Protestant religious affiliations furnished a vital ingredient in the identities of both the Smith and Shortt families. The Smiths were devout Anglicans, and this bond made an indelible imprint upon a youthful Elizabeth Smith. "Elizabeth's Anglicanism was essential to her sense of well-being. Faith in a benevolent but stern deity gave a moral framework to her life. Her principles rested on the confidence that the Protestant religion, and especially the Church of England, represented the surest guide to human experience."[1]

Not a great deal is known about Adam Shortt's early years and upbringing, but it is clear that religion in the form of the Free Kirk Presbyterian Church vitally affected his personal development. His father was one of three brothers who migrated during the 1850s to Canada, where they sought to employ the milling skills they had learned in their native Scotland. In 1858, George Shortt brought his bride, Mary Shields, to Kilworth, a small village eight miles west of London. Mary was very religious, and she imbued the Shortts' household with a pious tone.[2] At Kilworth, George established a milling enterprise, which a flood in 1863 largely destroyed. The family sold what remained of their property there, and George directed various milling operations within the province. Having accumulated sufficient capital, they moved to Walkerton in 1867, where two further attempts at achieving prosperity through the ownership of grain mills ultimately failed.

Over the next fourteen years as Adam gradually aged, the Shortts experienced both prosperity and hardship, and for some time their eldest son was denied access to the local school because of a tax dispute. The Presbyterian minister in the area, the Reverend George Bell, assisted in Adam's youthful instruction by encouraging him to read extensively at the town's Mechanics' Institute. This was supplemented by Sunday evening readings where Adam and his siblings were introduced to literary classics by authors such as Dickens, Scott, and Thackeray.[3] This unusual avenue to an early education was not without advantage. S. E. D. Shortt tells us that Adam later "attributed his distrust of commonly accepted views and penchant for original research to this unorthodox educational background."[4] Thus, intellectual autonomy became another crucial element in Shortt's personal cachet.

When Principal George Grant of Queen's University visited Walkerton in 1878 on a fundraising trip, his stirring address deeply moved Adam and his parents. By now Adam had nearly completed the necessary schooling to qualify for university matriculation. One year later he won a scholarship to Queen's, and his lengthy association with this institution began.

These events deeply affected the young Adam Shortt. As Ferguson asserts, "Shortt experienced in childhood and youth the vicissitudes of the miller's trade in a marginal agricultural area during the pioneer phase."[5] He was determined to avoid the insecurities of his father's business. As Bowden points out, he discovered an escape route in higher education. At first, this process seemed to lie in the Presbyterian-controlled faculty of theology at Queen's University, where, under his devout mother's prodding, Shortt initially studied for the Presbyterian ministry. He soon abandoned this maternal ambition,[6] but he never renounced his commitment to Protestant Christianity. Indeed, in 1893 Shortt asserted that his personal vision of political, social and religious advancement centred on a Christian notion of salvation: "Our destiny must be eternal progress with perfection as its goal. This I take to be the end at once of true national life and true religion."[7]

After his move to Ottawa in 1908, Shortt regularly attended St. George's Anglican Church, where he became a highly esteemed member.[8] But he also responded to the needs of the Presbyterian denomination that had nurtured his early Christian faith. For example, in 1910 Adam joined with William Lyon Mackenzie King, Oscar Skelton, and Robert Magill to produce a reader for that church on contemporary social issues.[9] Adam Shortt's dedication to Protestant Christianity was less overt and emotive than the frequent religious expressions of his wife Elizabeth—a fact made abundantly clear in their diary entries during their 1911 trip to Europe—but his world view was rooted just as firmly in Christian doctrine. It is not surprising that H. A. Innis admired the "very firm ethical, religious and philosophical context in which men like Shortt and [James] Mavor grounded their advocacy of reform."[10]

In the same year that Elizabeth Smith and Adam Shortt were born, traditional Christian dogma was challenged by the publication of Charles Darwin's treatise *On the Origin of Species by Means of Natural Selection: Or the Preservation of Favoured Races in the Struggle for Life*. This work suggested that an evolutionary method of creation, and not a transcendent God, was responsible for the original and ongoing changes in the natural environment. Moreover, the benevolent divinity in the Christian Bible seemed to have very little relevance in Darwin's world of natural selection, where amoral forces determined the survival, modification, or extinction of life forms. Another volume published by Darwin, *On the Descent of Man* in 1871, cast doubt on humanity's unique and superior place in creation as presented in the Book of Genesis. According to this British scientist, men and women had evolved from higher creatures in the animal world, which were "different in *degree* but not in *kind*" from their human descendants.[11]

These concepts had a revolutionary impact on Great Britain's social thought as well as on its scientific studies. Soon the country's Christian churches felt threatened by Darwin's apparently godless theories. It was not long before these controversial ideas were exported to the British colony of Canada, where McKillop reports that "the spectre of Doubt was abroad." Some Canadian thinkers totally rejected the new science and its implications, but others sought a reconciliation between it and traditional Christianity.[12]

Among the leading intellectuals pursuing the latter course was John Watson, an adherent of Objective Idealism, whose work was widely respected throughout the Anglo-Saxon world.[13] Watson and other Canadian idealists expressed an evolutionary approach in their metaphysical orientation, but for them it extended to both the spiritual and material realms.[14] In his inaugural speech as a professor of philosophy at Queen's University in 1872, Watson articulated the accommodation that many Canadian Christians had longed to hear: "Watson's stages in the progressive evolution of thought offered an alternative to the materialistic social evolutionism of Herbert Spencer[15] and his disciples. Moreover, and most important of all, the philosophy Watson espoused did not seem to undermine the Christian experience."[16]

After Adam Shortt arrived on the Queen's campus to pursue an undergraduate degree, he was soon captivated by the scholarly and moral perspective of the renowned Professor Watson. Indeed, a desire to study philosophy under Watson provided Shortt with a key reason for concentrating on that subject as his major, and the former became the young man's "academic mentor." More specifically, Watson endowed Adam with a deep and lifelong respect for science, as well as religion and philosophy. "Both Shortt and Watson were interested in the relation of science to philosophy, as demonstrated by Shortt's honours essay on Herbert Spencer.... Both men thought that science, religion and philosophy were not antithetical because science was a process, an attitude and not a theory of knowledge which could explain the nature of reality itself."[17]

During his undergraduate days at Queen's, Shortt encountered another person who was destined to have an even more profound effect on his life than Professor Watson. Elizabeth Smith was one of the first three women to seek medical degrees at the Royal Medical College in Kingston, which was affiliated with Queen's, where Principal George M. Grant had vigorously supported coeducation at the university level.[18] Miss Smith, Mrs. Alice McGillivray, and Miss Elizabeth Beatty met Mr. Shortt while all four were staying at the same boarding house near the university campus. It was not long before Adam became, in Miss Smith's words, "like a brother to us."[19]

The three female medical students sorely needed a brother's encouragement and assistance. Their entry into the Royal had caused a massive revolt by the male students at the institution led by no less a figure than the College's professor of physiology, Dr. Thomas Fenwick.[20] Only a handful of female physicians were functioning in Canada at this time. It was one thing to allow women into the undergraduate arts and science programs within the Dominion's universities, and quite another to allow females to enter professional schools like the Kingston medical college. "The three Rs, domestic science, art, music, and literature were generally accepted as appropriate subjects for women. Few objected to their training to be teachers or to be better wives and mothers. But opposition was acute to the idea of women entering the medical or law schools, for this suggested that women intended to be doctors and lawyers rather than wives and mothers."[21] Moreover, on a more practical level, as another historian has pointed out, male doctors had no desire to share their profitable and respected calling with female rivals.[22]

Thus, when Elizabeth issued an appeal for other women to join her in applying to the Royal, she was creating a radical gender upheaval in medical education. It was a response that had been encouraged by her family. In 1853, when Sylvester and Damaris McGee were married, they had used loans from their parents to buy a 170-acre farm near the Niagara

Escarpment and the town of Winona. There, the third generation of Smiths in Saltfleet Township specialized in grain and cattle production.[23] As Damaris Smith put it, "altogether, we got to be quite well-to-do-farmers."[24] In time, this land would be managed by Elizabeth's older brother Ernest, who enhanced not only the family farm but also his own estate in the same area. Here a concentration on the growth and sale of fruits and vegetables led to his eventual founding, in 1882, of one of Canada's major processing operations in the food industry, the E. D. Smith & Sons Company Limited.[25]

Six years before this significant development in Ontario's business community, E. D.'s younger sister also faced a weighty personal decision. Elizabeth had just completed a year and a half of high school, which was all the family could afford with five other children to look after. Therefore, she was presented with a momentous choice. She could remain at home, now dubbed Mountain Hall, and look after the three younger children while awaiting a possible suitor for marriage. Or she could prepare to study at a medical school on the understanding that most of the expenses there would be covered by income secured through public school teaching.[26]

It did not take her long to decide on the second alternative. A Smith family history notes that from her earliest days Elizabeth was determined to become a physician.[27] Damaris Smith had yearned for a similar career because she greatly admired her father, an army surgeon. Elizabeth would fulfill the ambition that her mother had found unattainable.[28] On the negative side, Miss Smith rejected the exclusive homemaker role, which so many young women of her generation at least publicly accepted. A return to a farm life and nothing more, she feared, would cause her "to rust mentally and wear out 'physically' in the drudgery of *all* work on a farm." However, a desire to pursue a medical career did not mean the abandonment of aspirations to marry in the future; on the contrary, earning a doctor's substantial livelihood would enable Elizabeth "to marry for love and not for mercenary motives."[29] The young Miss Smith was determined to control her own destiny.

After she had opted for medical studies, Smith generally relied on the motivation provided by the first woman to be licensed as a practitioner of medicine in Ontario, Dr. Jenny Trout. Indeed, as Strong-Boag reveals, Elizabeth became Dr. Trout's "special disciple."[30] Jenny supplied her protegé with the same linkage between religion and science that John Watson had furnished to Adam Shortt. "I thank God that a few noble women are preparing themselves to work in that part of 'The Master's' vineyard which needs their services so much.... I am glad that it is a matter of principle with you for it is the most noble work on this His Foot Stool, yes more noble than the ministry in one way. I believe in the old Christ-like apostolic way of healing the bodies and saving the souls of men by one and the same person."[31]

Such inspirational words were essential, for by 1882 Smith, McGillivray, and Beatty felt they were suffering in biblical proportion at the Royal Medical College. The ordeal finally ended in 1884, with the successful graduation of Shadrach (Smith), Meshach (McGillivray), and Abednego (Beatty), as the pious women had nicknamed themselves during the struggle.[32] The assumption of these religious tropes by the three young female physicians indicated their determination to integrate science and religion in their future careers. The episode also established the youthful Miss Smith as a leader in the struggle for women's rights, a role she retained for many years to come.[33]

Soon Beth's commitment to this mission had to be shared with another urgent involvement. By the end of her studies at the Royal Medical College, Smith's feelings for Adam Shortt had moved from the fraternal stage to close friendship, and finally into passionate love. By the summer of 1883, they were engaged to be married. Always a romantic, Beth acknowledged on 28 June 1884 that "love not only blossomed again, but grew to perfect blossom."[34] When she wrote these words, her engagement to Shortt had become a long-distance enterprise, which relied on extensive correspondence. In the spring of 1883, he had secured a B.A. from Queen's along with a gold medal for his outstanding performance in the university's philosophy classes.[35] The following September, Shortt left for postgraduate classes at both Glasgow (Watson's alma mater) and Edinburgh. He naturally concentrated on the philosophy courses, which had originally brought him to Scotland, but his growing interest in science caused him to pursue as well lectures in physics, chemistry, and botany. W. A. Mackintosh later pointed out that throughout his life, "he [Shortt] remained an enthusiastic and competent botanist."[36]

While at Glasgow, Adam sought a B.Sc. degree, but repairs to the laboratories there prevented him from completing a practical requirement in chemistry. Shortt then strove for a Ph.D. at Edinburgh, but his ambitions were thwarted once more, because he had only six months to write his thesis. The manuscript was considered "a fairly good piece of work, but one which was too slight to deserve the degree." The Edinburgh authorities offered Adam an M.A.,[37] but he preferred to receive the second degree from Queen's, where he had already submitted another paper for this purpose while in Scotland.

When Shortt returned to Kingston, where in 1885 he received the M.A. based on the studies in Scotland and his superior undergraduate performance,[38] Adam's formal education was complete. His mixture of philosophy and science created a diverse approach to life and thought. As S. E. D. Shortt has stated, "he was a transitional figure, related to the older idealistic scholarship of Maurice Hutton and James Cappon by his occasional metaphysical statements, yet usually a precursor of a later generation of pragmatic, realistic social scientists, which his University of Toronto counterpart, James Mavor, already represented."[39] Thus, religion, philosophy, and science became the three main pillars in Shortt's world view.

Adam assumed that the second degree and prizes won in a number of Scottish courses would lead to permanent employment at the university level by Christmas, 1885. However, only a few positions were open, and none suited his qualifications.[40] Watson again came to Adam's aid by persuading Principal George Grant to offer his protégé part-time work on the Queen's campus.[41] In 1886, among a myriad of responsibilities, Shortt was assigned the teaching of an unpopular course in political economy, "with Grant's polite hope that he [Shortt] would give the course a decent burial."[42]

However, Adam saw a unique opportunity in this dire situation. S. E. D. Shortt has asserted that, "born of his training in the empirical methods of science and the metaphysical speculations of philosophy, the teaching of political economy seemed to provide for Shortt the ideal career."[43] His students enthusiastically agreed, and in 1888 Adam was appointed a full-time lecturer in the field, which subsequently dominated the teaching phase of his career.

While Adam was struggling to secure an academic position at Queen's that would allow him to marry Elizabeth, she used her medical degree to make a comfortable living as a doctor with considerably more ease. It is true that her bid to teach at the recently created Women's Medical College in Toronto was rejected in 1884. However, later that same year she established a prosperous and generally satisfying practice in a two-story brick house at the corner of Main and McNab streets in Hamilton.[44] By the summer of 1886, Dr. Smith had paid off her debts and proudly informed Adam: "What do you think I did—I actually opened a bank account at the Savings Bank—deposited twenty five [dollars]."[45]

Toward the end of 1886, Shortt told his fiancée that his job prospects at Queen's were promising enough to permit their marriage in December, dependent on Elizabeth's acceptance of a teaching offer from another Women's Medical College in Kingston. This created a conflict for Dr. Smith.

Throughout her recent correspondence with Adam, Beth had repeatedly informed him that she did not want to live in Kingston. Moreover, by 1886, Elizabeth believed she had established herself as a competent and self-sustaining physician in Hamilton.[46] Nevertheless, after much discussion with her fiancé, she consented to move to Kingston and assume a teaching position at the Kingston Women's Medical College (KWMC).[47]

This decision established an important principle in the prospective couple's gender relationship. During the nineteenth century, "despite the changes taking place around them, women were told that they must continue to take their status from that of their husbands and inhabit the private sphere of the home. Women who avoided their roles as wives and mothers to stay in the paid labour force or who espoused the doctrines of 'women's rights' were the objects of criticism and ridicule. So too, were men who failed to maintain their wives in a domestic setting."[48]

Adam had heroically supported Elizabeth's entitlement to a medical education and her doctor's practice in Hamilton, but he placed strict limits on her pursuit of a physician's occupation. An 1884 letter from Shortt in Scotland clearly indicated his endorsement of the contemporary ideal of the male as a family's principal breadwinner. "I shall have no objections [to Elizabeth's working] provided always (& this is a point on which I am a little sensitive) that I had such a position as to leave no room for people to suppose that you were doing it from necessity—in order to help [make] a living. If there is one thing which I could not endure it would be to have people think that."[49]

While Dr. Smith defended her prerogative to opt for a medical calling, she agreed her fiancé's interests and image would take precedence in her own priorities. "She would not work outside the home to make money ... but to perform a useful role in society." Thus, she reluctantly accepted a return to Kingston, where her income and status would be inferior to those of her intended husband.[50] Nevertheless, Elizabeth would not be restricted to the narrow confines of her abode as were so many other middle-class women in late-Victorian Canada, where they were identified solely as wives and mothers.[51] The future Mrs. Shortt insisted on the right to become a feminist activist, on a part-time basis, outside the home.[52] With these understandings in place, Beth and Adam were wed on 24 December 1886.

When they began their marital life together, the Shortts encountered a new religious crusade, which deeply influenced their mutual development. As McKillop suggests, four notable Protestants furnished the basic principles that led to the creation of the Social Gospel campaign from 1890 to 1914.[53] One was Principal George M. Grant, who had inspired Adam to pursue his studies at Queen's while arranging for Beth's prospective employment by the KWMC.[54] Another member of the foursome was John Watson, who had served as Mr. Shortt's mentor and chief patron when he struggled to establish himself on the Queen's faculty. Thus, it was hardly surprising that the Shortts were drawn to the new religious initiative, which Grant ably defined. For the principal of Queen's, "preaching the Gospel [meant] ... the proclamation of the ever-living message of the love of God to all men, & the application of that message and the spirit which it implies to the ever-changing conditions of society."[55]

Elizabeth would enlarge the gender dimensions of this declaration to include women, but otherwise she warmly endorsed its essential message. In future years, such words often justified the myriad of social improvements that the deeply religious physician would advance. As McLaren succinctly puts it, for Mrs. Shortt, "the Social Gospel Movement opened up the possibility of making a career out of reform."[56] Elizabeth responded with enthusiasm to this activist calling during the years that Adam and she resided in Kingston and, later, Ottawa. Eventually she would specialize in medical improvements, which enabled her to use the M.D. she had struggled so hard to achieve. In the end, her achievements, rooted in the spirit of the Social Gospel, were remarkable, especially when one considers that they were effected within a part-time framework.

The Social Gospel had a similar impact on Mr. Shortt, who embraced the teaching profession with a religious zeal. One of his pupils, Andrew Haydon, echoed Principal Grant's emphasis on "the proclamation of the ever-living message of the love of God to all men" when he stated that Professor Shortt "won and held the respect and love of his students."[57] An analogous fervour inspired Adam's writings during his years at Queen's. For example, in 1908 Shortt published a biography on Lord Sydenham, governor general of the old Province of Canada between 1839 and 1841. Here he emphasized that Sydenham was a brilliant administrative reformer, who paved the way for Canada's self-government. Adam would not only write a well-received biography of Sydenham, but also seek to imitate his methods as a public servant. For example, while Adam served as a highly effective arbitrator for the federal government in 1907–8, Ferguson suggests that he was utilizing Sydenham's moderate techniques to forge unprecedented labour agreements.[58] Later he would attempt to employ the same approach when he grappled with the more formidable issue of national patronage. During these struggles, Adam found inspiration in Principal Grant's vision of the Social Gospel. As McKillop has asserted, "Principal Grant and the Queen's spirit of the 1890s inspired numerous individuals to engage in different forms of social service. Some, such as Adam Shortt ... and O. D. Skelton, became prominent federal civil servants."[59] The Social Gospel was, indeed, a key element in defining the world views and occupational goals of both Elizabeth and Adam Shortt.

Another historian of this movement, Richard Allen, has further suggested that the Social Gospel group could be analyzed in terms of "three emphases ... which might be labelled conservative, progressive and radical."[60] This perspective offers another useful tool in understanding the ideas and deeds of the Shortts. Beth's youthful determination to pursue a medical education constituted a radical departure within the gender and educational assumptions of late-Victorian Ontario. However, this was a rare decision for her. As a rule, she moved freely between conservative and liberal or progressive opinions. Such independence defied an easy ideological definition. For example, while studying at Queen's she eschewed a partisan stance in politics, an attitude she maintained throughout her life: "I believe there are good & bad in both parties & that each have principles worthy [of] the enthusiasm of its disciples & I think it blindest egotism in anyone to say anyone is less worthy of respect in the smallest little because an upholder of a policy opposed to theirs."[61]

Her husband also saw himself as a detached independent above the strife of party factions. For Adam, the most pressing need in Canadian politics was the creation of an intellectual elite that could devise a progressive agenda on leading political, economic, and social issues.[62] Intellectual leaders were required to control what Shortt arrogantly called "the stupidity which the common man exhibits when acting in bulk."[63] Owram notes that Shortt's elitism persisted as he sought moderate solutions to modern Canada's problems.[64] Democracy would succeed in the Dominion only so long as an intellectual aristocracy supplied it with vision and direction. This Shortt would seek to furnish as a university professor, public affairs analyst, historian, labour arbitrator, and civil servant.

On one significant occasion when he later sought to uproot partisan patronage in the federal bureaucracy, Shortt did adopt a radical perspective. However, like his wife's radical stand at medical school, this move constituted an unusual departure. Generally both Shortts were moderate reformers, who spurned partisan connections in developing an independent and at times elitist interpretation of the Social Gospel that was quite distinctive. These attitudes also provided one of the many bonds that united the couple.

As Elizabeth Shortt settled into marital life, she developed a more precise definition of the values that would give such a profound meaning to her life. Naomi Black has pointed out that social feminism recognizes a "focus on values and experience identified with women," such as "the so-called maternal feminism of the past and the radical feminism of the present."[65] In contrast, equal-rights feminism "stressed how much women resembled men, and how unjust it was that they should have fewer rights."[66] While the concepts are distinguishable, Black notes that "individuals may well subscribe to both."[67]

The equal-rights position aptly depicts the approach that Elizabeth and the other two Hebrew children employed in their successful drive for a measure of parity within Canada's medical education system. Here they demanded equal rights, but their struggle prevailed only because of "the wider public action on the part of women."[68] The support of sympathetic males like Adam Shortt was useful and welcome. However, it was the determination of Elizabeth Smith, Alice McGillivray, and Elizabeth Beatty, and the inspiration furnished by Dr. Jenny Trout, that won the battle at the Royal Medical College. The lesson was not lost on Mrs. Shortt.

In her future campaigns, Beth would utilize both equal-rights and social feminism, as many other contemporary women activists did. Nevertheless, she relied primarily on a social feminist approach, which, in the context of late-nineteenth- and early-twentieth-century Canada, meant that "women activists insisted on their responsibility to establish order and well-being, not just for their families, but for the country."[69]

Shortt's commitment to these values became apparent very soon after her marriage. During the early years in Kingston, Beth resembled many twenty-first century women, as she struggled to hold two jobs while assuming the pivotal role in the family household. In addition to her enormous domestic responsibilities, Mrs. Shortt was expected to teach two courses at the KWMC and conduct a part-time medical practice on the side. Such employment was an economic necessity for the couple in this period, but Adam "carefully maintained his role of primary breadwinner by determining how and when she could offer financial assistance."[70]

Even with her multiple burdens, Mrs. Shortt's teaching career at the KWMC was highly successful. Like her husband, she was cherished by her students,[71] who took Elizabeth's courses in medical jurisprudence and sanitary science. Her popularity was reflected in the fact that Mrs. Shortt, the lecturer, "soon entered the group of Queen's elect by being immortalized in a College song:

> O'Doctor, Cut my leg off
> O'Doctor, Cut my leg off
> O'Doctor, Cut my leg off
> Shortt, Shortt, Shortt!"[72]

When the KWMC closed its doors in 1893 to coalesce with the Toronto Medical College in the Ontario Medical College for Women, located in Toronto, Elizabeth could look back at the Kingston institution's brief history with satisfaction and pride. "And so after a cycle of twenty-five years we came round to the point at which we began but with a difference; the jaundiced eye which had regarded women was greatly cured, and women students were seen to be just individuals with an individual's desire and right of self-realization."[73] This miraculous change was ironically most evident in the personal history of Dr. Thomas Fenwick. As an instructor at the Royal Medical College in the 1880s, he had sought to drive the three Hebrew children out of medical education altogether. Yet in 1892, the same Fenwick, having apparently undergone a major conversion, became the third and last dean of the KWMC.[74]

Elizabeth Shortt had secured another major triumph in her lifelong effort to extend educational opportunities for women in Canada. As we shall see, by the second decade of the twentieth century she was promoting a wide variety of reforms in her pursuit of a feminist agenda. However, an emphasis on advancing the possibilities of education for females always remained at the top of her priorities. For example, in a 1913 presidential address to the Ottawa Women's Canadian Club, Shortt declared that "you should therefore make the education of your sex the chief object of your lives ... the best of all things you can do, is to help the members of your sex get a good education, for female education is the foundation for all national success and progress."[75]

Although Mrs. Shortt was a popular teacher, two events took place in 1889 that would eventually cause her to withdraw from this productive role. In 1889, the Shortts' financial burden, which had necessitated income from Elizabeth immediately after marriage, eased when Adam became a full-time lecturer in political economy at Queen's and his pay more than doubled as a result.[76] That same year the couple rejoiced over the birth of their first child—Muriel. But this welcome event also ushered in considerably more responsibilities for Mrs. Shortt on the domestic front. To quote McLaren, "childbearing and childrearing dominated her life for over 27 years from the time her eldest child was born in 1889 until her youngest left home to attend private school in 1916." In fact, the ambitious Adam Shortt became so career-minded that he was seldom at home.[77]

For four years, Mrs. Shortt struggled mightily to combine her teaching and part-time medical practice with full-time domestic work and child care. However, the birth of a son—George—in 1893 coincided with the closing of the KWMC, and Elizabeth decided it was now necessary to devote greater attention to her growing family. She never returned to the teaching profession and after the arrival of the third and last child—Lorraine—in 1897, Dr. Shortt abandoned her private medical practice, as well. By 1900, "she focussed her attention on the incredible demands of raising a young family and pursuing a career in reform work."[78]

It is difficult to appreciate in the twenty-first century the expectations that late-Victorian household responsibilities created. McLaren has ably summarized the wide diversity of activities that Elizabeth, a conscientious homemaker, was expected to assume. Here they can only be listed—cleaning the house, sewing, laundry and ironing, food preparation, child care, entertaining visitors, as well as making and receiving visits to and from other women in Kingston—all this Elizabeth was expected to perform without much assistance from her husband. Sometimes Adam's convivial nature led to further chores. For example, Adam's academic friends often stayed at the Shortts' Kingston residence while attending conferences on the Queen's campus.[79]

Mrs. Shortt had a female servant to help her complete these tasks, as did most other middle-class housewives in late-Victorian Canada. The maid, or "girl,"[80] was expected to cook and perform a number of other functions, which were negotiated with her mistress. Even the food preparation was shared with the householder, and kitchen responsibilities proved onerous for Elizabeth.[81] Having a single servant provided much-needed help for Mrs. Shortt, but it certainly did not remove the heavy strain flowing from her domestic activities. She made this evident in a letter to her daughter Muriel, just before her return to Canada from the Old World on 2 September 1911: "I expect we will have an awful pinch of money, but I really must have more servants even if we do without some other things."[82] However, the extra assistance never materialized, and Elizabeth continued to feel overburdened by her familial tasks.

Their spendthrift habits "cast an image of wealth but increased his [Adam's] anxiety about financial matters." His wife shared these fears, but, like her husband, did little to alleviate them. "Maintaining an image of prosperity was clearly more important to them than budgeting for their future. This attitude would have negative consequences for them later in life."[83]

Soon a pattern of reckless expenditure had been firmly established within the Shortts' household. For example, when they created their first home in Kingston, Adam originally budgeted $200 for the furnishings, but then revised this figure to $365.50 in order to accommodate a number of questionable acquisitions that he and his wife desired. The final tally for the furnishings is unclear, but still more items were added to the second projection before the process was completed. Sometime later, "continuing to live beyond their means, Elizabeth and Adam purchased an extravagant home in Kingston during the summer of 1896."[84] The Shortts appeared unable to develop a sense of fiscal responsibility and a reasonable family budget.

Closely related to this problem was another challenge, one often associated with the middle and upper classes in late-Victorian Canada. Bowden believes Adam's elitist approach to politics revealed "an unnecessary tone of superiority."[85] Out of this flowed what Ferguson identifies as Shortt's "social snobbery," which intensified as he grew older.[86] Richard Allen, in his biography of Salem Bland, notes that this contemporary of Adam, who drew much inspiration from his contacts at Queen's, had an ambivalent view of Professor Shortt in the late nineteenth century. Bland considered Adam eloquent, well-informed, and highly intelligent. But the more radical Salem found Shortt's disdainful comments about working-class movements and his simplistic dismissal of socialism as untenable positions. For example, at the Queen's Theological Alumni Conference in 1899, after Adam delivered a typical apologia lauding intellectual elites, Bland "charged Shortt with exhibiting the arrogance of an intellectual Brahmin and defended the wisdom of normal human experience and moral insight."[87] Elizabeth Shortt shared her husband's social snobbery. The negative features of this outlook were revealed during the early years of her medical practice in Hamilton: "Her practice was made up mostly of the 'poorer classes.' While she insisted that she could do the most good caring for these people, she measured her success by how many new patients she added from the 'better class.' She saw all poor people as displaying the same immoral behaviour—wife and child abuse, poor spending habits, juvenile delinquency and especially drunkenness ... her class-based attitudes led her to rely upon stereotypes about her patients and contributed to feelings of superiority toward them."

After Elizabeth relocated in Kingston, she displayed a "condescending attitude" toward the female servants the Shortt family engaged there, and often treated them like children. This resulted in a frequent loss of domestic help. For example, between mid-August 1896 and late November 1898, no less than four servants were hired to fill the single domestic position in the Shortts' household.[88]

It is only fair to point out that many other middle- and upper-class women who engaged domestics behaved in a similarly offensive manner. As Barber puts it, "while some domestics were well treated, many were exploited."[89] However, several women who, like Mrs. Shortt, defined themselves as feminists in late-nineteenth-century Canada were renowned for their more progressive approach toward women in the servant class. Nellie McClung,[90] Flora MacDonald Denison,[91] and Carrie Derick, who wanted domestic servants to be treated on the same professional level as nurses,[92] were all less haughty and more understanding to servants in personal, economic, and social terms. Thus, McClung, Denison, and Derick expressed a gender solidarity that flowed naturally out of the social feminism that they, as well as Elizabeth, often endorsed.

However, Shortt's "class based attitudes [which] led her to rely upon stereotypes about her [poor] patients [in Hamilton] and contributed to feelings of superiority toward them" also caused her to espouse reforms, which in many cases benefited women from the lower class. Indeed, McLaren completes the above observation with the perceptive comment: "they [the poor patients in Hamilton] also made the misery she witnessed more shocking to her which in turn fuelled her conviction about the need to reform society."[93]

It was this reforming zeal, based on the Social Gospel, which made Mrs. Shortt's contribution to the feminist movement one of great importance.[94] During the years in Kingston, Elizabeth launched three initiatives that articulated her positive and liberal commitment to social feminism.

The first reform emanated from Dr. Shortt's teaching stint at the Kingston Women's Medical College. While there she organized the female graduates into an alumni society and emerged as the group's president in 1885. When the women students at Queen's created their own student union in 1889, Elizabeth, as the first head of the Queen's Alumnae, was again at the centre of the agitation.[95] The Levana Society subsequently introduced social, religious, and humanitarian pursuits among the female students while seeking to correct the sexist image of women presented in the male-dominated *Queen's Journal*.[96] As McKillop asserts, this organization was a classic example of late-nineteenth-century social feminism in action: "They could use Levana as a means of forging an independent existence with its own structures and imperatives, one with priorities and activities that they alone would determine and organize and that would encompass the full range of university life."[97] In the process, the female scholars at Queen's had paved the way for similar improvements among women in other Canadian institutions of higher learning.[98] Mrs. Shortt had presided over another important triumph for progressive educational change.

In 1900, Beth resigned from her executive position as the president of the Queen's Alumnae to devout herself to additional feminist activities in Kingston. However, she always remained available to young female students at Queen's during her Kingston years. As a journalist for the *Ottawa Evening Citizen* put it, "and to the women students of whatever faculty, she was ever the kindest friend and adviser to whom one and all felt they might ever turn."[99] Alice Chown, for instance, was befriended by Mrs. Shortt while she studied at Queen's in the 1880s, and the latter continued to inspire and assist the former in the years to come. While Chown's subsequent radicalism and Shortt's continuing moderation at times strained the relationship, these feminists remained close friends.[100] Elizabeth also provided support for the wives of other faculty members. For example, she became a mentor for Mrs. Isabel Skelton, whose husband Oscar was a protegé of Adam Shortt and his successor as the Sir John A. Macdonald Professor of Political and Economic Science. When Elizabeth was about to leave Kingston for Ottawa in 1908, Isabel touchingly wrote her older friend that "Kingston's great attraction ... was that it held you and I could always appeal to you for big or little advice."[101] Beth, the social feminist, was generally available for intimate conversations with female friends.

Although she assumed all these personal obligations as well as her substantial responsibilities at home, Mrs. Shortt still found time for two other reform causes during her stay at Kingston. Each further defined her feminist perspective and distinct vision of the Social Gospel. By the 1890s, the Young Women's Christian Association (YWCA) had "adopted a maternal or social feminist stance, imbued with a strong sense of Christian morality."[102] It also furnished information centres, temporary residences, and educational facilities for young ladies seeking to relocate in urban areas.[103] Naturally drawn to the YWCA's philosophy and practical agenda, Elizabeth sought to breathe new life into the local "Y," which in Kingston had become "a dead thing here to what it is in other places."[104] The same year that she uttered these words—1898—saw her using the local chapter of the YWCA to campaign for domestic science classes in Kingston's public schools, which Adelaide Hoodless and other feminists were promoting around the same time.[105] As a physician and mother of three children, Shortt stressed that a more scientific approach to domestic work would generally improve the well-being of families in Canada while more specifically reducing the death rate of young children.[106] Dr. Shortt remained a woman of science as well as a devout Christian mother. However, McLaren mentions that the domestic science courses would also produce better-trained servants within the Dominion, a constant concern of middle-class housewives like Beth.[107] Thus, Elizabeth's campaign for domestic science classes in Kingston represented a personal mixture of altruism and self-interest, which often motivated her feminist initiatives.

Shortt's initial efforts to bring domestic science into Kingston's public school system were rejected. Nevertheless, the provincial government did allocate a grant to the local YWCA so that it could establish its own instruction in this field. When domestic science classes began at the Kingston Y in November 1898, no less than twenty-four fourth-grade girls signed up for the new courses. Elizabeth had secured yet another educational reform, this time on the public school level. By 1900, she had established herself as a major figure in Canada's evolving educational system, especially as an innovator employing feminist principles and organizations. In more immediate terms, Mrs. Shortt was rewarded with the presidency of the Kingston YWCA, where she again proved her executive prowess by guiding the association from 1904 to 1907.[108]

Around this time, Beth became interested in yet another feminist group in Kingston, the local chapter of the National Council of Women of Canada (NCWC). In time, the NCWC would become the organization with which she would be most closely associated. The NCWC's mandate was much broader than that of the YWCA and most other specifically defined feminist groups. It sought to unite all Canadian women in a common effort to achieve nothing less than "the redemption" of Canadian society. Its members, lacking a vote on the national level, began to refer to themselves as the "Parliament of Women."[109] In practice, the NCWC "promoted and followed the strongly held religious beliefs of the Protestant middle class majority" and "its programs, while cautious, nevertheless contained the seeds of significant reform."[110] It was only natural that Mrs. Shortt was interested in a group that was Protestant, middle-class, and moderately reform-minded. The NCWC was also a further example of the social feminist perspective that supplied an apt foundation for much of her activism.

In the beginning, however, she was drawn to the NCWC for the same reason that had, in part, attracted her to the YWCA: the organization's interest in obtaining well-trained and grateful domestics. Her strong emphasis on securing such help from Great Britain in 1904–5 "was likely among the harshest of those expressed by [Immigration] Committee members." It evoked a negative response from other leading feminists in the NCWC, such as Professor Carrie Derick of McGill. Derick placed a greater stress on dealing with the personal needs of the anticipated servants rather than the potential difficulties of their Canadian employers.[111]

Elizabeth took a more altruistic stand when she used her medical training to combat the contemporary ravages of tuberculosis. She addressed the annual meeting of the NCWC in Vancouver on 17 July 1907, with a call to deal at once with this "question of life and death." Shortt presented the female delegates with a five-point program that would serve as a beachhead for her personal war on TB: the circulation of more accurate information on the disease, greater hygiene and especially more sunshine and fresh air, better enforcement of existing municipal ordinances that could discourage the spread of the illness (e.g., anti-spitting laws), provincial legislation to include tuberculosis among the contagious illnesses that the medical health officer was mandated to correct, and the establishment of segregated facilities where this often fatal malady could be properly treated.[112]

It was an impressive beginning for Dr. Shortt as she launched her long-term assault on this major affliction in the Dominion. The following year, she was made the convenor of a newly created Committee on Public Health in the NCWC, which improved her ability to give further direction to this "life and death" struggle.[113] In 1908, a Hamilton newspaper observed that her paper on tuberculosis was already being "used as an authority on the subject,"[114] an accolade repeated by the Toronto *Globe* a few years later.[115]

By 1908, Elizabeth had established herself as a leading medical and educational reformer within Canada. More importantly, she had discovered a key role for the medical training Mrs. Shortt had fought so hard to complete. The Hamilton paper further reported, "Dr. Shortt's knowledge of medicine has been of much service to herself and to humanity in her philanthropic and other work."[116] When she prepared to leave Kingston for Ottawa in 1908, Elizabeth's credentials as a major social feminist and activist could not be contested. They would be further extended once she relocated in the national capital, where greater opportunities awaited Shortt's eagerness to introduce many more social improvements.

Meanwhile, during these years in Kingston, Adam Shortt was acquiring prominence throughout the country as a university academic, public affairs analyst, historian, and government arbitrator. When he began teaching

FIG. 1 Elizabeth Smith Shortt. This photograph is discussed in Mrs. Shortt's August 3 letter to her three children (para. 5). Courtesy of University of Waterloo Library, Special Collections & Archives, Elizabeth Smith Shortt fonds (WA10, file 2308, Head & shoulders of E. Smith-Shortt by Topley of Ottawa).

political economy on a full-time basis in 1888, Queen's University served a mere four hundred students.[117] These limited horizons were vastly expanded in the late nineteenth and early twentieth centuries. McKillop justifiably numbers Shortt among "the titans" who converted this small Presbyterian outpost in eastern Ontario into a first-class institution of higher learning with a favourable reputation throughout the Dominion.[118]

However, more immediately, Queen's humble origins meant that a newly arrived instructor like Adam would assume diverse tasks at the financially strapped university. Thus, from the very beginning of his career at Queen's, Professor Shortt was required to undertake administrative as well as teaching and publishing responsibilities. As Bowden recounts, during his twenty years at the school, Shortt served as "the editor of the

FIG. 2   Adam Shortt. Courtesy of University of Waterloo Library, Special Collections & Archives, Elizabeth Smith Shortt fonds (WA10, file 2305 Adam Shortt portrait).

Queen's *Journal* [the university newspaper], athletic director, co-ordinator of debates and organizer of the Political Economy club."[119] Thus, in various ways, he fostered the strong sense of togetherness that has been traditionally associated with the Queen's student body.

Nevertheless, Adam's contribution to the administrative evolution of Queen's was especially significant in four specific areas. He was a prime mover behind the growth of the university library, the founding and progress of the *Queen's Quarterly*, the early drive for the secularization of the Kingston institution, and the appointment of faculty and administrative personnel. These were all notable milestones in Queen's emergence as a major player in Canada's academic world.

In 1889, Shortt became the head of the Queen's library, which at the time was inadequate even in terms of the university's small student body.[120] He soon began to correct this regrettable situation with his characteristic vigour. In 1895, Shortt called for the introduction of a card catalogue system to facilitate student use of the library holdings. The change was later recognized by a grateful library as a turning point in its development.[121] More specifically, Hilda Neatby has disclosed that as a result of the catalogue, "circulation immediately doubled and books which had hitherto remained neglected on the shelves began to move."[122]

This improvement was accompanied by a dynamic acquisitions campaign, which greatly enhanced the number of materials available to the scholars at Queen's. One of them—Andrew Haydon—fondly acknowledged the debt that he owed to Adam Shortt the librarian, who amassed numerous works from libraries, stores, individual collections, and numerous other sources throughout the Dominion.[123] Thus began a calling for Adam that was of great importance to a definition of his personal identity. As Berger reports, Shortt became "an inveterate collector of old letters, books, autographs and other memorabilia."[124] During the 1911 trip to Europe, which will be examined in this volume, his dedication to the collector's mission became abundantly clear.

In 1896, Shortt declared that during the first year of his tenure, 473 volumes were added to the library's inventory. Moreover, during each of the following two years, more than 1,800 new works were ordered. As a result, student use of library resources also considerably increased. In the 1889–90 session, only ninety student checkouts were reported. By 1895–96, the number had more than tripled to a count of over three hundred.[125] Shortt's library policies were obviously producing desirable results.

However, the new additions to the library under Shortt's direction also revealed two other ways in which Adam influenced Queen's maturation. In garnering these works, he always stressed the need for primary sources, especially those with Canadian significance. For example, in 1894, he boasted that with recent purchases from the Bell papers, "Queen's now had the largest collection of early Ontario pamphlets anywhere to be found."[126] He utilized these sources in his own classes, in which the Canadian experience was uniquely stressed.[127] Wherever possible, he wanted his students to do the same, with particular attention to original papers. As we shall see, these predilections affected his teaching and writing, as well as his library responsibilities. When Shortt passed away, in 1931, it was not surprising that Dr. McNeill, then the vice-principal of Queen's, stated that, "Very fittingly his portrait will hang in the Douglas Library near the books he had helped to gather."[128] Adam had vitally contributed to the growth of an admirable library at his beloved university.

The image of that institution also advanced with the establishment of the *Queen's Quarterly* in 1893, which Shortt helped to found. He also remained on its management committee as an editor for a number of years. More importantly, he, along with Professor James Cappon, the chair of the English department, became a major writer for the quarterly over the next twelve years.[129] As Ferguson notes, this publication was "the first university-based intellectual periodical in the country." For Adam, it was a practical expression of an intellectual elite reaching out to the general public, as well as the students and alumni of Queen's. While this was a vital aspect of the intelligentsia's raison d'etre in the Dominion, the frequently cynical instructor of political economy questioned whether the journal would succeed in economic and intellectual terms.[130]

It was certainly not a financial success. The number of subscribers never exceeded the 750 level throughout Adam's stay at Queen's,[131] which saw the quarterly remain deeply mired in debt.[132] But it attained considerable praise in a larger sense. "It was," as Ferguson writes, "the only scholarly forum during the 1890s and one of the few for twenty more years in Canada to publish informed general essays on science, literature and public affairs."[133] Indeed, the *Queen's Quarterly* continues to fulfill the same mandate right down to the present. Shortt played a noteworthy role in creating this distinguished tradition.

Adam Shortt again teamed up with James Cappon[134] to achieve another important administrative change: the secularization of Queen's University. Ferguson has stressed that by 1900, Principal Grant, an ordained Presbyterian minister, was committed to the total end of his church's control over the university he led. Soon, Adam Shortt joined Grant in the effort to introduce secular management of Queen's.[135] Adam also brought to this campaign a powerful argument from history, which compared the contemporary advancement of Queen's to that of an increasingly autonomous Canada within the British Empire. "It is but the logical completion of the whole trend of the unwritten, as well as written constitutional development of Queen's to make the Board of Trustees representative of the new and larger corporation of the University [rather than the Presbyterian church]."[136]

Soon after Grant's death in 1902, Presbyterian leaders accepted the principle of secularization. Shortt rejoiced that the church which had nurtured his deeply rooted Christian beliefs had accepted this modernization of its university in Kingston.[137] The complicated process was not finalized until 1911, but it eventually did assist the progress of Queen's. In general terms, "secularization was important, for both autonomy and recognition could ensure that society took seriously the work and findings of the new social sciences," which Shortt was determined to promote there.[138] On a more mundane level, it fostered much-needed reforms, such as making the arts programs eligible for provincial grants.[139] Shortt had once again been a key figure in the evolution of the administrative structure at the Kingston institution.

Queen's also profited from Adam's sage advice about future faculty appointments. As we have seen, he was the first full-time instructor of political economy at the university. In 1891, this faculty position was solidified with the creation of the John A. Macdonald Chair of Political Science.[140] Before leaving Queen's, however, Shortt engineered an expansion of this academic sector that was vital to the further growth of all the other social sciences at the university. Oscar Skelton succeeded him in the Macdonald Chair, and William Swanson, a specialist in economics, was added to the fledgling department. As Crowley observes, the Department of Political and Economic Science at Queen's was beginning to acquire serious dimensions.[141] These modest steps by Adam Shortt had momentous consequences. To quote Ferguson: "From a single course in political economy offered in 1886, Adam Shortt built up a department of political and economic science and attracted a band of adepts who followed him in two major undertakings from 1890 to the Second World War. The first was to study, teach and write about Canadian economic and political questions using the tenets of the new political economy. The second was to move from comment on to participation in national affairs by becoming senior civil servants."[142]

Still more remarkable was Shortt's ability to influence further appointments at Queen's after he had left the institution. Haydon has noted that Adam served as a trustee of Queen's from 1908 down to his death in 1931, and his opinions were always seriously considered at board meetings.[143] Bowden further reveals that Shortt was later consulted on the selections of R. Bruce Taylor as principal and Duncan McArthur as a member of the history department.[144] In 1925, the Queen's trustees asked Adam and E. R. Peacock to explore the possibility of securing a new head of the English department within Great Britain. The mission ended in failure, but the episode indicated that even after leaving the university in 1908, Adam Shortt remained a major force in shaping his alma mater's destiny.[145]

Shortt's contribution to the administrative evolution of Queen's was certainly significant. I have dwelled on it here at length, since this subject has generally been understated in past publications on him. Nevertheless, for many of his students, it was Adam's role as a teacher that most profoundly affected their lives. One of these scholars, Andrew Haydon, believed that Shortt's work in the classroom represented his most important contribution, not only to Queen's but to Canada.[146] D. D. Calvin, in his centennial history of Queen's, bestowed a singular distinction upon Professor Shortt's teaching career: "no man on the staff of Queen's has had a stronger hold on his students."[147]

Adam shared with his wife Elizabeth an intense belief in the value of education. Indeed, for him, education was a necessity. As Professor Shortt, in a Darwinian tone, put it in 1905: "The human being enters life with little beyond capacity; he must be educated or perish."[148] Nature, as well as personal conviction, drew him into the teaching profession. Shortt's personal talents made the university classroom an appropriate setting for many of his adult years. There, Bowden points out, Adam skilfully combined strong powers of retention, a raconteur's ability to tell stories, and a flair for drawing meaningful comparisons.[149] Finally, Adam drew great satisfaction from instructing students at Queen's. As he revealed in 1904, "I am very much attached to the work of my class-room and the hours I spend with my students, especially my honour students, are the happiest of my life."[150]

During his teaching years at Queen's, Shortt gradually moved from a primary interest in political economy to a concentration on economic history.[151] Here we are mainly concerned with his work as a teacher; his writings on current affairs and history will be examined more closely when we explore Shortt's dedication to these two pursuits. However, in some respects, his pedagogical career was of greater importance than his publications in defining his place within the development of English-Canadian historiography. For example, Berger declares, "the substantial beginnings of the critical study of the Canadian past ... were laid in the years after 1894, when George Wrong was appointed to the Chair of History in the University of Toronto and Adam Shortt began his lectures on the early economic and social history of Canada at Queen's University."[152]

The very introduction of political economy as a significant field put Shortt into the vanguard of English Canadian professors. W. A. Mackintosh, subsequently a major figure in the instruction of economic history at Queen's, commented that, "As a teacher, more than anyone he helped to establish the place of Economics and Political Science in Canadian universities."[153] This also represented the beginning of the social sciences as a distinct division within these institutions.

However, Shortt's innovations in the classroom did not end there. He was also one of the first academics to use empirical methods, drawn from the scientist's laboratories, to examine social issues.[154] But it would be a mistake to see Adam as a fully dedicated social scientist akin to contemporary academics, like James Mavor, who utilized empirical methods and principles as the sole avenue to intellectual enlightenment.[155] From time to time, he made moral judgments that had little to do with the detachment of the scientist. For instance, Shortt lauded William Gladstone, the revered leader of late-Victorian liberalism, as an accomplished British politician. Gladstone was a superior leader not because of his skills as an empirical, pragmatic politician, but rather on account of his dedication to individual liberty and Christian morality.[156] McKillop correctly asserts that Adam blended the idealism of the philosopher and theologian with the empiricism of the scientist.[157] Science, empiricism, and moral judgments continued to interact in defining his world view, which proved to be a complex process.

Gradually Shortt stressed the historical approach, which, Crowley suggests, provided the Queen's academic with a better device to display the reciprocal interaction between economics and politics.[158] More specifically, greater emphasis was placed upon understanding economics through a detailed study of the past.[159] Indeed, in 1927, Canada's first great economic historian, Harold Innis, credited Shortt with founding within the Dominion the discipline that the former proceeded to cultivate so successfully.[160]

Another economic historian further contended that Adam was the initial professor in Canada to emphasize the significance of the domestic economy.[161] Bowden supports this view with particular references: "More than anyone else in his field in Canada in the decade after 1892 Shortt investigated the Canadian experience—the settlement of the prairies, development in British Columbia, early financiers, the changing structure of the banking system, tariff policy, fishing claims, and railway taxation."[162] Shortt was an avid champion of Canadian Studies long before this academic orientation was even designated.

His nationalist bent could also be observed in his support of promising students on the graduate level, because, among other things, he wanted to encourage Canadians with intellectual ability. Crowley emphasizes his impact on Oscar Skelton, whom Adam deeply affected. For example, Skelton endorsed Shortt's notion that social science leaders would eventually join business, political, and journalistic leaders in forming a benevolent ruling elite within Canada.[163] In this close relationship with the younger Skelton, Shortt was repaying a debt that he owed to another Queen's educator. As McKillop states, "Adam Shortt was to O. D. Skelton what John Watson had been to Shortt: an academic mentor who vitally affected the future career of his protégé."[164]

However, Skelton was not the only fortunate recipient of Professor Shortt's generous assistance to his students. Ferguson notes that in the 1890s and 1900s, several other promising scholars, such as W. B. Munro, Walter McLaren, and William Swanson, who pursued outstanding careers in teaching the social sciences on the university level, could also be considered Adam's "protégés."[165] He was building a firm structure for the social sciences in the halls of higher learning, and the foundation was unmistakably made in Canada. Many of these grateful students corresponded regularly with their former professor at Queen's. After reading the exchanges, Mackintosh perceptively commented: "From the letters one gets a pleasant impression of mutual confidence and high respect, which offers the best possible evidence of Shortt's success as a teacher."[166] There could be little doubt that Adam had become a distinguished educator during his years in Kingston.

In 1891, Professor Shortt extended his classes beyond this city to Ottawa, where he and James Cappon offered lectures on political science and English, respectively. Both courses proved "very popular," and Queen's became the first Ontario university to mount such an extramural program. On a personal level, Adam had once more broken new ground, and soon Queen's was presenting extension courses in remote areas, such as the Northwest Territories and Victoria on Canada's west coast. In the process, what had begun as a small regional university in eastern Ontario had started "to fulfil [Principal] Grant's dream of serving the growing communities on the prairies and in the far west."[167] Queen's was becoming a national institution.

Shortt's abilities as a teacher led naturally to an interest in public affairs, especially those emanating from the political capital in Ottawa. The professor of political economy urged his students to follow current events outside the classroom as an integral phase of their education.[168] With the founding of the *Queen's Quarterly* in 1893, he acquired a vehicle to express his own views on the issues of the day, and he utilized it to become a major analyst of the contemporary scene. However, Adam did not restrict his writings on these issues to the relatively safe confines of the Queen's publication. He gradually found new audiences in other journals, such as the *Dalhousie Review*, the Toronto *Globe*, *The News* in Toronto, the *Monetary Times*, the *Financial Post*, and the *Canadian Magazine*. As Bowden observes, "Very few scholars of his generation published so widely in periodicals which were read by academic, business and political leaders."[169]

Soon, the quality as well as the quantity of Shortt's articles and pamphlets on contemporary topics became evident. Berger, for example, reveals that Adam suddenly became a respected critic of public affairs with the publication of *Imperial Preferential Trade from a Canadian Point of View*, a 1904 tract where he vigorously opposed Joseph Chamberlain's program of economic centralization within the British Empire.[170] As far as Shortt was concerned, the only imperial structure worth having was an international community that recognized "free and independent development [among the self-governing colonies] … accompanied by constant intercourse and mutual interchange of ideas."[171] Though he did not use the term, he was groping for what became the essence of the modern British Commonwealth of Nations.

It is impossible in this brief introduction to do full justice to Adam's work as a commentator on public controversies. Nevertheless, these writings collectively document several tendencies that we have already identified as important aspects of his thinking. Shortt's personal independence, his moderate critiques, which at times reflected liberal and on other occasions conservative attitudes, and his general rejection of radical solutions could all be found in these publications.

In 1894, Shortt denounced a series of letters in the London *Times* that he believed encouraged "the European military curse" within Canada.[172] It was his opening censure of not only armed conflicts but also the very nature and necessity of modern warfare. This was an unusual position in Canada during the 1890s and 1900s. Socknat has indicated that in this period, most Canadians thought that North America was a peaceful oasis that remained immune to the frequent wars in the Old World.[173] And within the minority interested in foreign relations there were Canadian imperialists, like George Parkin, whom Adam sarcastically described as the author "for us [of] the glorious destiny of becoming a sort of military store or base of transit and supplies, in men and materials, which will enable Britain to enter upon that great future struggle with the United States."[174] Shortt was determined to resist greater military and economic integration with the mother country and most certainly another resort to arms with the American republic.

However, Shortt did criticize the American declaration of war with Spain in 1898, which he saw as another example of undesirable imperial expansion. But his moralistic critique of this military operation also revealed a religious foundation for his opinions: "The [American] people have been reminded with cruel frankness that war is laden not with airs from heaven but blasts from hell."[175] Adam also opposed both British and Canadian participation in the Boer War, which he traced to serious miscalculations by both the Afrikaners and the English.[176] However, once war had been declared, he believed it had to be fought to a successful conclusion; Shortt believed in peace but not pacifism. Thus, he welcomed the accord that ended the conflict in 1902, while reminding his readers that he had never endorsed the military option in the first place.[177]

After contemplating the tragedies of these two conflicts, Shortt sought out new ways to avoid future hostilities. In the process, he asserted his growing independence within English Canada's academic community. When Andrew Cory Courtice founded the Canadian Peace and Arbitration Society, the first Canada-wide peace organization, in 1905, Adam emerged as one of only four academics to endorse the proposition.[178] Moreover, his role in the group increased after labour adjudications assumed greater significance in its activities. Socknat informs us that "when a number of the society's members, such as Shortt, became successful mediators in industrial disputes, they became convinced that similar principles of negotiation could be applied to international conflicts."[179] More will be said shortly about Adam's work as an arbitrator in labour disagreements within Canada, but here it should be mentioned that he was equally confident that these peaceful methods could be employed on the international stage to avoid the "butchery" of war.[180]

Such views and commitments placed the independent Queen's professor within a peace movement, which was a definite minority in early-twentieth-century Canada. Two authorities—S. E. D. Shortt and Barry Ferguson—have more generally identified him with contemporary liberalism.[181] Certainly many of Shortt's attitudes, which we have already discussed, would further support their assertion. For example, Socknat places him and other members of the Peace and Arbitration Society among "the progressive peace reformers" of the era.[182] Similarly, his dedication to the secularization of Queen's could be described as a liberal assault upon traditional, conservative attitudes.[183] The very development of a social science sector within the university, which Shortt facilitated, could also be considered a progressive step in higher education. Adam also wanted more government intervention to solve labour disputes and to reform the federal civil service.[184] As we shall see, he became deeply immersed in future efforts to solve these problems by operating on the national level. Moreover, he vigorously supported the Laurier Liberals' opposition to Chamberlain's plans for a centralization of the British Empire in the early twentieth century.[185] Later, he upheld the same position in a conversation with Lord Percy on the voyage to Great Britain in 1911.

It would be misleading, however, to conclude that Shortt was nothing more than a Liberal partisan. He and his disciple, Oscar Skelton, became famous for their ringing criticisms of both major parties in the Canadian parliament during the first decade of the twentieth century.[186] In 1903, Shortt reduced national politics in Canada to one vital issue: "to obtain and afterwards to retain office is the absorbing interest in practical politics. Neither political party has reasoned political convictions by which it is willing to stand or fall.... In fact there is little true party government, it is simply a struggle of the ins and outs."[187] Like his wife Elizabeth, Adam saw no need to identify with this sordid system of party politics. He preferred to retain a highly critical and independent stance, which he enunciated from his neutral perch on the Queen's campus.

Sometimes conservative as well as liberal attitudes were voiced by the professor of political economy in Kingston. He had a traditional fear of mob violence. For example, in 1894, he ridiculed in a scornful fashion Coxey's march on Washington to aid the large number of unemployed workers in the United States. Shortt welcomed the failure of this poorly led movement, but he also feared that "the low, ignorant and inflammable elements of the people ... may become the tools of an abler demagogue than Coxey and work much damage to law, order, property and cause much damage before being suppressed."[188] He repeated this warning on other occasions,[189] and thought that the "ignorant rabble" could only be saved by accepting the leadership furnished by the political, economic, social, and intellectual elites, which would give them sensible guidance.[190]

He maintained conservative attitudes on several other major issues confronting the Dominion in the late nineteenth and early twentieth centuries. Although Shortt accepted government interventions in the social and economic sectors, such public mediations were meant only to be exceptional rather than the accustomed rule. In general terms, "while a government can do much towards injuring a country, it can do but little towards building it up, beyond smoothing the path of private enterprise."[191] This belief in laissez-faire government should only be altered in very dire circumstances, such as the granting of public assistance to those mired in acute poverty.[192]

Such views further buttressed Shortt's firm conviction that Canada's capitalist leaders were entitled to their privileged status and abundant wealth, a process that he justified in Darwinian terms: "the whole growth of economic organization, the subsequent development of the millionaire, and the final effort to avoid the ruinous waste of individual competition, are simply stages in the economic triumph of man over nature." There could be no overall prosperity in Canada without the guidance of the corporate elite.[193] Ferguson has further associated him with a conservative approach to specific economic and social questions of this era. "Behind Shortt's theorizing about economic growth and about labour-capital relations there was a conservative goal. Shortt aimed to sustain the effective economic machinery. To prevent inefficiency, distracting and deleterious labour conflicts and similar forms of business competition should be avoided."[194] Thus, Adam blended liberal and conservative views in his independent version of the Social Gospel.

One thing was clear: Professor Shortt was generally determined to avoid radical solutions to political, economic, and social questions. This brought him into conflict with more left-wing exponents of the Social Gospel, such as Salem Bland, who by the mid-1890s openly proclaimed himself a socialist.[195] In fact, McKillop defines Bland as "the most radical of the social gospellers in Canada."[196] Adam totally rejected the socialism being preached by Bland and others in North America at this time. Moreover, he associated such extremism with the lack of intelligence that had inspired the Coxey movement in the United States. Shortt wrote that socialism appealed only to "men who, in their ignorance, had been led to believe that they had been unjustly deprived of a great part of the wealth which properly belongs to them by a tyrannous and selfish upper class."[197] In 1908, Adam even speculated that the deluded socialists within North America might be psychologically unbalanced.[198] In the final analysis, he rejected all nostrums like socialism, which threatened the established order in Canada.

While the moderate professor at Queen's had risen to national prominence as a result of teaching political economy and interpreting current events, he also began to publish scholarly works, which earned him acceptance among a number of anglophone intellectuals both at home and abroad. For example, he developed several contacts with members of the Round Table movement in Great Britain who were interested in learning more about the histories of the self-governing Dominions. Before long, Lionel Curtis, Lord Milner, and Phillip Kerr established personal friendships with Shortt on various trips to Canada.[199]

During his Queen's years, Adam established a solid reputation as an innovative scholar with a clearly revisionist bent. Shortt, the university librarian, had been intent on acquiring primary materials for the students on campus. In 1899, he used the *Queen's Quarterly* to publish further historical records dealing with the Kingston area. The edition of July 1899 contained documents from the Court of Quarter Sessions in the District of Mecklenburg (later the Midland District), which met in the "Limestone City" beginning in 1789. Further primary sources appeared in print for the first time within six subsequent issues of the same periodical.[200]

By 1904, when he met Arthur Doughty, who had just been appointed the first Dominion archivist under the aegis of the department of agriculture, a revisionist Adam Shortt was well known for introducing primary sources dealing with political, social, and economic events drawn from Canada's history. Doughty shared Shortt's passion for finding original documents relating to Canada, as well as his strong urge to make them accessible to other scholars. In 1907, Doughty engineered the creation of a national historical manuscripts commission. Later that year, one of its first volumes appeared, *Documents Relating to the Constitutional History of Canada, 1759–1791*, jointly edited by Shortt and Doughty. It was a landmark publication that was reprinted in 1918, when a second edition expanded the scope of the study down to 1841.

These works were essential references in their field for many years to come. Bowden indicates that "Shortt and Doughty" became required texts for university students selecting pre-Confederation history courses, "at least until the publication of A. L. Burt's *The Old Province of Quebec* in 1933."[201] It represented the beginning of a lengthy and productive partnership between the two men, whose collaboration had a long-term impact on Canadian historiography. Berger points out that "the renaissance of Canadian history in the twenties and thirties would have been inconceivable without the preliminary work of Doughty and Shortt."[202]

While the collection and processing of original materials dealing with social and economic history represented Shortt's "major contribution" to Canadian historiography, he also published analytical papers and one book that expressed revisionist perspectives in the years from 1896 to 1908. During the first ten years of this period, Adam wrote no less than thirty-two articles for the *Journal of the Canadian Bankers' Association* on the evolution of Canada's currency and banking system. This marked the first time that these aspects of the Dominion's past had been treated in a thorough fashion.[203] These articles solidified his growing reputation as an economic historian. Moreover, his work drew high praise from the commercial sector of the economic elite, with which Shortt became closely associated.[204]

He was equally interested in promoting local history, and therefore Shortt also investigated Kingston's early development. For example, in 1901, he composed an article for the *Queen's Quarterly* on "Life in Kingston the Year after Waterloo," where he critically asserted that the city had become "an extravagant, fashionable, and even sinful town" following the Napoleonic wars. Here the religious underpinnings of Adam's world view were evident, as was his faith in the salvation of society through the efforts of redemptive elites. Thus, Adam lauded the "important minority of shrewd, well-informed and public spirited citizens," who eventually brought a more promising future to the urban centre where Queen's was eventually founded.[205] In fact, many of Shortt's own papers were initially read at meetings of the Kingston Historical Society, which proudly numbered him among its founders.[206] Professor Shortt was also innovative as a local historian with a critical viewpoint.

While social and economic history grew more important to Shortt as he became a noteworthy historian, he never totally abandoned his interest in the political side of political economy. For example, in 1902, he published the article "The Winning of Responsible Government" in the *Queen's Quarterly*. Here he introduced several revisionist positions. The coming of responsible government was traditionally associated with the report that Lord Durham had submitted to the British government in 1839. But for Shortt, Durham was a "gorgeous meteor" who "flared across the troubled sky of Canadian politics, and was suddenly snuffed out by an alarmed Home government, leaving confusion worse confounded."[207]

The task of creating a viable and responsible government was left to Durham's successor, Lord Sydenham, who became for Shortt the most significant governor in the pre-Confederation period. Many fundamental changes were enacted during Sydenham's relatively brief stay in central Canada as the Queen's representative from 19 October 1839 to 19 September 1841. These included administrative improvements, such as a resolution of the vexing Clergy Reserves question, a more stable and reliable colonial budget, the creation of municipal governments throughout the province, and, of course, on the constitutional level the introduction of "an organized system of parliamentary government, in connection with which was incorporated the principle of responsible government."[208]

Adam's main message was clear. Pragmatic, empirical solutions, such as those provided by Sydenham, were more important than the visionary statements of a "gorgeous meteor" like Durham. Shortt would soon become personally involved in administrative reforms within the federal government, which could be interpreted as a continuation of Sydenham's legacy of moderate, evolutionary political progress. As Berger asserts, "in this businessman/consul Shortt found a kindred spirit."[209]

He also found a subject for a full-length biography in the Makers of Canada series, which the Toronto publisher George Morang organized during the first decade of the twentieth century. This work further enhanced Shortt's growing recognition as an able historian. Berger considers the Sydenham biography the finest contribution to Morang's innovative undertaking.[210] By 1908, Adam Shortt had become a highly regarded historian in English Canada, but he never achieved the status of a great historian. That honour is reserved for scholars such as Harold Innis, who developed original perspectives on subjects like Canada's fur trade and fishing industry.[211] However, it must be noted that Shortt vitally contributed to the formation of a more creative Innis. Mackintosh properly asserts that, "if we ever come to the time when *Who's Who* includes the intellectual pedigrees of scholars, there will appear an item: Innis, H. A. by Veblen, out of Shortt."[212]

Nevertheless, by 1903, the ever-restless Professor Shortt was looking for new worlds to conquer. He was no longer satisfied with his ivory-tower existence on the Queen's campus in Kingston, and was eager to apply the theory of political economy to practical economic and political questions.[213] In particular, Adam wanted to introduce scientific detachment to the study of the Dominion's problems,[214] as well as widen the Social Gospel's scope in Canada, through public service.[215] The opportunity arrived in 1903, when the Ontario government appointed Shortt as chair of a three-man panel, which sought to simplify the thorny issue of railway taxation in the province. According to Bowden, "from that point on, Shortt divided his effort between traditional academic writing and a combination of discussing public issues and undertaking government service."[216]

The investigative trio visited twelve American states to collect data, and both of Shortt's colleagues were confused by the vast amount of evidence presented. Thus, they gladly left Adam with the sole responsibility for writing a final report. He then produced a moderate but meaningful compromise centred on an annual tax levy of three percent on the railways' earnings as a solution that both the private and public sectors could accept. Shortt's first job as a civil servant had solved Ontario's immediate tax problems in the pivotal railway industry. However, it also had a long-term significance. American state governments consulted the report for guidance on similar quarrels, while Queen's Park further utilized it as a guide to solving other taxation disputes with private corporations.[217] Shortt had successfully employed his empirical talents on the public stage.

Another opportunity emerged in 1907, when the Laurier government in Ottawa began to implement the Industrial Disputes Investigation (Lemieux) Act, which had been recently legislated. This act was meant to bring the process of arbitration, which Shortt had fostered on the international level, into the growing number of labour/management disputes within the industrial sector. When the machinists working for the Grand Trunk Railway threatened to disrupt the operations of this transcontinental line, F. A. Acland, the deputy minister of labour in Ottawa, suggested Shortt as the chair of a three-man negotiation team. Acland, whom we shall encounter in the Shortts' writings that follow, had been deeply impressed with Adam's skilful handling of the railway taxation controversy in Ontario.[218]

As the leader of the group, Shortt worked with representatives from the union and the corporation to achieve unanimity on their concluding report. As Ferguson notes, Shortt acted more like a conciliator than an arbitrator.[219] Moreover, Allen points out that this role admirably suited Adam's personality and experience, since "he was cut out to be a conciliator between parties in dispute, a manager above the fray."[220] In the end, all three members of the board accepted Shortt's final recommendations, which he had reached within a month of the group's initial session. This represented only the first in a series of agreements that the professor presided over as he became the most accomplished chair under the Lemieux Act.[221] During the next sixteen months, he averted work stoppages by devising ten more industrial accords, which management, labour, and government officials happily accepted.[222]

According to Mackintosh, his work on these government boards represented "his greatest single achievement ... aside from the pervasive and enduring influence of an ardent teacher." Furthermore, after he withdrew from this work in 1908, the legislation "never again achieved the success ... when Adam Shortt had wrought mightily with it."[223] In addition, the cash received from Ottawa for his participation on these government panels was very welcome to the Shortts, who continued to live beyond their means during the later stages of their residence in Kingston. Bowden recounts that Adam obtained $1,640, plus expenses, for the eight cases he chaired during 1908, which substantially augmented his annual salary from Queen's of $2,500.[224]

Finally, Shortt's assignments for the Laurier regime under the Lemieux Act became a bridge to a far more significant public role for Adam. A 1910 article in the Toronto *Globe* summarized the link between the two positions. "It was doubtless the repeated and unvarying success achieved in his work as conciliator-at-large for the Dominion which brought Prof. Shortt prominently into public gaze, and led to his appointment in September, 1908, as one of the joint civil service commissioners under the new act [to reform the federal bureaucracy]."[225]

Adam had often criticized the Laurier regime for its misuse of national patronage. In 1906, he suggested in the *Canadian Magazine* that an effective national bureaucracy could never be attained while party services rather than personal merit determined appointments and promotions within the federal civil service. Many other prominent Canadians, such as Principal George Grant, Goldwin Smith, and J. S. Willison, had expressed similar sentiments.[226] Nonetheless, the proposals were never seriously considered by most politicians in Ottawa.[227] Gordon T. Stewart, a leading authority on this topic, argues that "both national parties used patronage as the cement of party.... Patronage was the ballast which enabled the political ship to make headway."[228] Thus, the generally moderate Shortt was asking for nothing less than a radical transformation of the federal political structure when he called for a less partisan civil service.

It was a bold, courageous, and principled stand, which even the more progressive Salem Bland admired.[229] However, the call for a thorough overhaul of national patronage at this time was destined to be rejected. Owram summarizes the dire situation confronting Shortt after he accepted the Laurier government's offer to become one of two commissioners entrusted with this awesome task: "Shortt's actual experience fell below his expectations. The problem of civil service reform was massive and involved not only the restriction of patronage but also the restructuring of the civil service itself and the redefinition of relations between the permanent advisor and the politician. To achieve these goals would take decades, and Shortt was naive to think that they could be accomplished quickly under governments that were less than fully committed to the principle of reform in the first place."[230]

Nevertheless, if Adam failed to obtain his lofty goals as a co-commissioner of the Dominion civil service, his role in Ottawa was positive in general, as well as specific terms. The improvements were readily apparent as early as 1911, when Shortt once again broke new ground after he moved from the halls of academe to the turbulence of national politics. In the process, he established a tradition that deeply affected both university life and the federal government.

It gradually became evident that Professor Shortt had initiated a march of talented academics and university-educated students into the Dominion civil service, which few of them had previously considered. His own protegé at Queen's, Oscar Skelton, later made the same transition to serve as a highly effective under-secretary of state for external affairs from 1925 down to his death in 1941. Skelton's first job in Ottawa materialized when Shortt appointed him the examiner on economic questions within new tests that the commissioners introduced in 1909 for applicants to the national bureaucracy.[231] Owram considers Adam's personal example and hiring decisions an important part of his long-term legacy to the central government's public service: "the 1920s did see the emergence in the nation's capital of a new class of civil servants. Highly educated, certain of their own abilities and the need for efficient government, these men were the heirs of men like Adam Shortt. Before long, they began to bring social scientific training and a pragmatic interventionism into discussions of government policy."[232]

Moreover, the examinations that Skelton and other academics graded[233] also represented a significant first step in a gradual reform of the federal bureaucracy. The concept of using examinations to help qualify candidates for the public service in Ottawa had initially been introduced in the years between 1882 and 1885 by the Macdonald government. However, the tests were concerned with demonstrating the prospective employee's literacy, practical reasoning, and informational skills. For example, one question asked the applicant: "If a file is not in its envelope what means have you of looking it up?" Another requested the aspirant to "state what you know about the landing and civil and medical examination of immigrants at ocean ports."[234]

Commissioner Shortt wanted more vigorous intellectual standards in the selection of federal bureaucrats as a means of judging their ability and independence. For this purpose, the public service was divided into three divisions and on each level the candidates were expected to answer more probing questions than those presented during the Macdonald era. For example, Division II applicants on the November 1910 examinations, which were prepared by university teachers, were invited to "explain why Oliver Cromwell became supreme in England."[235]

The use of more demanding tests was criticized by many politicians in Ottawa and even Shortt's co-commissioner, Michel G. La Rochelle. Nevertheless, Adam, always a stubborn man, prevailed, and the harder examinations, which eventually led to the creation of a well-educated

Dominion bureaucracy,[236] remained a permanent feature of the federal civil service. This salient victory was won only at a high personal cost for its creator. Many members of parliament had resented Shortt's movement from the university setting into their world of practical politics. Now these hard-headed politicians contended that the personal interaction traditionally furnished by the patronage system was a more reliable method of selecting able civil servants than Adam's impersonal examinations.[237] Not long after his arrival in Ottawa, Adam confided in his diary that he "felt tired, seedy and discouraged with the amount of work the battles to fight and the slight effective support."[238]

However, in 1910, Shortt was still optimistic that he could accomplish a major reform of the national public service. He even spelled out his future plans in a 1910 interview with the Toronto *Globe*: "classification of the thousands of civil servants, [revising] the regulations for promotion, the working out of new courses of study for the competitive examinations, the method of choice in cases where academic tests are obviously inapplicable [and] the inclusion of the outside service" within the mandate of the Civil Service Commission.[239] The last item was especially urgent for Adam.

The cautious renovation of the public service by the Laurier ministry in 1908 was severely limited in scope. The bill only brought the "inside service" under the purview of the new administrative body. Thus, the initiatives of the two-man commission would merely affect "roughly those involved in headquarters positions as well as a few key officials in other locations. The great majority of civil servants remained under the older and much more arbitrary procedures that dated back to the era of Confederation."[240] If the Civil Service Commission was to introduce substantial change, it had to have the power to deal with the entire federal bureaucracy stationed throughout the country.

By 1911, Shortt was able to convince the ministry that this and the other problems outlined in 1910 deserved to be investigated more thoroughly. In specific terms, he suggested a four-nation tour of Europe so that he could personally examine the civil services of those countries.[241] A devoted empiricist, Adam sought data from public servants in the Old World so that he could repair Canada's ailing bureaucracy across the ocean. When Shortt procured financial and diplomatic support from his government for this task, the basis for the readings that follow began to take shape. Once Elizabeth Shortt convinced her husband that she should join him on the excursion, the stage was set for a more comprehensive reporting of this interesting and meaningful visit to Europe.

FIG. 3 Copesworth, the Shortts' comfortable middle-class home in Kingston. Courtesy of University of Waterloo Library, Special Collections & Archives, Elizabeth Smith Shortt fonds (WA10, file 2304, house in Kingston).

For Adam, the move from Kingston to Ottawa created a number of serious problems, as well as new opportunities. The same assessment could be made about Elizabeth Shortt's relocation in the nation's capital. By 1908, two of the couple's three children were away at schools outside of Ottawa, but Mrs. Shortt remained the more active parent, who looked after all the progeny as well as an elaborate household.[242] These responsibilities had led to financial distress in Kingston, and a similar result took place in the capital of the Dominion. The new job in Ottawa provided the Shortts with a much higher salary,[243] and the 1911 federal census recorded an income of $5,000 per annum.[244] However, the family's expenses in Ottawa increased at a still more alarming rate, and their habit of spending considerably more money than they brought in remained a fundamental problem for the household.

Both Adam and Elizabeth believed that the former's enhanced standing in the central government necessitated much greater expenditures: "Their status required even more outward show when Adam was appointed Civil Service Commissioner in 1908. He did not expect to be merely one more senior civil servant, for he was pioneering a new independent role, paid at the level of the most important Deputy Ministers.... Shortt believed

5 Marlborough Ave. 1934 Ottawa

FIG. 4   5 Marlborough Avenue, the more opulent residence in Ottawa that Adam and Elizabeth built. It later appropriately became the Swiss Embassy (see chapter 4). Courtesy of University of Waterloo Library, Special Collections & Archives, Elizabeth Smith Shortt fonds (WA10, file 2304, 5 Marlborough Ave., Ottawa).

himself to be head of an independent administrative body and more or less equal in importance to the Speaker of the House. In 1908, Ottawa was an expensive town for a man with these ideas."[245]

The exorbitant outlay for maintaining such a perspective was immediately apparent when the Shortts decided to construct a new house at 5 Marlborough Avenue. They bought a large lot, with a splendid view of the Rideau River, from Robert Borden, the leader of the opposition. The initial transaction "cost them more than the entire Kingston estate." The residence which they proceeded to erect on the property also displayed little concern for fiscal responsibility. The structure was "massive,"[246] and it later became and remains the embassy of the Swiss government in Ottawa. The mortgage was not paid off until the late 1920s, and the property taxes alone consumed almost ten per cent of Adam's salary in 1911.[247] McLaren justifiably concludes that the Shortts were again spending much more than they should have on housing.[248]

The Shortts were continuing their spendthrift habits in their efforts to associate with Ottawa's upper classes. However, the price of such social pretensions was much higher than it had been in the smaller city of Kingston. For example, Elizabeth and Adam were founding members of the Rivermead Golf Club, where they socialized with Ottawa's rich and famous. Elizabeth regularly attended a whirl of social events, which enabled her to interact with many women belonging to the most powerful families in the Dominion capital, such as Lady Aberdeen, Lady Laurier, and Lady Borden. As she looked back on this era, Mrs. Shortt fondly remembered that on several occasions she entertained their husbands, as well: "many interesting people [e.g., Sir Wilfrid Laurier, Sir Robert Borden, Sir George Foster, and Sir Clifford Sifton] were here and Sun[day] afternoons at 5 Marlborough became known to quite a few as a place to meet people." Elizabeth and Adam had always desired to mingle with the upper echelons of high society. This longing was largely fulfilled in Ottawa, where they persuaded the political, social, and economic elites that they were worthy friends. Unfortunately, this social snobbery also created financial insecurity for the couple and their family.[249]

On the other end of the social scale, Mrs. Shortt encountered severe problems with the servants who worked for the family in their fashionable home. From April 1910 to July 1916, no less than four domestics were employed there. Elizabeth regularly criticized their performance, "sometimes referring to them as animals."[250] In Ottawa, as well as Kingston, Mrs. Shortt could not seem to extend her keen sense of justice, which flowed naturally out of her commitment to women's equality, to the female help within her own household.

Such contradictions were common among middle-class women in early-twentieth-century Canada, and did not deter Shortt from pursuing her feminist objectives after arriving in Ottawa. Being in the federal capital placed Elizabeth at the centre of the struggle for the reforms that feminists were seeking to introduce on both the national and local levels of government.[251] In response to this challenge, Dr. Shortt thrived as a speaker, organizer, and club executive. Ultimately, she was much more successful than her husband in obtaining the public goals that had originally drawn the couple to Ottawa. One woman's magazine employing a measure of hyperbole declared that "Mrs. Shortt is the master mind amongst Canada's public women."[252] Whether this was literally true or not, there is no doubt that she was a major force in the NCWC soon after relocating in Ottawa. Eventually, Elizabeth became an inspiring model for younger recruits to this notable social feminist organization. "In her failure to practice her profession very long after marriage, Shortt may have heralded the entry of a slightly different type of member in Council affairs. This member, characterized here as 'the professional clubwoman,' was a decade or more younger than Shortt but she too was middle-class, university-trained, married and uninvolved in the paid labour force.... Although her club career peaked in the later 1920s and 1930s, 'the professional clubwoman' began to appear in strength about the time of the Great War."[253]

Some of the reforms that Elizabeth fostered in Ottawa were simply extensions of the causes she had initiated in Kingston. For example, she remained devoted to the campaign to eradicate tuberculosis throughout Canada. Now, however, her personal efforts became more successful, because she could work with other leaders who shared this commitment in the nation's capital. Charlotte Whitton observed that Dr. Shortt was a pivotal figure within the Anti-Tuberculosis League in Ottawa, which eventually led to the founding of the powerful Canadian Tuberculosis Association on the national level.[254]

However, Elizabeth was never content to limit herself to a single cause. Soon after arriving in Ottawa, she began agitating for two further improvements in the public health sector: the purification of both milk and water. Here Dr. Shortt, as *Saturday Night* magazine later acknowledged, was able to apply her medical training to practical social issues.[255] Her influence was strengthened in 1910, when she became the convenor of the NCWC's Public Health Committee, and she vividly denounced the growing problem of water pollution in no uncertain terms: "We have done the most astounding thing that a civilized and enlightened country in a century of preventive medicine could have done—we have emptied the sewage of our cities into the source of our drinking water."[256] By 1911, Shortt's drive to counteract milk and water contamination had not produced tangible results. However, she sowed the seeds of change, which helped to improve milk quality before the decade had ended. For example, in early 1914, Elizabeth used her influence within both the NCWC and the local anti-tuberculosis forces to present a petition to the federal government demanding an end to the distribution of milk from tuberculin cows. The Borden government enacted such legislation in May 1914.[257] Dr. Shortt had demonstrated her abilities as a lobbyist and networking activist at both the national and local levels.

On 1 March 1910, Mrs. Shortt delivered a lecture on hygiene to the parents and teachers of an Ottawa public school. In this address, she advocated for significant changes in the dress habits of Canadian women, which echoed her mother's previous calls for healthier forms of female attire. A year before, Mrs. Damaris McGee Smith, in a memoir on her pioneering life in Upper Canada, complained that the long dresses required of farm wives living amid primitive conditions on the frontier were "a few inches too long for cleanliness." She hoped this pernicious fashion would soon be abandoned. Mrs. Smith further denounced the use of tight corsets and high heels among the popular clothing options of the day.[258]

In her March 1910 speech, Elizabeth made certain that her mother's plea for a more progressive, more salubrious wardrobe for women would continue to occupy a place on the contemporary feminist agenda. Thus, Dr. Shortt decried the long dresses that were still common among many women at this time, since "no [better] carrier of bacilli, germs &c. could well be found than the trailing skirt in the street which is worn home and shaken off in the house." Shortt then attacked the contemporary use of tight waistbands, tight shoes, garters, and corsets, which led to unhealthy and unnatural contortions of the female figure. High heels were also condemned, as she employed her powerful sense of description to promote the cause: "Nature gave no indication that she needed high heeled shoes to complete the bodily machine and yet there are people who try to do their walking &c. with narrow pegs under each heel." Elizabeth ended her talk with a final appeal to undertake these reforms for religious as well as medical reasons. "But in order to develop that bit of the Eternal enshrouded in our mortal bodies, to its highest possible [extent], we must keep the body to its highest physical best."[259] As a feminist reformer, Shortt was continuing to respond to the message of the Social Gospel, as well as her scientific training in the medical field. She was also answering the social feminist appeal to maintain close relationships with other women, which for Beth originally emanated from an intimacy with her mother.

In dealing with dress modifications, Shortt was taking a very liberal stand. This was also true of another social change with which she became involved soon after her move to Ottawa: the creation of secure and properly equipped playgrounds for children. Here Mrs. Shortt was primarily motivated by the strong maternal aspects of the social feminist program of this era, and especially a mother's natural desire to obtain safe areas where her children could play. These benefits would particularly aid lower-class children. For example, Elizabeth pointed out that public playgrounds significantly counteracted the growing problem of juvenile delinquency in the Dominion capital.[260] As we have seen, Shortt sometimes expressed a social snobbery. However, her efforts to secure legislative changes generally extended to all classes, and many of these reforms were mainly relevant to the underclass.

In 1908, Mrs. Shortt joined others in founding the Ottawa Playground Association, which regularly lobbied city council to establish publicly supported playgrounds. Once more, very little was achieved before 1911. However, in 1912, the municipal government in Ottawa granted the Association access to a public park in the city where a playground could be established. Nevertheless, the Association was left with the costly problem of actually building the playground and supervising its operations.

The ever-resourceful Dr. Shortt employed her social connections with Ottawa's elites, such as the governor general, the Duke of Connaught, and the lumber baron, J. R. Booth, to secure the necessary funds. The project proved to be an instant success during the summer of 1912. By the following year, the municipal government was eager to assume responsibility for the popular enterprise and soon further playgrounds were being planned throughout the city.[261] Thus, Elizabeth played a pivotal role in securing social facilities that were essential to providing healthy childhoods, especially for Ottawa's less fortunate youngsters. Whitton has summarized well Shortt's ultimate contribution in this regard: "Worried by the deteriorating housing and the slums Ottawa's growth were breeding, Mrs. Shortt brought about the first supervised playground here, the nucleus of the City's present extensive public recreation system."[262]

All these campaigns for change reflected the Protestant, middle-class, and moderately reformist tendencies of the NCWC, with which Shortt became closely associated during her residence in Ottawa. As one journal put it not long afterward, "it would be well nigh impossible to imagine the National Council of Women without her."[263] But there was also a more conservative side to Elizabeth's feminist activism in the federal capital. Like her husband, Mrs. Shortt mixed conservative and liberal ingredients in producing her own unique and independent formula for social modification. This was evident in her reluctance to publicly support the increasingly popular movement for female suffrage in Canada.

McLaren argues that Shortt had privately backed "the desirability of the female population having the vote for at least 29 years before she actually took a public stand on the issue in January, 1913."[264] This position was understandable until the NCWC endorsed women's suffrage at its annual meeting in 1910.[265] As the principal historian of this social feminist organization has noted, "the Council was at best cautiously feminist. Policies were devised to elicit the broadest possible support among Canada's respectable community."[266] When Mrs. Shortt refused to approve publicly the NCWC's support of female voting rights for more than two years, she was, indeed, upholding an ultra-conservative opinion within the feminist movement.

Shortt also worked with other organizations in Ottawa that might be considered still more traditional than the "cautiously feminist" NCWC. Soon after Elizabeth arrived in the Dominion capital, she became president of the Mothers' Union. During her visit to England in 1911, Mrs. Shortt would have memorable visits with representatives of the Mothers' Union in the country where that association had been initially founded in 1876. Her November 1910 presidential address at the Rideau Hall residence of the governor general's wife emphasized the group's commitment to traditional values, such as "the sanctity of marriage [and] a sense of great responsibility in the training of boys and girls, the future fathers and mothers of the empire." Shortt was pleased to report that only 431 divorces had transpired in Canada since Confederation, while during the same period one million had occurred within the United States.[267]

However, such sanguine facts, the president warned, should not lead to complacency. Even within the conventional Mothers' Union, she argued for moderate reforms. Thus, Dr. Shortt urged the association's members to work for more effective medical inspections in the public schools, and adequate milk for infants, so that the high death rate of babies in Ottawa could be sharply reduced. When she stressed the need for a crèche, or daycare centre, in the city, Shortt was immediately informed by another participant at the meeting, a Miss Pierce of Ottawa's Settlement House, that her employer would open such a facility in a matter of days. Miss Pierce added that the service would especially help the poorer "children in thickly populated portions of Lower Town," since their parents would only pay "the small fee of five cents [per day] for each child." Thus this reform, like so many others advocated by Elizabeth, would primarily benefit the needy. Finally, Shortt utilized the immediate enthusiasm of the gathering to obtain additional forms of financial support for the enterprise. For example, "Lady Davies kindly signified her willingness to open her home for a drawing room concert to be given to augment the funds with which to conduct the new chreche [sic]." Utilizing wealthy contacts, a conservative tendency, had once more aided Elizabeth's pursuit of social improvements.[268]

During her first three years in Ottawa, Shortt combined liberal and conservative values as she defined her own distinctive interpretation of the Social Gospel. Her achievements are particularly impressive when one considers that Mrs. Shortt performed these tasks while remaining in charge of the family household and the requirements of the couple's three children.

By 1911, Mrs. Shortt had emerged as a major player in Ottawa's feminist movement, which exerted influence throughout Canada.

Mr. Shortt was encountering serious obstacles in his plan to fundamentally restructure the Dominion civil service, but he too was confident in 1911 that this ultimate objective could be attained. Indeed, a concern for such alterations furnished the pivotal reason for his trip to Europe. Moreover, 1911 saw a number of personal triumphs for Adam. He received an honorary doctorate from his beloved alma mater, Queen's University. There was now a second doctor in the Shortt family. He was also pleased to receive the honour of the C.M.G. (Companion of the Order of St. Michael and St. George) from King George V, who was about to be crowned in London. Finally, the Royal Society of Canada bestowed on him the J. B. Tyrell Historical Medal. It was a recognition that Dr. Shortt was, by this time, "well known throughout the Dominion as an author and historian."[269]

In 1911, Adam Shortt had reached the apex of his personal powers and influence. Elizabeth had also emerged as a potent force in the movement for women's rights within the strategic city of Ottawa. It was only natural that their commentaries on an important trip to Europe would become valuable documents in the cultural history of Canada during this period.

In my research for this book, two archives were especially significant in supplying resources and advice. The vast collection of materials in the Elizabeth Smith Shortt Papers, which are available at the Doris Lewis Room in the University of Waterloo's Dana Porter Arts Library, provided the project's single most important wellspring. The elaborate fonds was donated by Muriel Clark and Lorraine Shortt, the daughters of Adam and Elizabeth Shortt. It was received by the library in the fall of 1965; additional materials arrived the following year. Muriel Clark's papers were added to the collection in 1974.

Mrs. Shortt's diary from the 1911 visit to Europe is by no means her only form of writing within these extensive papers. For example, another diary gives parallel coverage of an earlier visit to the Old World in 1892, on which she was accompanied by the radical feminist, Alice Chown, as well as Adam. Her lifelong dedication to a lively correspondence was conducted with other significant figures during her early life, such as her mother, brothers, and sisters, as well as a spirited exchange of love letters with Adam while he pursued his studies in Scotland. Further notable correspondents in the later period include Augusta Stowe-Gullen, Dr. Jenny Trout, and Lady Aberdeen—and, of course, her two daughters, Muriel and Lorraine. The fonds also contain fifteen manuscript diaries authored by Elizabeth between 1872 and 1932, and around fifty manuscript addresses, reports, and speeches made by her throughout her adult years.

In the study that follows, Elizabeth's diaries furnished the principal source, along with letters that she wrote to her mother (who resided in Hamilton with Beth's sister, Gertrude) and the couple's three children in Ottawa. A few letters that Adam wrote to their children, while his wife convalesced after her serious eye operation, are also presented here. In general, the letters bring out personal touches, which are not as evident in the diary entries. There is a danger, of course, that such personal references will distract the reader from the more objective accounts in both Elizabeth's and Adam's diaries. Moreover, some of the details in the letters may appear esoteric and repetitive. Where the latter impediment became pronounced, I have sought to delete the redundant passages. However, in general, I thought the letters shed considerable insight on the diaries, and especially their context, and therefore merited publication in this volume.

Of course, Adam's diaries are reproduced here, as well. They were furnished by the equally obliging archives of Queen's University, which originally obtained them as part of Shortt's extensive fonds, which Mrs. Shortt donated to that institution soon after her husband's death in 1931. In 1959, Muriel Clark supplemented these documents with further records that her father had compiled. It will become obvious that Adam's diary entries are considerably more brief than Elizabeth's. Nevertheless, his commentary frequently offered significant insight into his wife's lengthier accounts. Moreover, presenting the perceptions of both Shortts gives this study a family dimension not often found in the life-writing field, making it particularly relevant to those interested in family history. Employing both diaries also facilitates our comprehension of gender differences between wife and husband. The family perspective is further reinforced by the sizeable number of letters sent by Elizabeth and Adam to their children during their travels abroad.

When one compares the writings of Adam and Elizabeth, gender implications become evident. The former's numerous articles and books were an integral part of his full-time academic career. Moreover, new publications appeared even after he assumed the massive responsibilities of a civil service commissioner in Ottawa. But Mrs. Shortt could not even think in such terms. Her full-time commitment as a wife and mother removed such thoughts from the realm of possibility. She made this evident in a letter to her dear friend and confidant, Isabel Skelton, who was dealing with a similar problem in her own marital life: "Whenever I set to work to write even a report ... I want a place & time I can concentrate on it. That is where the men have the advantage—i.e. when they are literary professionals—since they have no thousand humdrum details of sheets & towels & underwear & soup bones & salads to think of."[270]

Nevertheless, she remained devoted to a part-time activism as a feminist social reformer, an engagement that acquired much larger dimensions after the Shortts relocated in the national capital. This was reflected in her published writings, though the latter became much more copious during the post-1911 stage of her feminist pursuits.

The most notable publication in the early period was the pamphlet version of her 1907 speech to the NCWC, in which she exposed the dangers of tuberculosis and suggested methods to combat this dreaded disease. Soon afterward, Elizabeth emerged as a major figure in Ottawa's fight against TB and a respected medical authority within the feminist ranks. Shortt had assumed a prominence on the national stage that she would maintain for a long time to come.

Two further articles were published before 1911 that demonstrate other interests in her more specific campaign for women's rights. The first was a letter to the *Montreal Star* in March 1895. She began by correcting a speech by a Mrs. Carus-Wilson, reported in that newspaper back in January, which included the contention that only Bishop's College in Quebec currently granted medical degrees to women in Canada. Dr. Shortt pointed out that the Ontario Medical College for Women, with an annual enrolment of over forty students, had been supplying training for female physicians since it opened in 1893.

Elizabeth then censured those females in the upper class who categorically rejected medicine as an unfeminine pursuit. Like her husband, Mrs. Shortt could also display a highly caustic tone when confronting her antagonists: "It is not the woman who is simply 'a mirror of her social time and place' whose faith in her sex is strongest, but the woman who thinks for herself and whose plan of life is stamped by individuality and character. There is some reason for smiling when one hears women who can appear without even a strap over the shoulder at assembly or ball descant virtuously on the unwomanliness and indelicacy of women studying medicine—and almost without exception they do."[271] Shortt was drawn to many women in the upper class, but she was also highly critical of others, as the above comments reveal in no uncertain terms.

A second publication by Elizabeth appeared in the journal *Westminister* in August 1900. Once more she turned to the subject of women in education, and began her article with an ardent plea for feminist initiatives in this field: "Here and there women have been proving restive for years but felt that anything but quiet leavening of the lump of conservatism would be resented. Now so many women have been able to signal to each other that they have taken courage and have come to the forward stage of asking for some special remedies for special needs."[272]

Here the "special need" was the introduction of domestic science classes for girls at the public school level. In 1898, Mrs. Shortt was responsible for introducing such courses into Kingston's YWCA. Now she wanted them to become an integral part of the public school curriculum throughout Ontario. She strengthened her case with two convincing arguments. First, Shortt employed an equal-rights view, noting that a technical school for boys had already been established in Toronto, and four more were about to be launched in other urban centres of the province. Elizabeth logically asserted that such vocational education should be available for girls as well as boys.

Elizabeth argued further that training in domestic sciences would also prepare many young women for their future roles as wives and mothers within a family setting. She had no intention of challenging the male monopoly of the breadwinner's position in society, as another comment in the article revealed. "Make housekeeping and home-making more of an art, and fit the girls a little for the office nature and Mrs. Grundy desire them to fill."[273] Elizabeth was not generally a radical in her approach to gender relations, and she astutely closed her paper with a practical appeal for local school boards to enact the desired change.[274]

Elizabeth Smith Shortt accepted the main political, economic, social, and gender assumptions of her times. However, she was also determined to "hasten" the educational opportunities available to women, young and old, which would serve as a foundation for a gradual but steady liberation among women. And this social feminist would fight vigorously for many other reforms, such as the eradication of tuberculosis, which would more generally benefit society. In the period before 1911, her publications were slender, especially when compared with the massive outpourings of her husband. Nevertheless, Mrs. Shortt's writings introduced an agenda no less important than that of the civil service commissioner.

In order that the couple's words might be presented as originally written, I have sought to revise their texts as little as possible. However, several alterations seemed necessary in the interests of grammar, readability, and clarification. Therefore, I have provided conventional punctuation where such was not present. For example, in Mrs. Shortt's letter of 30 January, commas were substituted for the hyphens that she employed in the first sentence. Some apostrophes were introduced when the Shortts did not furnish them (e.g., Elizabeth's use of "doesnt" in the first sentence of her letter of 12 June), or to indicate the possessive case (e.g., her reference to "Mrs. Elders account" in the final sentence of Beth's diary entry of 1 July).

I have also italicized some foreign phrases that the Shortts did not acknowledge properly (e.g., Mrs. Shortt's reference to the "diner d'Adieu" in the last sentence of her diary remarks of 4 July) and translated others to provide greater clarity for the reader (e.g., the Latin phrase she employs in her diary on 7 August). Paragraph divisions were created on a number of occasions where they seemed appropriate (e.g., in Elizabeth's letter of 12 June, in which no paragraphs originally appeared). As mentioned previously, needless repetition was also avoided whenever possible. For example, in Beth's letter to her mother and sister of 3 July (which is presented in the material on 8 July), she repeats information about the Shortts' socializing with the Doughtys, Lord Percy, and Mrs. Ewart on the *Royal George*, which she had already mentioned in a previous diary entry.

More specifically, on occasion the material had to be chronologically reordered. For example, the comments in Mrs. Shortt's diary for 3 July were altered so that they preceded rather than followed the remarks for 4 July (they were reversed in the original manuscript). A few sentences that were not grammatically complete were joined to prior or subsequent statements where such links seemed pertinent. In Beth's diary for 10 August, her reference to "the sloping shores & many villas & the towering mountains beyond," etc., was initially presented as a separate sentence, lacking a verb. Therefore, I connected it to the previous sentence after adding a colon.

Sometimes I set letters, words, and phrases within brackets to define more lucidly a particular setting. For example, the recognition of Mr. Forin as the "sec[retary] to the [Civil Service] Commission" in Mrs. Shortt's diary for 27 June was inserted to provide greater precision. Some obvious errors in context, such as Elizabeth's citation of "6th Aug." at the outset of her diary entry for 22 July, were corrected in a parenthesis and then further clarified in an endnote. Some of Beth's letters also contained sentences on the side or very beginning of a page, which did not belong there.

Finally, I used "*sic*" to indicate grammatical and spelling errors in the original manuscripts, while the term "illegible," in brackets, reveals words or phrases that could not be deciphered. I and others who helped me have laboured long and hard to minimize the latter as much as possible. Misspellings of names were rectified, whenever possible, in endnotes.

Occasionally a single letter was added within brackets to adjust a misspelling (e.g., the frequent mentions of Dr. Flem[m]ing in Mrs. Shortt's writings).

While all of the above changes were employed to clarify various contexts for the reader, none were allowed knowingly to alter their meaning. The Shortts generally wrote in a lucid, informative, and entertaining fashion, and one of my primary concerns has been to retain the value and integrity of such cherished documents. I can only hope at this point that I have succeeded in this essential task.

I further contemplated the inclusion of comments on the lives and accomplishments of Adam and Elizabeth in the period after 1911. However, my main purpose in this volume has been to focus on the primary materials being presented. Any attempt to cover the post-1911 era would have been either so brief and general as to be virtually meaningless, or so long and detailed that it would probably distract the reader from my principal intention. This is particularly true with regard to the later life of Elizabeth Shortt. She lived another thirty-eight years after her 1911 trip to Europe, and in the 1930s and 1940s remained, as McLaren puts it, "Not 'A Nice Old Lady,'" whose story even in these late stages required some forty-eight pages to tell.[275]

Thus, I have remained content to deal with the Shortts only up to their European trip in 1911. There are other documents and topics awaiting future scholars, and I heartily recommend visits to the libraries at Waterloo and Queen's to pursue such interests. Meanwhile, in this book I confine my coverage to Elizabeth and Adam's 1911 journey to the Old World. I trust that others will enjoy and benefit from their experiences and observations as much as I did. *Bon voyage*.

Notes

1 Elizabeth Smith, *"A Woman with a Purpose": The Diaries of Elizabeth Smith 1872–1884*, ed. Veronica Strong-Boag (Toronto: University of Toronto Press, 1980), xiii. Strong-Boag is being cited here; see also Alison Prentice et al., *Canadian Women: A History*, 2nd ed. (Toronto: Harcourt Brace Canada, 1996), 163–64.

2 Bruce W. Bowden, *Adam Shortt* (Ph.D. diss., University of Toronto, 1979), 4, 8.

3 Bowden, *Adam Shortt*, 6–8.

4 S. E. D. Shortt, *The Search for an Ideal: Six Canadian Intellectuals and Their Convictions in an Age of Transition 1890–1930* (Toronto: University of Toronto Press, 1976), 96.

5 Barry Ferguson, *Remaking Liberalism: The Intellectual Legacy of Adam Shortt, O. D. Skelton, W. C. Clark, and W. A. Mackintosh, 1890–1925* (Montreal: McGill-Queen's University Press, 1993), 13.

6 Bowden, *Adam Shortt*, 3, 15, and 22–23.

7 Adam Shortt, cited in Ferguson, *Remaking Liberalism*, 46.

8 University of Waterloo, Elizabeth Smith Shortt Papers (hereafter cited as ESSP), WA10, file 2242, "Two Worthy Men."

9 Terry Crowley, *Marriage of Minds: Isabel and Oscar Skelton Reinventing Canada* (Toronto: University of Toronto Press, 2003), 58.

10 Doug Owram, *The Government Generation: Canadian Intellectuals and the State 1900–1945* (Toronto: University of Toronto Press, 1986), 274.

11 Peter J. Bowler, *Evolution: The History of an Idea*, rev. ed. (Berkeley: University of California Press, 1989), 17, 233.

12 A. B. McKillop, *A Disciplined Intelligence: Critical Inquiry and Canadian Thought in the Victorian Era* (Montreal: McGill-Queen's University Press, 1979), 138 and 137–41.

13 Robert C. Sibley, *Northern Spirits: John Watson, George Grant and Charles Taylor—Appropriations of Hegelian Political Thought* (Montreal: McGill-Queen's University Press, 2008), 42–43.

14 McKillop, *A Disciplined Intelligence*, 217.

15 For an explanation of Spencer's idea of evolution, see Bowler, *Evolution*, 237–41.

16 McKillop, *A Disciplined Intelligence*, 191; see also Suzanne Zeller, "Environment, Culture, and the Reception of Darwin in Canada, 1858–1909," in *Disseminating Darwinism: The Role of Place, Race, Religion, and Gender*, ed. Ronald L. Numbers and John Stenhouse (Cambridge: Cambridge University Press, 1999), 108.

17 Bowden, *Adam Shortt*, 21, 22.

18 A. B. McKillop, *Matters of Mind: The University in Ontario, 1791–1951* (Toronto: University of Toronto Press, 1994), 201, 21, 129.

19 Smith, "*A Woman with a Purpose*," 292.

20 Peter E. Paul Dembski, "Jenny Kidd Trout and the Founding of the Women's Medical Colleges at Kingston and Toronto," *Ontario History* LXXVII (1985): 192, 194–95.

21 Prentice et al., *Canadian Women*, 174; see also McKillop, *Matters of Mind*, 132.

22 Dembski, "Jenny Kidd Trout," 183.

23 Sean W. Gouglas, "A Currant Affair: E. D. Smith and Agricultural Change in Nineteenth-Century Saltfleet Township, Ontario," *Agricultural History* 75 (2001): 442.

24 ESSP, WA10, file 2258, Damaris McGee Smith, "Pioneer Wife," September 1944, 3 (originally published in 1909).

25 *Silas Smith, U.E.L., and His Descendants*, compiled by R. Janet Powell from history collected by Miss Gertrude Smith and other descendants (n.p., n.d.), 21. This work is available in the Doris Lewis Rare Book Room of the Dana Porter Library at the University of Waterloo.

26 Sheryl Stotts McLaren, *Becoming Indispensable: A Biography of Elizabeth Smith Shortt 1859–1949* (Ph.D. diss., York University, 2001), 42, 56.

27 *Silas Smith*, 52.

28 McLaren, *Becoming Indispensable*, 42.

29 Smith, "*A Woman with a Purpose*," 219, 184.

30 Smith, "*A Woman with a Purpose*," xxii.

31 Jenny Trout, cited in Smith, "*A Woman with a Purpose*," xxv.

32 A. A. Travill, "Early Medical Co-Education and Women's Medical College Kingston Ontario 1880–1894," *Historic Kingston* 30 (1982): 71. Shadrach, Meshach, and Abednego were three Jewish officials of King Nebuchadnezzar of Babylonia. According to chapter 3 of the biblical Book of Daniel, the three refused to worship a gold statue established by their ruler. They were consequently sent to die in a blazing furnace, but were saved by the miraculous intervention of the Hebrew God and his angelic delegates. The king recognized the special status of Jehovah and promoted his three disciples to more important positions within his own realm.

33 McLaren, *Becoming Indispensable*, 55.

34 Smith, "*A Woman with a Purpose*," 297–98.

35 Andrew Haydon, "Adam Shortt," *Queen's Quarterly* XXXVIII (1931): 611.

36 W. A. Mackintosh, "Adam Shortt, 1959–1931," *Canadian Journal of Economics and Political Science* IV (1938): 165; see also Haydon, "Adam Shortt," 611.

37 Bowden, *Adam Shortt*, 35.

38 Ferguson, *Remaking Liberalism*, 13.

39 S. E. D. Shortt, *The Search for an Ideal*, 102; see also ibid., 107.

40 Bowden, *Adam Shortt*, 50–51.

41 S. E. D. Shortt, *The Search for an Ideal*, 97.

42 Ferguson, *Remaking Liberalism*, 14.

43 S. E. D. Shortt, *The Search for an Ideal*, 97.

44 McLaren, *Becoming Indispensable*, 150–52.

45 Elizabeth Smith, cited in McLaren, *Becoming Indispensable*, 168.

46 McLaren, *Becoming Indispensable*, 186, 190.

47 McLaren, *Becoming Indispensable*, 172, 186, 188, 190, 192.

48 Alvin Finkel and Margaret Conrad, *History of the Canadian Peoples: 1867 to the Present*, vol. II, 3rd ed. (Toronto: Addison Wesley Longman, 2002), 12.

49 Adam Shortt, cited in McLaren, *Becoming Indispensable*, 182–83.

50 McLaren, *Becoming Indispensable*, 183, 188–90.

51 Prentice et al., *Canadian Women*, 175.

52 McLaren uses the term "career" to describe the activist dimensions of Smith Shortt's life; McLaren, *Becoming Indispensable*, 167, 199, 265, 438–39. This term is generally accurate, but it needs to be qualified as "part-time" to distinguish it from the full-time opportunities available to many contemporary males, such as her husband Adam, as McLaren acknowledges; ibid., 238.

53 McKillop, *A Disciplined Intelligence*, 217.

54 McLaren, *Becoming Indispensable*, 188.

55 George M. Grant, cited in McKillop, *A Disciplined Intelligence*, 217.

56 McLaren, *Becoming Indispensable*, 439; see n. 52 and Prentice et al., *Canadian Women*, 164.

57 Haydon, "Adam Shortt," 613.

58 Ferguson, *Remaking Liberalism*, 124.

59 McKillop, *A Disciplined Intelligence*, 218.

60 Richard Allen, *The Social Passion: Religion and Social Reform in Canada 1914–28* (Toronto: University of Toronto Press, 1971), 17.

61 Smith, "*A Woman with a Purpose*," 252.

62 Owram, *The Government Generation*, 66.

63 Adam Shortt, cited in Owram, *The Government Generation*, 44.

64 Owram, *The Government Generation*, 66.

65 Naomi Black, *Social Feminism* (Ithaca: Cornell University Press, 1989), 1.

66 Prentice et al., *Canadian Women*, 190.

67 Black, *Social Feminism*, 53.

68 Black, *Social Feminism*, 11.

69 Prentice et al., *Canadian Women*, 190, 189.

70 McLaren, *Becoming Indispensable*, 197.

71 "Famous Kingstonians Abroad," *Kingston British Whig*, 20 May 1920.

72 Travill, "Early Medical Co-Education," 85.

73 ESSP, WA10, file 2065.

74 Travill, "Early Medical Co-Education," 83.

75 ESSP, WA10, file 2055.

76 Bowden, *Adam Shortt*, 269.

77 McLaren, *Becoming Indispensable*, 198–99, 236.

78 McLaren, *Becoming Indispensable*, 214, 198. See n. 52.

79 McLaren, *Becoming Indispensable*, 220–28, 232–41.

80 Marilyn Barber, *Immigrant Domestic Servants in Canada* (Ottawa: Canadian Historical Association, 1991), 8, 4.

81 McLaren, *Becoming Indispensable*, 224.

82 ESSP, WA10, file 493, Smith Shortt to Muriel Clarke, n.d. [2 September 1911].

83 McLaren, *Becoming Indispensable*, 107, 206–7, 213; see also Bowden, *Adam Shortt*, 269.

84 McLaren, *Becoming Indispensable*, 205–6, 212.

85 Bowden, *Adam Shortt*, 91.

86 Ferguson, *Remaking Liberalism*, 57.

87 Richard Allen, *The View from Murray Tower: Salem Bland, the Late Victorian Controversies, and the Search for a New Christianity* (Toronto: University of Toronto Press, 2008), 213, 217.

88 McLaren, *Becoming Indispensable*, 170, 271, 229.

89 Barber, *Immigrant Domestic Servants*, 27.

90 Mary Hallett and Marilyn Davis, *Firing the Heather: The Life and Times of Nellie McClung* (Saskatoon: Fifth House Publishers, 1993), 76–77, 216–20.

91 Deborah Gorham, "Flora MacDonald Denison: Canadian Feminist," in *A Not Unreasonable Claim: Women and Reform in Canada, 1880s–1920s*, ed. Linda Kealey (Toronto: Women's Press, 1979), 54–55.

92 Veronica Jane Strong-Boag, *"The Parliament of Women": The National Council of Women of Canada 1893–1929* (Ottawa: National Museums of Canada, 1976), 160.

93 McLaren, *Becoming Indispensable*, 170.

94 "Mrs. Shortt Leads Canadian Women in National Thought," *Everywoman's World*, January 1918, and Charlotte Whitton, "Dr. Elizabeth Shortt Played a Great Part," *Ottawa Evening Citizen*, 15 January 1949.

95 *Ottawa Evening Citizen*, 11 October 1941.

96 Crowley, *Marriage of Minds*, 16.

97 McKillop, *Matters of Mind*, 146.

98 Strong-Boag, "*The Parliament of Women*," 129.

99 *Ottawa Evening Citizen*, 11 October 1941.

100 105 Alice A. Chown, *The Stairway*, introduction by Diana Chown (Toronto: University of Toronto Press, 1988), xv.

101 Isabel Skelton, cited in Crowley, *Marriage of Minds*, 34.

102 Prentice et al., *Canadian Women*, 198; see also Strong-Boag, "*The Parliament of Women*," 64.

103 Prentice et al., *Canadian Women*, 197.

104 Elizabeth Shortt, cited in McLaren, *Becoming Indispensable*, 244.

105 Terry Crowley "Madonnas before Magdelenes: Adelaide Hoodless and the Making of the Canadian Gibson Girl," *Canadian Historical Review* 67 (1986): 520–47.

106 Elizabeth Shortt, cited in *Daily Whig* (Kingston), 5 May 1898.

107 McLaren, *Becoming Indispensable*, 251.

108 McLaren, *Becoming Indispensable*, 248.

109 Strong-Boag, "*The Parliament of Women*," vii, 2.

110 Prentice et al., *Canadian Women*, 203.

111 McLaren, *Becoming Indispensable*, 254, 256, 257.

112 ESSP, WA10, file 2150, "Address to the National Council of Canadian Women, 1907."

113 McLaren, *Becoming Indispensable*, 259.

114 ESSP, WA10, file 2246, clipping from a "Hamilton newspaper in 1908."

115 Jean Graham, "Representative Canadian Women: Mrs. Adam Shortt," *The Globe* (Toronto), 23 November 1912.

116 ESSP, WA10, file 2246, clipping from a "Hamilton newspaper in 1908."

117 S. E. D. Shortt, *The Search for an Ideal*, 63.

118 McKillop, *Matters of Mind*, 440; see also H. Pearson Gundy, *Queen's University at Kingston* (Kingston: n.p., 1967), 22–23.

119 Bowden, *Adam Shortt*, 292.

120 Bowden, *Adam Shortt*, 56, 292.

121 Douglas Library Notes, Queen's University, VIII (1959): 1.

122 Hilda Neatby, *Queen's University*, vol. I, 1841–1917: And Not to Yield (Montreal: McGill-Queen's University Press, 1978), 190.

123 Haydon, "Adam Shortt," 615.

124 Carl Berger, *The Writing of Canadian History: Aspects of English-Canadian Historical Writing, 1900–1970* (Toronto: Oxford University Press, 1976), 26.

125 Library Report, *Queen's Quarterly* IV (1896): 72.

126 Library Report, *Queen's Quarterly* II (1894): 74.

127 Bowden, *Adam Shortt*, 75.

128 Dr. McNeill, cited in Haydon, "Adam Shortt," 618.

129 Bowden, *Adam Shortt*, 292.

130 Ferguson, *Remaking Liberalism*, 16, 17.

131 Ferguson, *Remaking Liberalism*, 16, 17.

132 S. E. D. Shortt, *The Search for an Ideal*, 62.

133 Ferguson, *Remaking Liberalism*, 17.

134 S. E. D. Shortt, *The Search for an Ideal*, 61–62.

135 Ferguson, *Remaking Liberalism*, 19.

136 Adam Shortt, "Should We Revise the Constitution of Queen's," *Queen's Quarterly* VIII (1900): 114.

137 Adam Shortt, "Queen's and the Church," *Queen's Quarterly* X (1902): 123.

138 Ferguson, *Remaking Liberalism*, 29.

139 S. E. D. Shortt, *The Search for an Ideal*, 62.

140 S. E. D. Shortt, *The Search for an Ideal*, 97.

141 Crowley, *Marriage of Minds*, 33.

142 Ferguson, *Remaking Liberalism*, 3.

143 Haydon, "Adam Shortt," 618.

144 Bowden, *Adam Shortt*, 292.

145 Frederick W. Gibson, *Queen's University*, vol. II, 1917–61: To Serve and Yet Be Free (Montreal: McGill-Queen's University Press, 1983), 54–55.

146 Haydon, "Adam Shortt," 614.

147 D. D. Calvin, *Queen's University at Kingston: The First Century of a Scottish-Canadian Foundation 1841–1941* (Kingston: Trustees of the University, 1941), 136.

148 Adam Shortt, "The University Man in Business Life," *Queen's Quarterly* XIII (1905): 189.

149 Bowden, *Adam Shortt*, 291.

150 Adam Shortt, cited in S. E. D. Shortt, *The Search for an Ideal*, 98.

151 S. E. D. Shortt, *The Search for an Ideal*, 97.

152 Berger, *The Writing of Canadian History*, 1.

153 Mackintosh, "Adam Shortt, 1959–1931," 175.

154 Owram, *The Government Generation*, 13.

155 S. E. D. Shortt, *The Search for an Ideal*, 120.

156 Adam Shortt, "Book Notices, Morley's Life of Gladstone," *Queen's Quarterly* XI (1904): 423–24.

157 McKillop, *Matters of Mind*, 196.

158 Crowley, *Marriage of Minds*, 41.

159 Owram, *The Government Generation*, 194.

160 S. E. D. Shortt, *The Search for an Ideal*, 102; and Berger, *The Writing of Canadian History*, 90–100.

161 C. D. W. Goodwin, *Canadian Economic Thought: The Political Economy of a Developing Nation, 1814–1914* (Durham: Duke University Press, 1961), 187.

162 Bowden, *Adam Shortt*, 75–76.

163 Crowley, *Marriage of Minds*, 19, 45.

164 McKillop, *Matters of Mind*, 201.

165 Ferguson, *Remaking Liberalism*, 14.

166 Mackintosh, "Adam Shortt, 1959–1931," 169.

167 Neatby, *Queen's University*, 228.

168 Haydon, "Adam Shortt," 612.

169 Bowden, *Adam Shortt*, 293.

170 Berger, *The Writing of Canadian History*, 25.

171 Adam Shortt, cited in Allen, *The View from Murray Tower*, 302.

172 Adam Shortt, "The [London] Times Letters on Canada," *Queen's Quarterly* II (1894): 78.

173 Thomas P. Socknat, *Witness Against War: Pacifism in Canada, 1900–1945* (Toronto: University of Toronto Press, 1987), 37.

174 Adam Shortt, "The Times Letters on Canada": 76.

175 Adam Shortt, "Peace and After," *Queen's Quarterly* VI (1898): 156; see also Shortt, "Peace in South Africa," *Queen's Quarterly* X (1902): 121.

176 182 Adam Shortt, "The [Boer] War," *Queen's Quarterly* IX (1901): 149.

177 Adam Shortt, "Peace in South Africa," *Queen's Quarterly* X (1902): 121.

178 Socknat, *Witness against War*, 29. The three other academics who joined Shortt in endorsing the Canadian Peace and Arbitartion Society were "J. E. McCurdy of Toronto, Charles Zavitz of Guelph and Lewis E. Horning of Victoria College"; ibid., 30.

179 Socknat, *Witness against War*, 30.

180 Adam Shortt, "The Exposure of War," *Queen's Quarterly* XIII (1905): 77. In this article, Shortt specifically advocates arbitration as a means of evading war; ibid., 76–77.

181 S. E. D. Shortt, *The Search for an Ideal*, 106; and Ferguson, *Remaking Liberalism*, xv.

182 Socknat, *Witness Against War*, 35.

183 Ferguson, *Remaking Liberalism*, 15.

184 Owram, *The Government Generation*, 47.

185 Adam Shortt, "The Colonial Conference," *Queen's Quarterly* X (1902): 242–45.

186 Ferguson, *Remaking Liberalism*, 118.

187 Adam Shortt, "Party Politics," *Queen's Quarterly* X (1903): 510.

188 Adam Shortt, "The Coxey Movement," *Queen's Quarterly* II (1894): 76.

189 Adam Shortt, "The King as a Statesman," *Queen's Quarterly* XII (1905): 322–23.

190 Adam Shortt, "Peace in South Africa," *Queen's Quarterly* X (1902): 120.

191 Adam Shortt, "Immigration," *Queen's Quarterly* IX (1902): 322.

192 Adam Shortt, "Some Observations on the Great Northwest II Social and Economic Condition," *Queen's Quarterly* III (1895): 22.

193 Adam Shortt, "In Defence of Millionaires," *Canadian Magazine* XIII (1899): 496–98.

194 Ferguson, *Remaking Liberalism*, 96; see also Berger, *The Writing of Canadian History*, 25–26.

195 Allen, *The View from Murray Tower*, 388.

196 McKillop, *A Disciplined Intelligence*, 219.

197 Adam Shortt, "Recent Phases of Socialism," *Queen's Quarterly* V (1897): 12–13.

198 Ferguson, *Remaking Liberalism*, 101.

199 S. E. D. Shortt, *The Search for an Ideal*, 113–14.

200 Adam Shortt, "Early Records of Ontario," *Queen's Quarterly* VII (1899): 51–59, 137–52; VII (1900): 202–14, 243–50, 324–31; VIII (1900): 65–72, 145–52; VIII (1901): 223–30.

201 Bowden, *Adam Shortt*, 220–21.

202 Berger, *The Writing of Canadian History*, 31.

203 Berger, *The Writing of Canadian History*, 26, 21.

204 *The Globe* (Toronto), 2 April 1910.

205 Adam Shortt, "Life in Kingston in the Years after Waterloo," *Queen's Quarterly* VIII (1901): 181, 190.

206 Bowden, *Adam Shortt*, 207.

207 Adam Shortt, "The Winning of Responsible Government in Canada," *Queen's Quarterly* X (1902): 153.

208 Adam Shortt, "The Winning of Responsible Government in Canada," 153–54.

209 Berger, *The Writing of Canadian History*, 28.

210 Berger, *The Writing of Canadian History*; see also Bowden, *Adam Shortt*, 224.

211 Bowden, *Adam Shortt*, 298.

212 Mackintosh, "Adam Shortt, 1959–1931," 176.

213 S. E. D. Shortt, *The Search for an Ideal*, 99.

214 Berger, *The Writing of Canadian History*, 74.

215 McKillop, *A Disciplined Intelligence*, 218.

216 Bowden, *Adam Shortt*, 83.

217 Bowden, *Adam Shortt*, 85.

218 Bowden, *Adam Shortt*, 126.

219 Ferguson, *Remaking Liberalism*, 121.

220 Allen, *The View from Murray Tower*, 218.

221 Bowden, *Adam Shortt*, 131, 126.

222 Ferguson, *Remaking Liberalism*, 121.

223 Mackintosh, "Adam Shortt, 1959–1931," 271.

224 Bowden, *Adam Shortt*, 132.

225 *The Globe* (Toronto), 2 April 1910.

226 Owram, *The Government Generation*, 46–47; and Adam Shortt, cited in ibid., 47.

227 Bowden, *Adam Shortt*, 151.

228 Gordon T. Stewart, *The Origins of Canadian Politics: A Comparative Approach* (Vancouver: UBC Press, 1986), 74.

229 Allen, *The View from Murray Tower*, 218.

230 Owram, *The Government Generation*, 71.

231 Crowley, *Marriage of Minds*, 57.

232 Owram, *The Government Generation*, 129; see also ibid., 333.

233 For example, McKillop observes that, "it was to [John] Watson that Shortt sent the philosophy questions to be marked." *Matters of Mind*, 198.

234 Bowden, *Adam Shortt*, 166.

235 Bowden, *Adam Shortt*, 167.

236 Owram, *The Government Generation*, 129.

237 Bowden, *Adam Shortt*, 163, 169.

238 Adam Shortt, cited in S. E. D. Shortt, *The Search for an Ideal*, 100.

239 *The Globe* (Toronto), 2 April 1910.

240 Owram, *The Government Generation*, 70.

241 Ferguson, *Remaking Liberalism*, 126.

242 McLaren, *Becoming Indispensable*, 264.

243 Ferguson, *Remaking Liberalism*, 37.

244 1911 Census of Canada, Ontario, Ottawa [District 105], St. George's Ward [Enumeration District 35], p. 10, line 43, http://automatedgeneology.com/census11/. As of 28 February 2011, there is a transcription error: the Shortt family name is listed as "Shorst" (lines 43–47). I have submitted a correction.

245 Bowden, *Adam Shortt*, 273.

246 McLaren, *Becoming Indispensable*, 269.

247 Bowden, *Adam Shortt*, 274–75. The exact cost of property taxes for the Shortts was $493 per year; ibid., 275.

248 McLaren, *Becoming Indispensable*, 269.

249 McLaren, *Becoming Indispensable*, 270–71, 269. Elizabeth Shortt, cited in ibid., 271.

250 McLaren, *Becoming Indispensable*, 295.

251 *Ottawa Evening Citizen*, 11 October 1941.

252 "Mrs. Adam Shortt Leads Canadian Women."

253 Strong-Boag, "*The Parliament of Women*," 162.

254 Whitton, "Dr. Elizabeth Shortt Played a Great Part."

255 "Canadian Women in the Public Eye," *Saturday Night*, 29 November 1919.

256 Elizabeth Shortt, cited in McLaren, *Becoming Indispensable*, 301; see also ibid., 299.

257 McLaren, *Becoming Indispensable*, 299–302.

258 ESSP, WA10, file 2258, "Pioneer Wife," October 1944, 12–13. See n. 24.

259 ESSP, WA10, file 1864, "Lecture on Hygiene to the Parents and Teachers of Osgoode St. School in Ottawa."

260 McLaren, *Becoming Indispensable*, 298.

261 McLaren, *Becoming Indispensable*, 298–99.

262 Whitton, *Ottawa Evening Citizen*, 15 January 1949.

263 "Mrs. Shortt Leads Canadian Women."

264 McLaren, *Becoming Indispensable*, 318.

265 Prentice et al., *Canadian Women*, 216.

266 Strong-Boag, *"The Parliament of Women,"* 422–23.

267 ESSP, WA10, file 2188, *Ottawa Evening Citizen*, 3 November 1910, "Mothers' Union at Rideau Hall."

268 ESSP, WA10, file 2188, *Ottawa Evening Citizen*, 3 November 1910, "Mothers' Union at Rideau Hall."

269 *Silas Smith*, 44–45.

270 Elizabeth Smith Shortt, cited in Crowley, *Marriage of Minds*, 172.

271 Elizabeth Smith Shortt, "Medical Women," *Montreal Daily Star*, 9 March 1895.

272 In the Elizabeth Smith Shortt Papers is an article by Elizabeth on "Women in Education." She designated the piece as originating in the "Westminister," but no further publication information is provided except for a publication date of August 1900 (probably either 4 or 9 August). ESSP, WA10, file 2290.

273 Mrs. Grundy's name originated in Thomas Morton's 1798 play, *Speed the Plough*, though she never appeared on stage. However, another character in the drama, Dame Ashfield, was vitally concerned about receiving the moral sanction of her neighbour, Mrs. Grundy, who was considered the area's foremost authority on ethical behaviour. Afterward, Mrs. Grundy became synonymous with "the censorship enacted in everyday life by conventional opinion" and "a criterion of rigid respectability" (see www.britannica.com/ EBchecked/topic/247423/Mrs-Grundy).

274 ESSP, WA10, file 2290.

275 McLaren, *Becoming Indispensable*, 388–435.

Chapter 1

Prelude to a Journey, the Crossing to England, and Near Tragedy

Prelude

Elizabeth's Decision to Go

Adam Shortt had been authorized by the Canadian government in 1911 to study the public bureaucracies in England, Switzerland, Austria, and Germany as a foundation for possible reforms in the Dominion. The prospective trip caused Elizabeth Shortt to think of joining her husband for practical reasons (31 March), but more importantly as an escape from the dual role of a busy middle-class housewife and social feminist in the nation's capital (28 May and 12 June).

As we know, the second responsibility had expanded after the Shortts moved to Ottawa in 1908. A letter presented here documents this point. To quote Elizabeth: "When I came here I thought I would take life easier & not worry about other people, but I am more in demand than ever & I must say I feel I am more use doing & talking for others than in just calling & going to teas." For this conscientious activist even her expected attendance at the purely social teas in Ottawa had assumed a political significance. "Of course both in calling & teas there are chances of interesting other people in public affairs" (24 February). By 1911, Mrs. Shortt was a considerable force in the feminist movement within Ottawa. That year, she was elected president of the local council of the NCWC, the most significant organization fighting for women's rights on the national level. Elizabeth had acquired a power base, which she used skilfully to advance her feminist agenda down to 1918.[1] At this juncture, both Mr. And Mrs. Shortt were major figures in the federal capital.

Elizabeth's Correspondence

30 January *Elizabeth to "Mother and Gertrude" (Smith)*[2]

You will be surprised when I tell you we (Adam & I) have taken berths to sail on June 28th, but I do not know at all whether I can go, for I have no arrangement in hand for the children. George[3] will be just ready for his exams then I suppose. However I am just trusting that some scheme will come into the range of possible by that time. If Violet[4] were only not so far away.

1 February *Elizabeth to "Mother"*[5]

I have been very gay lately going to luncheons & dinners & meetings. Last evg. we were at a very elegant affair at Mrs. Ami's[6] across the way. I wore a new dress I had made in London this summer & felt very fine—like a peacock. Lots of shell pink satin underdress with pale grey chiffon overdress & trimmed with silver and pearl lace and fringe & I had my hair done up its nicest best.

24 February *Elizabeth to "Mother and Sister" (Gertrude)*[7]

It is amazing what a lot of calls come to me from all sorts of societies to be patroness of the Orpheus Musical club, to preside at a prayer meeting, to belong to this & to that & to do this & to do that. When I came here I thought I would take life easier & not worry about other people, but I am more in demand than ever & I must say I feel I am more use doing & talking for others than in just calling & going to teas. Of course both in calling & teas there are chances of interesting other people in public affairs. This last week there were two teas on Wed., two on Thurs. & two on Friday, tho. I could only get to one each day—& there was also one on Tues....

I have not solved the question of what I can do with the children in the summer yet. George will have to be here till about the middle of July for his exams. It is very lovely of you Gertrude to ask them to stay with you. We will see how things turn out later. We would like to take Muriel[8] with us, if we could do it....

31 March *Elizabeth to "Gertrude"*[9]

If we do go as we suppose we will on 27 of June I would not be able to get up this summer & perhaps not very soon after our return. You see it is much cheaper for me to go with Adam (because I share his room) or I would send Muriel & go to keep house with you & mother. For awhile we talked of taking Muriel & then when Lorraine[10] looked so frail after her illness it all came over me that I could not take Muriel & leave Lorraine on this side. So we talked it over again & think we will let Muriel go next summer with friends. May Chown & her Aunt, Miss Arming, are going for a trip next summer & Muriel could go with them.

I do not know yet what plans we can make. Possibly Mr. & Mrs. Cowley may take our house for the summer & then Muriel can pay her cousins visits as she is anxious to do before the girl cousins get scattered. Lorraine's heart is set on spending part of the summer in Kingston with Marjory & Mrs. Garnoley has kindly written to ask her to. I think I could let her stay safely there for some wks. if Mrs. G. will let me make some return. I do not yet know, as I say. If the Cowleys do not want the house perhaps Muriel & George will have to stay & keep it open for the summer. The plants are here to take care of as usual—something to necessitate keeping house.

28 May *Elizabeth to "Mother" and Gertrude"*[11]
I feel rather crowded because there are a lot of things to do, if I am really going to Eng. in a few wks.. Things look as tho. we would [*sic*] not be able to rent the house & that probably Muriel will stay & keep house with the servant but that may all change before four weeks go over.... Sometimes I think I will chuck the Old Country trip & go & stay a month with you and yet it seems so hard to let Adam go so far away, & for so long & stay behind. And I do want to get away from [preparing] three meals a day & have good meals & freedom from care. I feel so in need of it and I fear that if I just kept on the same round here till winter that I would not be as ready for the winter's duties. I am not entirely set on anything tho. our passage is taken for 28th June. I hate to leave the children on this side of the ocean & yet I would never go if I waited to take them all.... Of course I am not getting any clothes to go over with, as I hope to get them there & save some toward the expense of the journey.

12 June *Elizabeth to "Mother"*[12]
Much keeps going on here & hardly a night that someone doesn't turn up. Tonight since I began this letter Prof. Mathieson & Rev. Mr. Kidd have been in most of the evg.. Sat. night Principal Murray of Saskatoon[13] & Rev. Mr. Rowand of Stratford. Tomorrow George Wilson (Mary's brother) is coming to lunch & Assembly people [from the NCWC] are in occasionally. Principal Gordon[14] was in to dinner on Sunday. Prof. Andrew Tearoson from California was in one evg.—two evgs. I think—last wk. & yesterday Dr. Doughty[15] & Dr. Hewitt[16] & Mr. McGillivary from Halifax. Tomorrow

night is a Queen's dinner. They want me to speak at it to the women graduates &c.. I do not know till morning whether I shall be physically fit but I don't feel like it now & wish they didn't want me to do it.

I am firmly convinced of this—that I must get away from every care & responsibility for awhile. I am not sure that a trip to England is the very best, but as Adam is going anyway, I can try it. I have weighed & considered all sorts of alternatives & I feel I cannot go on doing & thinking as I have been or I will not live very long. I have never felt the broken feeling, the prostration I have this last time of being down.

I would like to come & stay a month with you, if I were just that little bit stronger that I could be sure of being able to do things everyday but I might fail some days & be no good....

Martha & Mary each write urging us to let George visit them but then as I do not want to rent the house & there are a lot of plants to be kept & moths to see after—it seems as if it were best to keep the house open. Muriel does not mind staying. If George stays here all summer (he will not be through his exams till 11th July), he wants to go camping for two weeks after school closes & then Adam says he will give him something to do in the archives....

25 June   *Elizabeth to "Mother"*[17]

We finally got matters settled & Muriel is going to keep house & George is going to do work for his father in the Archives and get paid for it by his father. He will not be through his exams till the middle of July. Lorraine is to go to Kingston with Miss Stewart about the 18th & pay a visit to Marjory & then come back & stay with Muriel the rest of the time. The servant is to sleep [here] too. I think I will ask Sara Gibson to stay August with M. (Muriel). Miss Gibson (Sara) has no place she calls home & she might stay here a month, for I think Muriel does not like the idea of being without someone, tho. she says he [sic] wants to do some literary work & she thinks Miss Gibson would amuse herself & leave her free to do her work. She has a great deal of writing to do in connection with the Memorial Residence scheme[18] & she is going to take up a section of Canadian History & work at it. She thinks she will rather enjoy being alone to that extent & has a lot planned for the time.

Two months will very soon go by and yet it seems a big wrench to get up & go so far from the children & you dear ones. We expect to sail for home after Sept 7th, so it will be about 2½ months [away]. I have had one of the most rushing times trying to get ready, both to leave & to get myself ready. I am sorry Muriel cannot go up & stay part of the summer with you. If I had been here, she & I could have seen you through a part of the summer while a good housekeeper was being formed. I was glad to hear that one is coming on 4th July & I do hope she will be very satisfactory. It is very trying to have people come into one's clean house & do things in an imperfect way but, after all, we can live through it as the great majority live in that way. It is one of the most trying things in my life—never to have anyone who will do their work as thoroughly & well as I do it, even when overburdened with fifty other phases of everyday life which they have not.

June (no date given, but apparently late June)   *Elizabeth to "Gertrude"*[19]

The only address [in London] I know now is care of Canadian Commission or Canadian office 17 Victoria St. I hope the crowds will be out of London by the time we get there & the place cleaned up.[20]

If there is anything you want to tell me now, a letter sent tomorrow evg.—to the *Royal George*, CN Steamship, Montreal—would get [to] us Tues.. We sail Wed. morning at eight. I expect to go down Tues. afternoon & go on board that evg..

Dr. Doughty was married yesterday & sails with us by [the] *Royal George*. His wife is not half as interesting as he is—she was [working] in the archives.... I feel on a measure as if I were running away from you when you were in stress & yet I could not stay on indefinitely.

Adam's Preparations

Adam, having been commissioned by his federal employers, restricted his preparations to the practical issues involved in his departure. His diary displays none of the angst and emotional turmoil in his wife's writings on the same event. For the head of Canada's civil service, the excursion was primarily a business trip.

However, one aspect of Shortt's diaries just before the trip merits special attention. In the midst of the frenzy of preparation for his transatlantic journey, Adam found the time to attend a church service "with Muriel and Lorraine." He further indicated that his was "the last time before going" (25 June), suggesting that this was a frequent occurrence for him and his two daughters. It confirmed that in his own quiet way, Mr. Shortt was a devout man who strove to share his religious fervour with his children.

Adam's Diary[21]

24 June

Busy at office. Got Doughty's Bride present. Cheque for $500 from Glasgow[22] and $1,200 from government for travelling expenses. Got letter of Credit, Traveller's Cheques &c.

Lunch at Rideau Club[23] with Mr. Acland[24] and Prof. ——— from Cambridge. Talk on Trade and Empire.

Golf Club in evening and to dinner. Talk with Ruddick[25] re condensed milk expert.

25 June

To Church with Muriel and Lorraine, last time before going. Wrote some letters and got some things in shape for leaving.

26 June

Rush of things at office. LaRochelle[26] went to Sorel and promised to sign papers. Got as many things wound up as possible. Wrote letters all evening but did not get them all finished.

The Crossing to England

During their voyage to the mother country, Adam and Elizabeth travelled first-class. He was an important civil servant in Ottawa, where the Shortts mingled socially with members of the political and bureaucratic elites. Moreover, by 1911, Mrs. Shortt had also acquired a personal prominence in the capital's increasingly more significant feminist movement.

The couple took part in many of the activities extended to first-class passengers on an Atlantic trip. The wonders of nature (28 and 29 June and 3 July); a couple of concerts (1 and 3 July); a religious service (2 July); an afternoon of sports on deck, as observers not participants (4 July); occasional readings (29 June and 4 July); frequent conversations (2, 3 and 4 July); and card games (29 June and 5 July) helped to distract the Shortts from bouts of seasickness (30 June and 1 July). The latter were "an all too common experience" for those sailing to Europe.[27]

Elizabeth and Adam were pleased to accept the captain's invitation to inspect the various details of the *Royal George*'s operation. Mrs. Shortt was especially intrigued by the navigation devices that directed the ship. Meanwhile, her husband noted that the accommodations throughout the vessel, as well as its kitchen facilities, were excellent. Mr. Shortt was particularly interested when the ship's engineer guided the party through the engine and furnace quarters, where he explained in detail the operation of the turbine engines (4 July). Consistently attentive to the latest technological developments, a scientifically minded Adam was thrilled with this visit to what Morgan has called the "touring of the ship's depths," a privilege extended only to first-class travellers.[28]

Elizabeth also found time to read during the long voyage, and her choice of material tells us something about her personal interests at this time. She chose to concentrate on *The Awakening of Helena Richie* (1906), Margaret Deland's latest novel (June 29). The work was an enormous success in the United States, where it was first published: "*The Awakening of Helena Richie* was a runaway best seller. It was on the Bookman's list of the top six books nationally for three months and continued on regional best-seller lists much longer. It was the only one of the six top sellers that autumn to receive the unanimous approval of the reviewers of *Literary Digest*. Critics praised it, *Harper's Weekly* calling it 'a masterpiece of fiction.'"[29]

The book, however, did not endorse the common notions of feminism in this period. The independent Deland believed that women deserved greater economic and educational opportunities, but feared that enhanced personal freedom would cause some females to abandon social responsibility whenever it clashed with strong individual desire. This, in turn, could precipitate dire consequences, like an increase in the divorce rate, which might ultimately lead to the disintegration of the modern family. For Deland, as well as Mrs. Shortt, such prospects threatened the very foundations of society.[30] In the novel, Helena Richie follows this undesirable course when, after leaving an abusive husband, she pursues an illicit affair with a young widower, Lloyd Pryor. To make matters worse, Pryor is falsely presented to others in Old Chester as her devoted brother. Slowly and painfully, the novel's heroine recognizes the error of her ways. "Helena's awakening to the weakness of her position and to her foolishness in accepting Lloyd's assertions that they are above morality leads to her development as a women."[31] Once she has confessed her sins and promised to mend her ways, a redeemed Helena re-enters the mainstream of society. Moreover, she is allowed to regain parental control over a young orphan, David, whom she has come to love dearly during her clandestine life in Old Chester. A reformed Helena then creates a new life elsewhere centring on her maternal devotion to David.[32]

Mrs. Shortt certainly would have agreed with most of the main assumptions in this popular work. For example, both she and Deland "welcomed the disappearance of the empty-headed helpless young woman of the past." However, Elizabeth appeared more optimistic about their common hope for the triumph of the "new woman who was physically active and intellectually independent" through further education.[33] More importantly, opting to read this book on the passage to England meant that she was in touch with contemporary literature and the rethinking of gender relations that authors like Deland were promoting.

Tuesday, 27 June

Adam's Diary[34]
Great rush all morning. Skelton[35] called will be in town for a week. Got tickets arranged. Left on 3.15 train for Montreal. Mr. and Mrs. Hunter (Dept. Public Works)[36] on train. Had long talk on many things. Dined with them and went on board.

Elizabeth's Diary[37]
Adam & I bade the dear three children goodbye with mixed feelings. It certainly is a wrench to leave the children behind—but it is a part of the stoical sense of duty & the conclusion of reason that drives one on doing things in spite of sadness or parting—that enabled me to start off on a long journey with my husband & thus leave my children at home.

Children is a misleading term perhaps, for Muriel is of age and George is nearing eighteen & Lorraine my baby will be fourteen before I see her again. None of them are irresponsible—none wild & each has occupations of duty & amusement. So God send, it may all be for the best in the end. On board the Pullman when we left behind Mr. Forin, Mr. Haydon[38] & Mr. McArthur,[39] we found the Deputy [Minister of Public Works James Hunter], Miss Hunter & wife who were also going to Montreal.

Mr. Haydon good soul came to see me off & he had been our friend & legal advisor & so we left him to the children as such. Mr. Forin, sec. to the [Civil Service] Commission came down to see his chief off & McArthur our mutual friend with Dr. Doughty came for various reasons. Muriel came down to see us off & they [McArthur and Muriel] went away together. I wonder if they are anything more than good friends.

We had a pleasant enough trip to Montreal & the scenery at Vaudreil & St. Anne was very lovely. Arrived in Montreal—the heat was still great. We had dinner at the Station with Mr. & Mrs. Hunter & there saw a German capitalist that Adam knew and Jack Murray also. Just as we started off in a cab the rain began & we had a heavy shower but as the wharf was under shelter we arrived all right. I sat in the rotunda of the ship watching people coming on board while Adam looked after the trunks. While I was waiting a terrible thunder storm came on & there was one terrific crash that I found after had struck St. Peter's [church] in Montreal & burnt it down.

Adam saw Dr. & Mrs. Doughty come on board but I saw no one I knew. Our room was warm & of course being in the harbour we did not sleep very well, the constant noise of loading & hoisting preventing [it]. Next morning just as I began dressing I saw the tender pulling the nose of the boat round & we were soon off on our real journey—the Atlantic trip.

Wednesday, 28 June

Adam's Diary
Doughty and wife turned up also Lord Percy, A.D.C. on way home. Arranged to sit at same table for the five of us. Beautiful day down river to Quebec and below. Long talk with Percy on Imperialism. I defended course of Sir W. Laurier.

Elizabeth's Diary
The first person I saw when I came out of our room was Lord Percy talking to Adam and so when the Doughtys joined us we formed a table by ourselves—Lord Percy at the head & I & Dr. D. on one side & Adam & Mrs. D. the other, the end being against the wall, a number of tables down each side of the dining room being so placed. I sent off a letter to Muriel at Montreal & Quebec wh. we reached that afternoon. It was a perfect day— warm and beautiful, the shore being most picturesque, hills & broken higher hills behind, wild Laureels [*sic*] nestling on the shore at every valley formed by the hills. We were outside all day except for meals. Mrs. D. & I secured a couple of chairs & later Dr. D. & A. secured [an] other two on the other side so we could drop down on either side. Lord Percy had one next ours also.

Thursday, 29 June

Adam's Diary
Another beautiful day down the river below Rimouski to Gaspe. Not very large Cabin list. Mrs. Ewart and daughter[40] on board, also Mr. Millar of Saltcoats. Several very ordinary people but not mixing much. Game of Five Hundred. Saw Capt. Very kind. Changed room.

Elizabeth's Diary

Another beautiful perfect day spent on deck walking or sitting, reading or talking, the shore being much of the same beauty all the way to Gaspe. Hills & higher hills behind, beautiful shades of green & nestling hamlets, fishermen's hamlets along shore in the valleys between hills. Found the first day on that Mrs. Ewart & daughter Gladys & Miss Cross the violinist were on board. Have afternoon tea with Mrs. Ewart when I am able to take tea at all. This evening Lord Percy, Dr. & Mrs. Doughty & A. & I wanting to have a game to ourselves, the Captain showed us down to the nursery & we had an absurd game of 500. Then Mrs. D., not feeling well & retiring, we had a game of bridge—Lord Percy & I against A. & Dr. D.. I read the *Awakening of Helena Richie* & found it very interesting, especially the boy David who when asked to add "Bless Mr. Pryor" to his other prayers for blessings said "God could bless him if he liked but he needn't do it to please him" &c..

Friday, 30 June

Adam's Diary

Across the Gulf. Another long talk with Percy re trade policy of Britain and Colonies, single tax &c. &c. He mixes with none beyond our party. Very fine fellow when you get within his shell. All at table so far. Some fog, little wind.

Elizabeth's Diary

Rain & fog greeted us & a constant drizzle. The deck was wet & "slipperly" & I did not go out. Felt nauseated all day, tho. able to be about part of the time but skipped luncheon. Really ill about noon, but went down in the evg. to dinner for looks.

Saturday, 1 July

Adam's Diary

No enthusiasm over Dominion Day. One man got a couple of flags put up. Fog all day but not rough. Little interest in passengers. Read papers, talk and sleep. Good music by Miss Ewart and Cross.

Elizabeth's Diary

Rain & fog & fog horn all night & all day. Feeling miserable nausea but between reading & listening to music & going down to meals the day goes quickly by. They could only find two flags to put on the tables to celebrate Dominion Day. A. had a notion of dressing for dinner to celebrate but everything was so depressing including his own stomach that he gave it up. The ladies change their dresses, but it's only even in a few cases—half dressing. Some men do—not many. A. finds a Mr. Mullen on board who is known to us by Mrs. Elders' account of the family with whom she lived in her experience out west.

Sunday, 2 July

Adam's Diary
Service by Mr. Johnston [*sic*] of Minneapolis. Episcopalian.[41] Pretentious sermon. Had long talk with the parson afterwards. Better than he sounded but not very connected in his thought. Long walk and talk with Percy. Good chats at our alcove table.

Elizabeth's Diary
Rain & fog and foghorn again. Adam feeling very uncertain & I none too well. We were at late breakfast & then down to Sunday service. A Rev. Mr. Johnson from Min-ta. gave the sermon & a clergyman travelling 3rd class read the lessons. Miss Ewart played the piano. Second class fares came in for the service & scattered in the dining room. They all made up quite a congregation. We had good old hymns & the singing was hearty. Miss Ewart & Miss Cross give us beautiful music & seem the only musical performers among the 1st class. There is a very small list of 1st class—I think about 70. I do not fancy they are very interesting tho. no doubt some of them would be if talked to. Quite a percentage of them are English & the [English] tone seems to predominate tho. there are quite a number of Americans on board also.

Lord Percy who was A.D.C. to Lord Grey is going home to be married—next month I think. If he lives I suppose he will be Duke of Northumberland. He is very nice—intelligent & shy. He feels it was worthwhile having his Canadian experience. He is a Hotspur in looks, not in character, I think.[42]

Monday, 3 July

Adam's Diary
Long talk with Bristol man on British trade. Another long talk with Percy on Loyalists and heredity. Saw three groups of porpoises. Concert in second cabin. Some fair numbers but not much.

Elizabeth's Diary

July 3rd was a quiet one, tho. I had a promenade before breakfast & after & again in the afternoon. In the evg. we went down to the second [class] cabin to hear their concert & who should I see there but Robert Laidlaw[43]— the dear boy—& he said there were two others of the teachers from St. Andrew's. I have not been able to see him yet because I wanted to ask the Capt., as there are some regulations about first & 2nd class mingling on account of the possibility of infectious disease & quarantine but Commander Harrison said I might have Robert come up. So I shall hope to see him tomorrow. Last night about eleven Adam & I went out to see the porpoises out [on the water]—little animals [which] light up the water. Truly the works of the Lord are wonderful.

Tuesday, 4 July

Adam's Diary

Lord Percy and I were taken through ship by Captain. Accommodation for all classes very good. Kitchen and pantrys [sic] well fitted. Engineer took us through engine and furnace rooms and explained the turbine engines. Sports in afternoon and cards in evening.

Elizabeth's Diary

Up betimes for breakfast & found on going down to the dining room that some of the Americans had decorated their tables with stars and stripes. Read part of the forenoon. After luncheon the Americans got up a program of sports. The Bull of Bashan (Rev. Mr. Johnson of Minneapolis) was manager in general. Were on deck about this till four & then went to the tearoom & spent [time] till six taking tea & talking to Mrs. Ewart. Then dinner—the Captain's dinner, presumably our *diner d'Adieu*, but we may be on so late tomorrow as to necessitate another dinner.

Near Tragedy

At a farewell party for the Doughtys and Shortts in Lord Percy's cabin the evening before reaching England, Elizabeth contracted an eye disease that threatened to alter drastically the entire trip for her and her husband. Despite assistance from others, the disorder worsened and it was only under "mortifying" circumstances that Elizabeth left the *Royal George* and made her way to London (5 July). After the Doughtys offered to share their lodgings with the Shortts at the Savoy Mansions, Adam and Elizabeth consulted Dr. Percy Flemming, a leading eye specialist in London. He informed the astonished couple that Elizabeth was suffering from glaucoma, which required an immediate operation to save her sight in the injured right eye (6 July).

The following day, Dr. Flemming performed a successful operation, though the Shortts were deeply troubled by the high costs of the procedure and a prolonged stay recuperating at Miss Lancaster's private and expensive hospital (7 July). Adam assumed the role of family correspondent with the couple's relatives, a responsibility ordinarily carried out by his wife (8, 9, 10 and 14 July). After a brief excursion to Windsor with the Doughtys (9 July), Adam's daily visits to the hospital to see "Beth" were accompanied by a growing concentration on appointments with British officials to fulfill the business side of the civil service commissioner's trip. Shortt arranged meetings with important, though not the most significant, members of London's political and bureaucratic elites, while also finding time to take tourist outings to the London zoo (15 July) and Hampton Court (16 July). Meanwhile, Elizabeth convalesced at Miss Lancaster's establishment.

Wednesday, 5 July

Adam's Diary[44]
Beth suffering from neuralgia in eyes from draught evening before. Miss Doer[45] very kind to her. Beautiful day up Bristol channel. Landed late and with much discomfort, especially to Beth whose eye was very painful. Went through to London at 2 a.m. Very disagreeable.

Elizabeth's Diary[46]
"I must just narrate as I can the course of events in retrospect, since circumstances did interrupt the course of my daily narration" (12 August in Spiez, Switzerland)

The morning was bright & fair & smooth rippling sea. The evening before (Tues. evg.), a sort of farewell party—Dr. & Mrs. Doughty and Adam & I met in Lord Percy's room & had an evg. at cards of five hundred & quite a merry time. His room was a very nice stateroom & the window and door were open & [permitted] a good draught of air through. Mrs. D. sat in the full current & I at one side of it, but I got so cold at last that I asked to have the door closed. After twelve mid-night I felt sort of neuralgic pain in my temple (I had had it the previous night between 12 & 3 but it had passed off).

In the morning my right eye was suffused, still a neuralgic pain in the temple. I went to breakfast, wiped my eye frequently. After breakfast Dr. D. wanted to put some drops into it & did. It seemed about the same in suffusion but it was either worse in pain or was wearing. I went about & went with our party—L. Percy, Dr. & Mrs. D. & Adam—to the Capt's bridge & saw the part of the apparatus for guiding & steering the ship [and] everyone was most kind. Later I borrowed Mrs. D's hot water bag & put my neuralgic eye on it. It seemed to make it worse but I persisted & even dosed off for awhile. The eye grew worse in the afternoon both in pain & suffusion.

It was a perfectly lovely day outside & in the afternoon we began to see land & later it was beautiful sailing up the Bristol channel & seeing the English villages on the shore. I was too ill to go outside but I peeped out of the window at times in spite of misery of nausea & pain &c.... We had dinner again—I think I did not go down. Then we were finishing up. Mrs. Ewart came in to see me & helped put a sort of bandage over my eye to go on shore, but I couldn't stand it either [way]. Adam & Mrs. D. came sometimes to see how I was getting on. Once in my misery I heard some noise & looking up with my left eye I saw an apparition with straw color hair & linen coat—something looking like a darkie of the [American] South & it seemed to say "books." It took several brain waves to conclude it was "boots" & [he was] waiting [for] his tip. I had not seen him before nor had he done anything for me. Each one—head steward, bath steward, woman steward, boots [polisher], elevatorboy, Dining room waiter &c &c—all had to have tips, each steward &c.. It is a biggish handing out when a man is of any consequence or a woman hopes to be helped.

We did not reach Avonmouth till about 8 o'clock & were put off on a tender at between eight & nine. It was really objectionable & there were no conveniences on the tender. We seemed sort of rounded up like cattle. I was seasick just before leaving the *Royal George* & again on the tender. Imagine my chagrin. I could scarcely walk by this time. Fortunately it was dusk & did not seem quite so bad, but it was mortifying even in ghastly misery to be with Lord Percy & Dr. & Mrs. D. under the circumstances. Lord P. was instrumental in getting me a glass of water which seemed impossible under the conditions, & as I had whiskey, I took some to carry me through.

Then came the landing at Avonmouth & the Customs delay so that it was twelve o'clock before we could get on. As Avonmouth is not exactly Bristol & it would mean going up by a train & then again to London, we concluded to go through to London. There again God's hand was leading me, for we had intended to wait till morning. When we reached London, & shall I ever forget the misery of the train motion—(I was so seasick) & the pain too, well I was just at the fainting point & saved from it by another unloading of the stomach just beside the train as I sat on the step of the first class compartment. We came in ([for] which [a] big tip [for services] was left to Adam & to me [to pay] & I was able to lie down).

Thursday, 6 July

Adam's Diary
No room at Ry. Hotel, went to Albert hotel. Doughty found Bigger,[47] got rooms at Savoy Mansions. Arranged for Beth to see Dr. Percy Flemming, Eye Specialist.[48] Diagnosed trouble as Glaucoma requiring serious operation. Prepared to take her to private Hospital in morning.

Elizabeth's Diary
After a long delay, with Dr. D. supporting me on one side & Mrs. D. on the other, Lord Percy said goodbye & was off. No doubt he saw Lady Gordon-Lennox, daughter of the Duke of Richmond,[49] next day & Adam looked after the luggage. Dr. D. at last settled me on a valise & Mrs. D. & I stayed by the hand luggage while Adam wrestled with the trunk baggage & Dr. D. went in search of an hotel. Two of the best near ones were full but we succeeded in getting two rooms in a decent hotel nearby & I was in bed just at daylight—4 o'clock or thereabouts.

Our window looked down a real characteristic London street. A "mews," or place for conveyances &c., was in sight & nothing of that kind is seen on our side of the water. After a few hours sleep I wakened still in misery—nausea & pain & found I could not see at all with my right eye. Dr. D. was up & off to get in touch with Mr. Biggar (H. P.) who is co-adjutor in archive work but who stays in London & [surrounding] Parts (chiefly London) & who had secured rooms—a suite for him. When Dr. D. went to see them, he found we could share them. There were two bedrooms, a bathroom, washroom, bunk room & sitting room & our meals could be served in our sitting room. It was the suite on the end of the Savoy Mansions, near the Strand on Savoy St., quite close to the Savoy theatre & hotel.

So we went over there with our baggage in a taxicab. Then Dr. D. & Mr. Biggar, after failing to get an appointment with one eye specialist, secured one at 5:30 with Flem[m]ing, 70 Harley St.. When Adam & I went there in a taxi, we were unsuspecting of any serious trouble. It seems odd to me, but was still a special Providence, that I had not worried over my eye but felt I only needed a couple of days to get over it.

Dr. Flem[m]ing said I had glaucoma & was blind in my right eye & it could only be saved to me by prompt operation. He said the nausea was due to that chiefly & yet vomiting of course strained the eye. He said it was often brought on, when there was impending tendency, by seasickness or influenza or biliousness &c. That it was a trouble that not infrequently occurred to long sighted people. The eye ball seems to harden & tries apparently to push the pupil thro. the Iris, the pupil looking quite large. Then some active conjestion [*sic*] chokes the eye as it were by the tightness of the impact. The remedy is to cut out a piece of the eye & lessen the strain. Then it would not occur again.

He said he thought he could save the left eye by drops from coming to the stage of operation but it was a close shave, for I saw rainbows round every light with the left eye, as we stood on the Tender that previous night & it seems that is a symptom of glaucoma. Well, I went back to our rooms & went to bed & had quite a good night's sleep (tho. I was still seasick & was quite ill in the taxi returning from Dr. Flem[m]ing's). Adam unpacked the things & put them in the wardrobe & bureau & put the big trunk out in the hall.

Friday, 7 July

Adam's Diary
Took Beth to Miss Lancaster's Home or Private Hospital, 29 Wimpole St.. Dr. Flemming operated at 5.30 and reported operation successful. Fee 42 guineas and 3 guineas for anaesthetic. Room and nurse 10 guineas per week. Rode out to East End on bus.

Elizabeth's Diary
Next morning Adam put a few things in the black bag for me & we went to a private hospital under the care of Miss Lancaster on Wimpole Street. I was put to bed at once in a very comfortable room up two flights of stairs, which comfortable room was 10 guineas a week, if you please. Miss Lancaster is head of one of what is called Nursing Homes in London but what we call in Canada, private hospitals. It seems necessary to round up the people who can procure the services of high [highly qualified and paid] specialists into these houses near the residences of the big specialists, as they could not get to see many scattered ones in the time they have. Miss Lancaster's establishment consisted of 2½ houses of a terrace (I think four flats high) &

for this space she said she paid £1,350 rent & nearly a quarter as much more in rates & taxes. She kept 15 servants & ten nurses.

The hospital only could take in 20 or 21 patients & they were of all kinds of cases—eyes, appendix, kidney, anything—operations going on every day of the most serious nature. It had a good record too, for one of the nurses told me they had only had one death since 1st Feb. i.e. [over the last] five months. The ten guineas included everything but medicines, dressings &c. &c.

About five that day they began operations by giving me a hypodermic of morphia. I had eaten nothing since I came to London but some lovely strawberries which I had returned up with ether the day before. The only thing I had had was Horlick's malted milk which stayed down & seemed to be a comfort. Then, they gave me chloroform, a Dr. Rood giving it. They differentiate so much in London that, tho. physicians do give anesthetics for one another, they call a lot of them, Anesthetists. I think they made two mistakes. I should have had a liver cathartic at once, when Dr. F. said I had to be operated on, & then I should have had strychnine sometime before the chloroform.

I knew no more till nearly eleven o'clock. I was so very dead with morphoria & chloroform & weakness & fatigue. As soon as I regained consciousness I put my hand gently to my head & found my eye very severely bandaged up & knew that it was all over. My one prayer when I went under the anesthetic was that, if I was not to regain my sight, I might die under the chloroform. I knew life would not be happy under another such serious limitation. I knew God knew all about it & it was in His hands.

As soon as I was conscious I was conscious of horrible smothering around my heart & my throat filled with phlegm till it seemed I would strangle & choke & smother all at once. It was like the most horrible nightmares I've ever had & I could only get my right hand to help by first working my throat & then trying to raise my ribs. They had pinned each sleeve of my nightdress to the mattress to keep my hands down but, thank God, the sleeves were loose enough to let my hands & arms work through them. Anyway I would have torn them loose, so great was the terror of smothering.

I could not make anyone hear for a long time & then all she could do was to give me a drink. She knew nothing of wiping out the mouth with camphor water or anything to ease one, but a drink. I hope no one beloved by me will ever be left to waken alone out of chloroform or other anesthetic & feel so utterly helpless & alone as I did. I had been so entirely bowled over that I hadn't prearranged anything & Adam, having always left all these medical things to me, never thought of it.

Saturday, July 8

A Letter from Adam to Mrs. Smith[50]
[Elizabeth begins the letter, writing to her mother and sister, Gertrude, on 3 July.] Here we are on the Atlantic and they say we shall see the Irish coast tomorrow. It is a quick passage & it has not been rough. The weather & scenery from Montreal till the end of Gaspe was perfect, the river so fine & the shore so very picturesque. We were outside most of those days except for meals. They were days of the lotus eaters. It was in a sense always oblivious—nothing to do but dream & enjoy. Those two days were perfect, but on waking next morning (Friday), we were in the fog off Newfoundland & it continued to be fog & rain every day. Mon [July] 3rd there was not quite so much during the day, but it is settling down again.

I have only missed going down to meals once tho. I've been nauseated a lot. So yesterday I got some of the famous *mal-de-mer* remedy, Mothersill, & took a dose. I have been on deck again quite a lot today. I read & listen to the music. We have a good piano player & violinist on board from Ottawa. The violinist is going to Vienna to study—Margaret Cross. She is going alone & without knowing how to speak German either.... [The rest of this incomplete letter deals with the Shortts' socializing with the Doughtys, Lord Percy, and Mrs. Ewart aboard the *Royal George*.]

[On 8 July, Adam completes the unfinished dispatch from the Savoy Mansions in London.] I have delayed sending this letter of Beth's owing to an unexpected trouble she developed in her eyes the last day we were on the boat. It appeared like an attack of neuralgia in the right eye with the other somewhat affected. As it was still bad when we got here I at once looked up an eye specialist & took her to him where he found that she had a very serious condition of her right eye, known as *glaucoma*, a trouble which if not soon relieved causes permanent loss of sight.

I at once arranged, under the Dr's. direction, to have her placed in a private hospital yesterday morning and the operation was performed yesterday evening. The Dr. reported everything as favourable as could be expected & this morning the matron reports that she spent a good night! I will see her in a couple of hours.

It will be some time before she can be round much but I hope to have her back here to our rooms in a week or ten days where I can look after her as much as necessary. She will have to keep quiet and not use her eyes much for a time. It has quite upset our plans & I can't say as yet what changes we may have to make apart from the programme which I will have to go through in connection with my official duties. It appear[s] that this trouble of the eye, though gradually led up to, comes on suddenly in the end. It is a misfortune, indeed, but it would have been much worse if we had been somewhere beyond reach of the best skill. I will let you know tomorrow or next day when I get some more definite information as to her prospects.

A Letter from Adam to Muriel Shortt[51]
I have delayed sending this off as your mother during the last day on the boat, had a bad attack of what appeared neuralgia of the eye and was quite ill the night we landed.... [The remainder of the paragraph essentially repeats the information in the letter to Mrs. Smith, above, concerning Elizabeth's operation and prognosis.]

After taking your mother to the hospital I went to the High Commissioner's & got some letters, among them yours enclosing the two others. The one which was not opened was from Authors & Co. about George's legs. You must have forgotten that I told you to open the letters and, if they seemed to require an answer from me or to contain information I should have, to send them on but, if not, to keep them & inform the writers I had gone to England.

It seems that Authors & Co. were very busy and could not get the legs finished for some days. I hope they got them down in time for George's exams so that he would not have to wear the old ones but from their letter this seemed doubtful. If you had opened the letter you could have answered it and got some satisfaction. Our address is: Savoy Mansions, Strand, London, Eng.. With love to you all & hoping George did well on his exams.

Adam's Diary[52]
Saw Beth in morning, did shopping and ordered clothes &c. Visit from Mr. Ed. Peacock[53] and mother. Dined with them in evening and had long talk on British and Canadian politics. He will arrange for me to see some old and new friends.

Elizabeth's Diary[54]
I got through the night somehow, dozing & smothering & then in the morning, daylight & the day nurse helped a little. Dr. F. came at nine & looked at the eye & said the sight would come back if I had it before the

glaucoma, that the operation was successful, if I could keep the eye still & let it heal. I was not allowed to turn off my back for some time & then the nurse had to turn my head & body gently to my left. It was weeks before I was allowed to lie on my right side. As soon as Dr. F. said the operation was successful & that I would have my sight if I had it before, I did not worry about my eye.

I had a time of it to get the things I needed when I needed them, for the nurses were more or less perfunctory & did things as they were indexed— not as needed. For instance she always cleaned my teeth before meals because it was more convenient & fitted in with her time for other things. I have fortunately a sense of the ridiculous which helped me many times. My bowels, not being allowed to move & having all that floating bile which had been a trial since the first days of seasickness, I had a constant feeling of gas round the heart, a feeling as if the pleura was filled with gas & crowded the heart & stomach which kept up a feeling of nausea.

The bill of fare was all right. For somedays it was cut or made so fine that I was not expected to chew it, for fear of agitating my eye. Having the nausea & not having my bowels moved I could not use as much food, as they wanted to give me. The operation was Friday. Sat. evg. she fed me strawberries & cream & I could sometimes taste the berries were not fresh but as I could not see them, they were put in as they came by the nurse who fed me. [Elizabeth remained at Miss Lancaster's Private Hospital from 9 to 16 July. Her diary treats her stay there as one whole, rather than day by day. Elizabeth's material, here, is thus presented in this fashion, while Adam's accounts for this period continue in a chronological manner.]

Sunday, 9 July

Adam's Diary[55]
Spent most of forenoon with Beth. Dr. very hopeful of the case. Dr. and Mrs. Doughty and I went out to Windsor by train. Perfect day, attended even song service in St. George's Chapel, beautiful singing of boys in choir. Saw Beth in evening. Wrote Muriel.

A Letter from Adam to "Muriel & George"[56]
I have just come down from the private hospital where your mother is and the Dr. had just been in to see how her eye was getting on. He was very pleased with the way it was healing up after the operation & reports

favourably about the left eye on which he did not operate, but which was in poor shape also.

We are hoping that she may get back to the rooms here before the end of this week and then she may rest for a time. I was out at Windsor Castle today & heard the even song service in St. George's Chapel in which a number of boys with very fine soprano voices took part. The views from the castle are very fine.

Last night I had dinner with Mr. Peacock and his mother and we will see them again before they leave for Canada. Today Dr. Doughty saw Mrs. D. Gibson of Ottawa and she is going to see your mother. I have seen Mr. O'Halloran[57] on the street, Dick Waldron of Kingston, Mr. M. Mackenzie, M.P.P. of Macleod Alta. & a couple of men from Calgary, also Prof. Howard Murray of Dalhousie University, Halifax,[58] and one or two other Canadians. Tomorrow I will start in regularly on my work here as there are only another three weeks of the month left! I have not called on many people yet, but will look up some right away. You can still send letters to the High Commissioner's at Victoria St., as they will have any change of address which we may make.

I see by the papers that they have been having it very hot in America including Montreal & Toronto & I suppose you have not escaped it in Ottawa. It would come just in the midst of George's exams & if he had to depend on his old legs for some days it would not be very pleasant. I hope you had a cab to take him back & forth to the examination hall. Before this [letter arrives], of course, he will have his legs back & I hope they were much improved.

Outside of the heat, we get very little Canadian news here. Forin promised to send us a paper now & again. I have been so taken up with your mother's eye trouble that I have not had time to get my typewriter in order but expect to send my next letter to you on it. Lorraine I expect is enjoying her holiday and will be nearly ready for Kingston by the time this reaches you. Tell her I have not yet seen any of the pins with the kittens on them but may find one later on.

We are in the very centre of London here being just off the Strand, between it & the Thames Embankment where there is a sort of park along the riverfront between Waterloo Bridge & the Houses of Parliament. Waterloo Bridge is just a block from us and the Parliament buildings & Westminister Abbey about three & four blocks. We are two & a half blocks from Trafalgar Square & the National Gallery and right in the midst of the theatres & hotels. I hope you are not finding the house-keeping too strenuous or the youngster [Lorraine] too obstreperous. With love to you all & hope to hear soon how you are getting on.

Monday, 10 July

Adam's Diary[59]
Making connections on phone. Mr. Peacock rang up to say that Mr. Steel-Maitland[60] invited us to lunch, Thursday, and Mr. Oliver[61] to dinner same day. Letter from Lord Percy with note from Duke of Northumberland to keeper of Westminster. Afternoon with Mr. Stanley Leather [*sic*][62] of C.S. Commission.

A Letter from Adam to Mrs. Smith[63]
Just a line to say that Beth is getting on nicely. The Dr. is now quite sure that the sight of her [right] eye will be saved though she will have to be careful of both eyes and especially the left from this time on. She is in very comfortable quarters, but we hope to have her back here by the end of the week.

We have had it very warm here until this morning,[64] but you seem to have had it still warmer in Canada. It was too bad that George should have such weather for his examinations. As Beth has not been able to go round any since our arrival we have not seen much of London as yet except what I have been over on business. Yesterday, however, Sunday, I went out to Windsor & walked around the outside of the Castle & heard a musical service in St. George's Chapel.

Although Beth will not be able to go about as much as she expected, yet when she is able to go out at all we will see some of the special buildings &c.. Meantime I have many official people to look up, & other business to attend to.

With kindest regards for Gertie

Tuesday, 11 July

Adam's Diary[65]
To Bank, Lunch with Prin. Gordon and Miss Minnie.[66] Interview with Mr. Larren a Rhodes Scholar for Assistant [professorship] in English at Queen's. Took long walks, got some books and portrait of Lord Durham. Visited Beth and read letters from Muriel and others. Saw much of city today.

Wednesday, 12 July

Adam's Diary
Out book hunting after writing. To House of Commons in afternoon. Heard Lloyd George, Harcourt,[67] Austin [*sic*] Chamberlain,[68] Hon. Walter Long[69] and several others. Chamberlain poor speaker; Long and George very good.

Saw Beth, getting better fast.

Saw John Burns.[70]

Thursday, July 13

Adam's Diary
Out with Doughty book hunting. To lunch with Mr. Steel-Maitland,[71] Mrs. S-M, Mr. W. Maitland of Rl'y. Dept., India office,[72] Mr. Meiklejohn, Mr. Askwith's [*sic*] private secty,[73] and Peacock.

Dinner with Mr. —— Oliver,[74] Mrs. O., L. Curtis,[75] Col. —— and Peacock.

Saw Beth in afternoon.

Friday, 14 July

Adam's Diary
Book hunting in morning, small success. Royal Academy in afternoon, some very fine pictures and few extremes. Some very fine water colours and etchings. Portraits numerous and mostly very good.

Evening with Beth. Still improving.

A Letter from Adam to "Muriel and George"[76]
As I stated on my card we received your letter of the 1st which I read to your mother. I have just returned from a visit to her. She is getting on quite well though the healing of the eye & the recovery of the sight after the operation is a slow matter. We hope to have her down here again on Monday 17th or Tuesday at latest. But even then she will not be able to go out for a week or so. Dr. & Mrs. Doughty have been up to see her a couple of times and Mrs. Peacock also. Otherwise she is alone except when I am there.

I have seen quite a number of people and yesterday I was at lunch with Mr. Steel-Maitland who was out in Canada with Lord Milner[77] & is now next to Mr. Balfour in the direction of the Liberal-Unionist party. Then I was at dinner with Mr. Oliver who is a writer of some distinction and quite a power in politics. In both cases Mr. Peacock went with me. In the later case I saw Mr. [Lionel] Curtis who was at our place in Ottawa. I was in the House of Commons one afternoon & heard Mr. Lloyd George, Mr. Austin [sic] Chamberlain, Mr. Walter Long and several others. Just before going into the gallery I saw my friend, Hon. John Burns,[78] who invited me to call on him next week. I have seen several people also on Civil Service business. The other day, too, I met Col. Taylor who used to be the Commandant at the R.M.C. in Kingston and had a good talk with him about Canadian & other matters.

We are having quite ideal weather here, no rain for over two weeks and some days almost too warm for comfort but a breeze up from the sea every night. Your mother wants to know what kind of a watch you [Muriel] want, a black one, silver one, or a gold (9 carats). [In] the latter case he had on [it] a leather bracelet for $15 or a gold bracelet of the same standard for about $20. Today I got the set of golf sticks and a bag and now I will be able to play if we go into the country where there are golf links; then I can take them home without duty.

I see you have been having it pretty warm in America with serious bush fires up in northern Ontario. I hope George got on all right with his exams and is down to regular work at the Archives. Lorraine will be in Kingston by the time this reaches her. I am enclosing with this 300 miscellaneous stamps for George which I got for a couple of Shillings. Tell Lorraine when you write that after much search in the stores, I got a pin with two kittens on it. Love to you all.

Saturday, 15 July

Adam's Diary[79]
Called on Sir Hoffman Jost [sic] at Colonial Office.[80] He will get me introductions to other Depts. Called on Sir Chas. Lucas, also of Colonial Office. He is getting out Durham's Report and Appendixes.[81] Lunch with Mr. Biggar;[82] O'Halloran[83] and Doughty present. Went with latter to zoo.

Sunday, 16 July

Adam's Diary
Took river steamer to Hampton Court but it stuck in river and waited for tide. Very interesting trip, racing craft, pleasure boats. Beautiful gardens up

river and luxurious house boats. Came back by train. Saw Beth, will get out tomorrow.

9–16 July

Elizabeth's Diary[84]
Well, Sun. [9 July] they consented to give me a little calomel about ten o'clock [a.m.]. In less than an hour I felt a great need of unloading & called the nurse, but I could never find the bedpan a substitute for the natural methods & on account of my eye I was not free to make any effort. I explained to two diff. nurses & had one of them go to Miss Lancaster & explain my needs—a very small injection of water. No, the time was not due, the hour was not auspicious. I had to suffer six hrs. before they gave way, when I flatly refused to eat another bite until they gave me relief. I think the day nurse in a great temper gave in. At once great relief, great cause for everything. The strawberries being half decayed had set up a great fermentation & consequences ensued. There was a humorous side, but I was annoyed under all my other difficulties to have to lie helpless & absorbing poisonous matter which would have to be eliminated again for [after] six hours.

I asked Dr. Flem[m]ing when he came that afternoon if he thought by the time we were as old as India we would be as helplessly bound up in complications? I narrated a case of one of our women missionaries who on being called to a case of Placenta Previa in a young wife & finding instead relief necessary, so informed the husband through the women in charge. The husband went to the priest & the priest consulted the oracle & the reply came back through the diff. stages again, to say it could not be done today for it was not an auspicious day. On the Dr's. telling her [the woman in charge], it must [be done] to save the 18 yr. old life—& that she would die if it was delayed—still the answer came back that it was not an auspicious day & she could come back tomorrow. So in spite of the entreaties of the young wife to save her, she had to turn her back on her & go away. Next day on inquiring she was dead! I did not explain my illustration, but I thought, if there were any explanations between the nurse and him [Dr. Flemming], he would find the analogy.

I had the best hour of each day, barring Adam's daily visit, with Dr. F. during his half hour call at nine [a.m.] & at 5:30 or six [p.m.]. He came very promptly & faithfully twice a day & I had quite a lot of fun—in talk—with him. He said I was getting younger every day & I think it was just at the last he said: "I had been the most cheerful glaucoma patient he had ever had." Said he didn't think I had worried about my eye as much as he had. I told him I hadn't since he said I would have my sight again—that I had had before. He said once it was getting better in spite of me because I did not keep still enough & moved my head too much. But I said I didn't like that way of putting it for I felt I was getting my eye healed right, with my able assistance.

I was urging to go back to Savoy Mansions at the end of the week. It was so expensive but he said he had never let them go short of ten days & two wks. was short enough. I said I didn't see why I couldn't go to him every day in a taxi after one wk. & he said that showed how little I realized how necessary the most rigid care of my eye was necessary.

By this time I was allowed to sit up in bed & anyone who has tried that knows how tiring it can be. So I said to him next day you chaff me about going to you once a day in a taxi with Mr. Shortt's assistance. Now do you think that is any worse than being suspended by the back of the head on four pillows & bracing your feet on a sliding surface to keep from going downstream? He just laughed. I told him the expense worried me a lot, & one day after he insisted on the 10 days stay, I had had [sic] recalled to mind Maud's[85] injunction:

> Ah take the cash & let the credit go
> For she who spent her coin on flannels red
> And she who took pneumonia instead
> Will both be underground in fifty years
> And prudence pays no premium to the dead

He seemed much taken with the parody.

Mrs. Peacock came up twice to see me, but as she was in the country for some days, she did not get [here] more frequently. The Doughtys were in twice to see me & Adam came every day but that was all my visitors & not being able to sleep but little & generally not till one o'clock [a.m.], the hours seemed very long. I think I was never so lonesome since I first went away to school. I could not read nor write nor move nor even play cards & yet I had all my senses except sight. I thought of starting another society—one to go & read to strangers who took ill away from home. Adam of course was busy most of the day & when he came in the evg., he told me what he had been doing & read the letters. Letters were never more welcome & especially from Muriel & George & Lorraine.

Each day went on pretty much the same—the nausea getting less after I had the wee bit of calomel, but not entirely so. It was a long week. Sat. afternoon I was allowed up for half an hour. Sun. I was up & dressed from 2 to seven & tried to walk across the room & was soon able to do so. The day nurse was in intelligence like Miss Lloyd & like thousands of others. One day when I was fainting with the pressure of gas round my heart & she was advising me to eat & I was trying to sit up, hoping I might be able to eat, she said as to a child: "you know I'll be quite worried if you do not eat" but she had to bring me hot water & tea, all the same before my heart regained its full beat.

I think the Canadian nurses have quite abit more individuality & we do know somethings they do not in England & no doubt the converse is true too. English people overwork the word "quite" and Germans do the same by "so" & perhaps we use the word "yes" in quite a few cases of their meanings of these words, an expression often [over-]used. I remember the night nurse who was a modern Sarah Gamp[86] saying one night, when she was setting me for the night, & I did not feel the pillows fit my head: "your pillows are quite all right." No doubt they were the right number & they were lying one on top of the other, but it did not matter whether they were comfortable to the patient.

She was expected to move my head very carefully at night when I turned, but I had to look after that myself & take it in my two hands & firmly and gently turn it over myself when she turned my shoulders. She frequently advised me to take aspirin to make me sleep. I knew enough not to do so, but I thought how a baby would fare [badly] in her hands at night.

Notes

1 University of Waterloo, Elizabeth Smith Shortt Papers (hereafter cited as ESSP), WA10, file 1034, Smith Shortt to Damaris I. McGee Smith, 30 January 1911; see also Sheryl Stotts McLaren, *Becoming Indispensable: A Biography of Elizabeth Smith Shortt 1859–1949* (Ph.D. diss., York University, 2001), 267.

2 See "Frequently Mentioned Names" on p. xix for information on Mrs. Damaris Isabella Smith and her daughter Miss Gertrude Smith.

3 See "Frequently Mentioned Names" on p. xix.

4 See "Frequently Mentioned Names" on p. xix.

5 ESSP, WA10, file 1034, Smith Shortt to Damaris I. McGee Smith, 1 February 1911.

6 Mrs. Clarissa Ami was a neighbour and close friend of the Shortts, and her husband was Henri-Marc Ami, a leading paleontologist and prehistorian in Canada. By 1911, his savings and his wife's dowry enabled him to resign from the Geological Survey, where he had worked since 1882, principally as a geologist, to pursue his private interests in prehistory. Raymond Duchesne, "Henri-Marc Ami," in *The Canadian Encyclopedia*, 2nd ed., vol. 1 (Edmonton: Hurtig Publishers, 1988), 70.

7 ESSP, WA10, file 1034, Smith Shortt to Damaris I. McGee Smith, 24 February 1911.

8 See "Frequently Mentioned Names" on p. xix.

9 ESSP, WA10, file 1051, Smith Shortt to Gertrude Smith, 31 March 1911.

10 See "Frequently Mentioned Names" on p. xix.

11 ESSP, WA10, file 1034, Smith Shortt to Damaris I. McGee Smith, 28 May 1911.

12 ESSP, WA10, file 1034, Smith Shortt to Damaris I. McGee Smith, 12 June 1911.

13 Walter Charles Murray was the president, not the principal, of the University of Saskatchewan, beginning with his appointment in 1908; Sir Charles G. D. Roberts and Arthur Leonard Tunnell, eds., *Canadian Who's Who, 1936–1937* (Toronto: Murray Publishing, 1936), 819.

14 See "Frequently Mentioned Names" on p. xix.

15 See "Frequently Mentioned Names" on p. xx.

16 Charles Gordon Hewitt was an English professor of zoology at the University of Manchester until his appointment as Canada's dominion entomologist in 1909, where, like Adam Shortt, he became an influential member of the federal bureaucracy; *Canadian Who's Who, 1910* (London: Times Publishing Company, 1910), 106.

17 ESSP, WA10, file 1034, Smith Shortt to Mother, 25 June 1911.

18 This was Elizabeth and Muriel Shortt's project to create a residence for women at Queen's University based on a grant from a wealthy benefactor such as Lord

Strathcona in England; see, for example, ESSP, WA10, file 423, Smith Shortt to Lord Strathcona, 16 November 1910.

19 The finding aid lists this letter from Elizabeth to Gertrude Smith in file 1051 as "n.d., 1912," but the context clearly relates to the period shortly before the Shortts' sailing from Montreal to England; ESSP, WA10, file 1051, Smith Shortt to Gertrude Smith, "n.d., 1912."

20 On June 22, the coronation of King George V took place in Westminster Abbey, and a considerable cleanup was required in its aftermath. For example, even within the confines of the Cathedral, "the cleaners who swept up the Abbey afterwards resisted the temptation to pocket three ropes of pearls, twenty brooches, half a dozen bracelets, twenty golden balls dislodged from coronets and three-quarters of a diamond necklace, in all a haul worth 20,000 pounds, most of which was eventually returned safely to its owners." Juliet Nicolson, *The Perfect Summer: Dancing into Shadow in 1911* (Toronto: McArthur, 2007), 117.

21 Queen's University Archives, Adam Shortt Papers (hereafter cited as ASP), box 11, Adam Shortt Diary, typed transcript, 24 June 1911.

22 In 1906, Robert Glasgow founded the publishing firm of Glasgow, Brook and Co., which began to publish the Makers of Canada series that included Adam Shortt's *Life of Lord Sydenham*; Carl Berger, *The Writing of Canadian History: Aspects of English-Canadian Historical Writing, 1900–1970* (Toronto: Oxford University Press, 1976), 28.

23 The Rideau Club was in 1911 a men's club, founded by Sir John A. Macdonald, which brought together members of the political, bureaucratic, and business elites in Ottawa; John Robert Colombo, *Colombo's Canadian References* (Toronto: Oxford University Press, 1976), 445.

24 Frederick A. Acland was a journalist in England, the United States, and Canada who became the secretary to the Department of Labour in 1907, and then the deputy minister of Labour, the highest civil service position in this federal ministry, the following year; *Canadian Who's Who, 1910*, 1.

25 John Archibald Ruddick was another prominent national official who had served as Canada's dairy commissioner since 1905, following a lengthy career in the public services of both New Zealand and his native Canada; *Canadian Who's Who, 1910*, 200.

26 With Adam Shortt, Michel G. Larochelle was the co-commissioner of the Dominion civil service, positions that had been created in 1908. Prior to the appointment, Larochelle was a Quebec lawyer and former secretary to Wilfrid Laurier, and soon conflicts between Shortt and Larochelle developed; Barry Ferguson, *Remaking Liberalism: The Intellectual Legacy of Adam Shortt,*

O. D. Skelton, W. C. Clark, and W. A. Mackintosh, 1890–1925 (Montreal: McGill-Queen's University Press, 1993), 125–26.

27 Cecilia Morgan, *"A Happy Holiday": English Canadians and Transatlantic Tourism, 1870–1930* (Toronto: University of Toronto Press, 2008), 38.

28 Morgan, *"A Happy Holiday,"* 40.

29 Diana C. Reep, *Margaret Deland* (Boston: Twayne Publishers, 1985), 15.

30 Reep, *Margaret Deland,* 14.

31 Reep, *Margaret Deland,* 64.

32 Reep, *Margaret Deland,* 64–65.

33 Reep, *Margaret Deland,* 13.

34 ASP, box 11, Adam Shortt Diary, 27 June 1911.

35 Oscar Douglas Skelton succeeded Adam Shortt as the John A. Macdonald Professor of Political and Economic Science at Queen's University after the latter left for Ottawa and the Civil Service Commission in 1908. Skelton and his wife, Isabel, were close friends of both the Shortts, from whom they purchased their Kingston house; Terry Crowley, *Marriage of Minds: Isabel and Oscar Skelton Reinventing Canada* (Toronto: University of Toronto Press, 2003), 16, 25–26, 29–34, 44–45, 57–58.

36 James Blake Hunter entered the public service in 1899, and by 1908 was appointed deputy minister of Public Works, an office he continued to hold in 1911; *Canadian Who's Who, 1910,* 112.

37 ESSP, WA10, file 1772, Smith Shortt Diary, 27 June 1911.

38 Andrew Haydon was a former student of Adam Shortt's at Queen's. Haydon collectively and affectionately referred to Shortt's students as the professor's "boys"; Andrew Haydon, "Adam Shortt," *Queen's Quarterly* XXXVIII (1931): 613. Haydon became a leading lawyer in the Ottawa area and an influential Liberal Party activist; *Encyclopaedia Canadiana,* vol. 5 (Toronto: Grolier of Canada, 1975), 98.

39 Duncan McArthur was another of Shortt's "boys" at Queen's, where he attained a B.A. in 1907 and an M.A. in 1908. In 1911, McArthur was employed at the Dominion Archives in Ottawa under A. G. Doughty, with whom he would later collaborate in the publication of several historical materials; *Canadian Who's Who, 1936–1937,* 727.

40 See "Frequently Mentioned Names" on p. xxi.

41 The passenger list of the *Royal George* can be found in the Smith Shortt Papers and reveals that the Episcopalian minister was Rev. Irving Johnson from Minnesota; ESSP, WA10, file 2052.

42 Hotspur (Henry Percy, 1364–1403) was an heir to another Duke of Northumberland, who led a rebellion against King Henry IV and was defeated at the

battle of Shrewsbury, where he was killed. Hotspur was immortalized in Shakespeare's play *Henry IV*, which depicted him as an youthful and attractive but ultimately tragic hero.

43 Rev. Robert Simpson Laidlaw was the Presbyterian pastor of St. Andrew's Church in Belleville, Ontario, from 1904 to 1909, until his appointment as the head of St. Paul's Church in Brandon, Manitoba, where he continued to be stationed in 1911; *Canadian Who's Who, 1936–1937*, 606.

44 ASP, box 11, Adam Shortt Diary, 5 July 1911.

45 Miss Clara Doerr (note the incorrect spelling in the transcription of Adam's diary), of Minneapolis, Minnesota, was a fellow first-class passenger on the *Royal George* who assisted Mrs. Shortt in her time of distress; ESSP, WA10, file 2052.

46 ESSP, WA10, file 1772, Smith Shortt Diary, 5 July 1911.

47 Beginning in 1905, H. P. Biggar was Canada's chief archivist for the Dominion Archives in Great Britain and Europe; *Colombo's Canadian References*, 41.

48 Dr. Percy Flemming was a professor of ophthalmic medicine and surgery at University College, London, a leading practitioner in the field; *Who's Who, 1915* (London: A. & C. Black, 1915), 741.

49 Lady Helen Gordon-Lennox was the youngest daughter of the 7th Duke of Richmond. She married Lord Percy in 1911; *Who's Who, 1915*, 1696.

50 ESSP, WA10, file 1035, Smith Shortt to Damaris I. McGee Smith, 3 July 1911; and Adam Shortt to Mrs. Smith, 8 July 1911.

51 ESSP, WA10, file 1245, Adam Shortt to Muriel Clarke, 8 July 1911.

52 ASP, box 11, Adam Shortt Diary, 8 July 1911.

53 See "Frequently Mentioned Names" on p. xxi.

54 ESSP, WA10, file 1772, Smith Shortt Diary, 8 July 1911.

55 ASP, box 11, Adam Shortt Diary, 9 July 1911.

56 ESSP, WA10, file 1245, Adam Shortt to Muriel Clarke, 9 July 1911.

57 George Finlay O'Halloran was deputy minister of agriculture and deputy commissioner of patents for the Canadian government, and, like Shortt, a member of Ottawa's bureaucratic elite; *Canadian Who's Who, 1910*, 175.

58 Howard Murray was dean of Dalhousie College in Halifax, Nova Scotia, and had taught classics at the same institution since 1890; *Canadian Who's Who, 1910*, 170.

59 ASP, box 11, Adam Shortt Diary, 10 July 1911.

60 Arthur Steel-Maitland had been the Conservative Member of Parliament for East Birmingham since 1910, and chair of the Unionist Party organization, which united the Conservatives and some dissident Liberals who had left that party after Gladstone endorsed Home Rule for Ireland in 1886; *Who's Who, 1915*, 2034.

61 Frederick Scott Oliver was a barrister and political author in England who wielded considerable influence within the Unionist Party ranks; *Who's Who, 1915,* 1627.

62 Stanley Leathes (note the incorrect spelling in the transcription of Adam's diary) had been a British civil service commissioner since 1907, and the first commissioner beginning in 1910 after teaching and serving as an administrator at Cambridge University; *Who's Who, 1915,* 1261.

63 ESSP, WA10, file 1426, Adam Shortt to Damaris I. McGee Smith, 10 July 1911.

64 As Nicolson points out, by early July, "The oppressive weather was becoming hard to tolerate. On Saturday 8 July stuffy theatres reported matinee attendance well below average, while four people were admitted to St. Bart's Hospital and another four to Guy's, suffering from heatstroke.... To the young novelist D. H. Lawrence, from the Midlands, London seemed like 'some hoary massive underworld, a hoary ponderous inferno'"; Nicolson, *The Perfect Summer,* 127.

65 ASP, box 11, Adam Shortt Diary, 11 July 1911.

66 Miss Minnie Gordon was the daughter of Principal Donald M. Gordon of Queen's University, and she looked after her father and his household following the death of her mother, Eliza, in 1910; D. B. Mack, "Daniel Miner Gordon," in *The Dictionary of Canadian Biography,* vol. xv (Toronto: University of Toronto Press, 2005), 415. As part of this responsibility, Miss Gordon accompanied her father on their visit to London.

67 The Right Honourable Lewis Vernon Harcourt was the Liberal member from Rossendale Division, Lancashire, since 1904, and secretary for the colonies in Asquith's cabinet, beginning in 1910, after a stint as the first commissioner of works in the same ministry from 1908 to 1910; *Who's Who, 1915,* 949.

68 Sir (Joseph) Austen (note the misspelling in the transcript) Chamberlain was the eldest son of British stateman Joseph Chamberlain, and a Conservative member of the House of Commons from 1892. By 1911, he was a notable figure in the Tory opposition ranks, and later that year was seriously considered as a potential party leader until his withdrawal from consideration in favour of Bonar Law; *Encyclopaedia Britannica,* vol. 3, 64.

69 Walter Hume Long was the other main contender for the Conservative leadership in 1911, until Bonar Law emerged as a successful compromise candidate. He had served the party in the House of Commons since 1880, and as a cabinet minister from 1895 to 1905, while remaining a wealthy land owner who possessed approximately 15,500 acres throughout Great Britain; *Who's Who, 1915,* 1315.

70 John Elliott Burns was an active trade unionist and socialist who was originally elected to the House of Commons in 1892. He subsequently broke with the Independent Labour Party, founded in 1893, and twelve years later entered

Campbell-Bannerman's Liberal ministry as president of the Local Government Board. He remained in that position within Asquith's Liberal cabinet down to 1911; *Encyclopaedia Britannica*, vol. 2, 662.

71 See ch. 1, n. 60.

72 William James Maitland was the former deputy governor director of the Indian Guaranteed Railways, and by 1911 a relatively minor player in British political circles; *Who's Who, 1915*, 1419.

73 Roderick Sinclair Meiklejohn was a British bureaucrat who had served in the War Office and the Treasury before becoming private secretary to Sir E. Hamilton, the Duke of Devonshire, and then to H. H. Asquith (note the misspelling in the transcript) during his tenure as both the chancellor of the exchequer and prime minister; *Who's Who, 1915*, 1475.

74 See ch. 1, n. 61.

75 Lionel George Curtis fought in the South African War, and after its conclusion became secretary to Sir Alfred Milner, the British high commissioner in South Africa. Here, Curtis developed a concept of the British Empire evolving into a "Commonwealth" of equal partners that he propagated in the Liberal imperialist journal *Round Table*, which he founded in 1910. Curtis is generally credited with coining the term *The Commonwealth of Nations*, which became the title of his first major book in 1916; *Encyclopaedia Britannica*, vol. 3, 805.

76 ESSP, WA10, file 1245, Adam Shortt to Muriel Clarke, 14 July 1911.

77 Viscount Alfred Milner was the governor of the Cape Colony during the outbreak of the South African War, and his refusal to bargain with the Boers is generally cited as an immediate cause of the conflict. Milner was equally inflexible in the postwar reconstruction period, which he largely directed, and British criticism of his intransigence led to his return to England and a retirement from public life; *Encyclopaedia Britannica*, vol. 8, 140.

78 See ch. 1, n. 70.

79 ASP, box 11, Adam Shortt Diary, 15 July 1911.

80 Despite the incorrect spelling in the transcription of Adam's diary, this reference apparently is to Sir Hartmann Wolfgang Just, who had been the assistant under-secretary of state for the colonies since 1907. As part of the responsibilities of this office, he served as secretary at the Imperial Conferences held during this period; *Who's Who, 1915*, 1168.

81 Sir Charles Prestwood Lucas was a career official at the British Colonial Office, where in 1911 he served as assistant under-secretary of state in charge of the Dominions Department. Lucas had by this time authored several works on Canadian history, in particular, and the British Empire, in general; *Who's Who, 1915*, 1329.

82 See ch. 1, n. 47.

83 See ch. 1, n. 57.

84 ESSP, WA10, file 1772, Smith Shortt Diary, 9–16 July 1911.

85 This probably refers to Mrs. Maud Service Rankin, a close personal friend of Elizabeth Shortt, especially during the period 1876–81; ESSP, WA10, files 363–68.

86 Charles Dickens satirized Mrs. Sarah Gamp, a fictional domiciliary nurse, in his mid-nineteenth-century novel *Martin Chuzzlewit*. As Hayward has pointed out, "Sarah Gamp and Betsy Prig [another nurse in *Martin Chuzzlewit*] accurately portrayed the appalling character of the professional nurses of the time. Dickens' exposure of the cruelty, drunkeness and ignorance of these women had much to do with their final disappearance"; Arthur L. Hayward, *The Dickens Encyclopaedia* (Hamden, CT: Archon Books, 1968), 66. Anne Summers later agreed with the negative image epitomized by Sarah Gamp in *Martin Chuzzlewit*, but challenged the soundness of Dickens' judgments on the work of such domiciliary nurses and the reasons for their passing; Anne Summers, "The Mysterious Demise of Sarah Gamp: The Domiciliary Nurse and Her Detractors, c. 1830–1860," in *Victorian Studies* 32, no. 3 (Spring 1989): 365–86.

Chapter 2

At Home in the Mother Country

After Elizabeth's release from Miss Lancaster's hospital, the Shortts began their systematic probe of England's capital. For Beth, the freedom to roam around London represented a personal emancipation, and her first walk since the eye surgery "was like getting out of prison" (20 July). Meanwhile, Adam continued to focus on the business side of his visit and valuable contacts with British politicians and bureaucrats who could advise the Canadian commissioner on how to reform the Dominion's civil service (18, 19, 20, 21, 22, 24, and 25 July). On one occasion, the couple had to forgo a social invitation in order to accommodate Mr. Shortt's work obligations. As Mrs. Shortt reported to their children on 21 July, "we are invited to a tea at Headquarters Staff at Bisley today but your father is too busy to go." Elizabeth had more personal time at her disposal, but she also had feminist objectives to discuss, which became evident when women activists such as Mrs. Maud of the British Mothers' Union (22 July) and the Countess Dowager of Chichester (31 July; see ch. 3) called on the prominent social reformer from Ottawa. Shortt learned a great deal about the British Mothers' Union from Mrs. Maud, who was the secretary of the organization's central council. Beth was especially pleased to discover that Maud's conceptions of this group's work "were liberal as mine almost," and not as imperious as Shortt had anticipated. "She read me Mrs. Campbell's letter from Toronto which gave me that [dictatorial] impression & I've no doubt my own would have had much the same ring" (22 July). Shortt's ability to utilize self-criticism often yielded valuable insights.

The Shortts, however, did find time to deal with interests beyond their professional agendas while moving about an England where, in 1911, "the exuberance and self-congratulatory spirit ... was in many ways illusory."[1]

Momentous changes were taking place underneath the placid surface of British society, and it was an exciting time for two Canadians to descend on the imperial centre. Adam, for example, obviously enjoyed his visit to Lord Strathcona's estate (17–18 July), whose owner had "earned a reputation for his lavish hospitality."[2] He also relished several excursions to London's bookshops (c. 18, 22, 23, 24, 26, and 27 July).

Beth lamented her physical inability to attend Strathcona's opulent reception (21 July), but she eagerly accepted a dinner invitation from the Desboroughs, which Mrs. Shortt buoyantly described as "my first social dissipation since I left the boat" (22 July). Several other soirées provided by the same gracious hosts followed (23, 25, and 26 July). Even before these social get-togethers began, Elizabeth had sought out Mrs. Desborough's advice on where to buy clothes, and her first purchases were made at Penberthy's on Oxford Street, which her London guide had recommended. The gloves and stockings that Mrs. Shortt bought in this stylish English store were "not so very cheap but were very good" (20 July).

When further shopping trips revealed that high costs were widespread among London's clothiers, Mrs. Desborough explained that "things were never so dear," because the city's merchants were hoping to realize exceptional profits from the affluent visitors who had poured into the British capital for the recent coronation (26 July). More specifically, she suggested that Beth should contact Desborough's dressmaker, who could provide both lower prices and yet high quality, an offer which Shortt readily embraced (25 and 26 July and 3 August; on the latter, see ch. 3). Mrs. Desborough was not only a fine hostess, but also an apt consultant on London's inflated clothing markets. Like many other English Canadian women in this period, Mrs. Shortt "saw London as the arbiter of standards for fashionable dress."[3] Aided by Desborough's wise counsel, Elizabeth bought a large quantity of apparel there, which, we shall see in the conclusion, could be deemed excessive.

Shortt was grateful to the Desboroughs for both their company and practical help (2 August; see ch. 3). However, Elizabeth was also intent on utilizing her medical training and knowledge, which caused her to rebuke Mrs. Desborough's smoking habits. Beth's critique had almost a late-twentieth-century ring to it: "She is not very well & [yet] she smoked a cigarette. I hope it will keep on making her sick. She is so delicate & certainly it will not do her any good" (25 July).

The journey to Oxford was more positive for the Shortts. Here Elizabeth met the recently wed Mrs. Maude Grant, who favourably impressed her more than any other person she encountered on the trip for the first time. That same day, the well-read Mrs. Shortt discovered that the model for the famous heroine in *Alice in Wonderland*, Alice Hargreaves (née Liddell), "had married and become not even interesting above the usual," an opinion confirmed by more recent scholarship.[4] Meanwhile, in the evening Adam dominated a "very lively and interesting talk on Imperial problems" at the university, which he "enjoyed ... very much" (28 July). For both the Shortts, in varying degrees, the stay in England was a rewarding mix of work and play.

Monday, 17 July

Adam's Diary[5]
Brought Beth back to the room at Savoy Mansions, much better. Stayed in fixing things up. Took train at 1.55 at St. Pancras station for Lord Strathcona's garden party at Heliden [*sic*] Hall, Essex.[6] Large number of Canadians there, very enjoyable and lavish hospitality.

Elizabeth's Diary[7]
Well Mon. came at last—the 10th day & I was up & dressed before the Dr. came & ready to go away. The extras—dressings, bandages, &c. added to the 10 guineas & her [Miss Lancaster's] overcharge of ½ day made it just 8 dollars a day & came to $80. The anesthetist 15 dollars, Dr. F's first fee, 10.00, his later fee, 40.00 & my glasses, 8+. Of course, my expense for room at Savoy Mansions was still going on. At least Adam used the room & of course there was no reduction on my not being there. So the eye trouble cost over [$] 300.00 & two wks. loss of time & loss of courage & weeks of bother with my eye. I am wondering & trying to find, if there is any Belladona oil extract in Mothersill, as I took doses of that on the Mon. & Tues., the nights of which the trouble came up. Dr. F. said when there is an impending glaucoma or a tendency to it that Belladona would bring it on. I must find out if possible.

I went to our rooms in Savoy Mansions on Mon. 17th, the day of Lord Strathcona's garden party at Debden Hall. Adam went & had a very nice time. Saw Mrs. Fielding,[8] Mrs. Ewart & others who when hearing of my affliction were of course very properly sorry & sent all kinds of nice messages.

Tuesday, 18 July

Adam's Diary
Did not go out till late. Took a long turn through the South side of London over the river by Brixton and Camberwell. Saw Dr. Gordon and Mr. Macartney candidate for English. Saw some old books and prints and spent evening at rooms. Wrote to Muriel.

A Letter from Adam to Muriel and George[9]
Last night we received two letters from Muriel with enclosures and one from George & Lorraine. One of the letters was from Author and Co., again explaining about the legs and how they had been shipped. Like the other it should have been opened of course as it was no good to us since it was too late to reply with instructions &c.. Another [letter] forwarded without opening was a worthless advertisement. Fortunately they have followed my instructions at the office so we get from there only what they cannot answer or what is worth sending on.

We were very glad to get the news from you all, even though you have been having extreme heat. George's letter about his exams came this evening dated July 9th, though the one dated July 1st came only last night. I hope he has got on better with his last two papers on French & German. It was too bad about the Geometry which I thought was one of his good subjects. Tell him he should not put such a string of letters after my name. Neither should he write LL.D. with a period after the first L.. Finally, he should not spell Golf, "*Golph*." That reminds me that I got Muriel her set of golf sticks and a bag and much cheaper than in Ottawa. It was not very easy, however, to get a left hand set, as not many English people play left handed, though many Scotch people do.

Your mother was well enough to come back to the rooms yesterday and has been getting on quite well with the aid of dark glasses & will have to remain inside for a week yet. It is too bad, for we have not had a drop of rain, since we landed, and it is usually very wet & foggy in this region. About the time she may go out we are likely to have rain according to the prolis. Dr. & Mrs. Doughty are going over to France tomorrow for the rest of the week so we will be here alone for a few days. In about three or four days your mother expects to be able to write a bit by using her right eye. I have no doubt the weather is more tolerable there now. You did not say whether the great rain storm cut away any of our [ground] bank at the side.

I have been seeing a good many people & have been to some lunch [*sic*] and dinners. Yesterday afternoon I went to Lord Strathcona's At Home at Debden [Hall] near Cambridge. He took the people out by special train & sent them back in like manner. He has a beautiful place there & it was a delightful day. Among the people you would know who were there were Mr. & Mrs. & Miss Ewart, Senator & Mrs. Power,[10] Senator Watson,[11] Hon. Geo. E. Foster,[12] Lt. Gov. Gibson of Ont.,[13] Mr. O'Halloran,[14] Wilfrid Campbell,[15] Mrs. Fielding[16] & two of her daughters (one, Mrs. Macfield). Also many other Canadians & folk from other colonies.

I have done most of my shopping but your mother has hers all to do yet. Fortunately the cheap sales are still on and likely to remain on for the rest of the month. I got Lorraine her kittens [pin] the other day after quite a search. I wrote her a card to Kingston, saying they were for her birthday. I have not been to any shows or entertainments except the annual exhibition of pictures at the Royal Academy which was very fine. On Saturday the Doughtys and I went to the Zoo in the afternoon. I have seen Dr. Gordon twice lately, once this afternoon.

I have not had any golf since coming over here, but may have some when we leave London for a few days in the country. There could not have been much pleasure in playing golf during the heat in Canada. Although the crowds are still unabated in London many people are now leaving for the country & seaside resorts & fashionable life is on the ebb.

The shops here are quite a sight. It seems as though one could buy here whatever is produced in any part of the world, and yet when one has travelled about somewhat there seems to be an endless amount of repetition, and one wonders how they all live and pay their way.

I hope Lorraine got safely down to Kingston and that she will have a good time. George I suppose is now regularly at work at the Archives and taking his exercise on the lawn & at golf, when his half holiday comes round. I don't expect he will reduce his score as rapidly as he expected when I left. Have you had any visitors yet? Your mother wants you to keep an eye on the parlor sofa for moths. She has seen some nice old furniture here which causes her to wish she could take some of it back with us. It is mostly mahogany carved and inlaid.

I think your mother will not be able to go over to the continent with me. The Doctor advises against it at any rate & whether she will stay in London or go somewhere in a quieter atmosphere is not settled yet. In a letter from Prof. Morison she was invited to spend some time there.[17] We will probably leave here by Aug. 6th at the latest! The Doughtys talk about going home then. Well I am off to bed. Probably your mother will write the next letter.

Elizabeth's Diary[18]
I went uptown with Adam & bought a few things & looked at a few shops & found I was not able for a lot, & that wearing goggles & not seeing very well, I had not much courage about crossing sts. & getting buses. I bought some underwear & gloves at Penberthy's on Oxford St.[19] & they are good.

Wednesday, 19 July

Adam's Diary
Beth quite ill at stomache [*sic*], did not get out in consequence. Went to lunch with ——— at the Junior Service Club and had an interesting talk on Canadian History re Treaties. Interview with Dr. Gordon and Mr. Somerstone one of the candidates in classics.

Elizabeth's Diary
Mrs. Peacock came in in the afternoon & stayed quite awhile & again on Friday & they (she & E. R.) sailed on Sat. for home in Toronto. Adam had been dined & wined & suppered & tead by quite a few men but the season [for entertaining] was over. He had a lunch & a dinner with Philip Kerr who had been in Ottawa, the heir to the Marquis of Midlothian,[20] & he likes him well. He had dinner with Steel-Maitland,[21] Leader of the Unionist party & had a good talk. He also had dinner with Mr. & Mrs. Oliver,[22] the author, & tea with Lord Primrose,[23] as he couldn't go to dinner &c. &c..

Thursday, 20 July

Adam's Diary
Saw Sir Ed. Troup[24] at Home Office and his secty. Then saw Mr. ——— of Mines section and Sir ——— of Factory inspection. Both agreed that written exams are poor method of selecting best officers. Saw ——— Flux,[25] formerly of McGill and now in Board of Trade, also Mr. King, Mr. and Mrs. O'esborough [*sic*][26] called.

Elizabeth's Diary
It was hot outside till thurs. 20th, when I went [on] my first walk in London along the embankment gardens and the fronts of the big hotels—the

Cecil, the Adelphi & Savoy &c.. It was like getting out of prison. I had had goggles fitted the Sun. before I came out & the bandage was off for good. Thurs. afternoon Dr. F. came to see me & said my eye was coming on. The day before I had suffered much from getting rid of the accumulated bile, but once left to myself to deal with it I soon got rid of that & nausea.

Capt. & Mrs. Desborough came to see us Thurs. evg., but Dr. & Mrs. D. [Doughty] left that day for Paris. They [the Desboroughs] wanted us for dinner on Sat. evg. to meet Sir Hoffman Just who had been at our home in Ottawa.[27] It was Mrs. Desborough who gave me the name of Penberthys' as a good firm for gloves, stockings &c.. They were not so very cheap but were good.

Friday, 21 July

Adam's Diary
Saw Sir Hubert L. Smith of Board of Trade[28] but chiefly Mr. —— Lister[29] who explained general principles of appointment &c. and Mr. —— Barnes[30] who went over in detail the Companies Act and attempts to render it uniform throughout Colonies. Attended reception to Western Canadian teachers at King's Room, Holborn Restaurant.[31]

Elizabeth's Diary
It was this 21th that I went up town to the shops with Adam and bought also a beetle green tunic & two scarves, all very pretty at Marshall & Snelgrove's. I had no intention of buying a tunic but Adam liked it & it was such a reduced price I did take it.

A Letter from Elizabeth to the "Children"[32]
This is my first letter & I must not be long. I wrote a card to Lorraine & to George this A.M. & sent [it] S.D. to 2 Hales Cottages. I said when I knew I could see again—"Bless the Lord O my soul & let all that is within me bless His Holy Name." I could not & did not realize that I was blind. I could not see my hand at all before my face, but it came on first like an inflamed eye & I thought with a few days rest & care it would be all right.

[Elizabeth then recapitulates how she became aware of her illness and the subsequent ordeal leading to a successful operation.]

Of course I have not been able to read any of your letters till just now I ventured on one of George's typewritten ones. I read them all gradually for tho. your father read them all to me, he had a hard time with Muriel's. It set me laughing last time till I thought he feared I was getting hysterical, but he labored & labored & guessed & skipped & went back & came up at it again & it was getting on very late.

You will not be sorry for having written as often as you have for if you knew how eagerly I looked for them you would understand. I can not answer your letters till I get a chance to read them myself. Dr. & Mrs. D. are in Paris for two or three days, will be back Sunday. Alas, alas, they took all my money. Dr. Flem[m]ing charged over $200 for the operation & the hospital was $80 & the man who gave chloroform 15. It has been a dreadful blow & I will have to give up going to Geneva & Berlin & stay in a boarding house here while your father is away & dread it very much, for the Ds [Doughtys] go home Aug. 6th or 7th & Mr. & Mrs. Peacock go tomorrow & I feel so unequal to going about London.

I have to wear goggles on the st. & in the house for another week yet. We had such a nice letter from Prof. Morison, asking us to visit them in his home, tho. he sails back [to Canada] Aug. 9th. Principal Gordon is in town & your father has seen him a number of times about candidates &c. for positions at Queen's. I could not go to Lord Strathcona's last Mon.—the fates were in it. It was the place I most wanted to go. Your father went & had a fine time. We are invited to a tea at Headquarters Staff at Bisley today but your father is too busy to go. He is going to a reception tonight, but I guess I will not venture [out], but I expect to make my first dissipation by going to Capt. & Mrs. Desborough's to dinner tomorrow.

Thank the Lord for me dear children. I will be able to see as usual. I was led in a wonderful way to Dr. Flem[m]ing. I will tell you more of the hospital later. I escaped last Monday as your father wrote & Dr. Flem[m] ing was here to see me yesterday & said I might use my eye a little with the colored glasses & the others [spectacles]. He allowed me out last evg. for a walk & I felt indeed like a prisoner let loose. I was out for an hour & a half today too. If ever I needed friends it was here. Just think of sitting in London for two weeks (or in bed either as I was for ten days) & neither able to read nor jot, nor write nor even play solitaire—just "sitting & thinking" & sometimes just sitting. Oh if I had only had someone to read to me.

With so much love to each of you poor sufferers from the heat. It is a record breaker here, but nothing like yours. Your budget of July 11 just rec.—will write tomorrow.

Saturday, 22 July

Adam's Diary[33]

Forenoon with Sir H. Jost [*sic*],[34] Mr. Canning, Secty to Hon J. Baras[35] and Mr. F. A. Flux,[36] very hot. Rested in afternoon and explored, got some interesting books and old Queen Ann Candlesticks. To Capt. Desborough's for dinner, Sir Hoffman Jost [*sic*] there. Had very enjoyable evening and conversation.

Elizabeth's Diary

We went to dinner at the Desboroughs & it was my first social dissipation since I left the boat. It was just dinner & talk & smoking all but Adam & me, for Mrs. D. is a dreadful smoker—cigarette after cigarette. They have no children & Capt. D. was fifteen years in the military in India. He is not a very militaristic sort of man, but unassuming & well informed. He is related to the Duke of Richmond. His grandfather was Sir Peregrine Maitland who ran away with the daughter of the Duke of Richmond just after Waterloo & was afterward Gov.-Gen. of Canada.[37] Lady Peregrine Maitland's picture is in my *Types of Canadian Women*.[38] Well I found I was quite a bit used up by being out till eleven & after & did not get an early start Sun..

Mrs. Maude [*sic*], Sec. of the Central Council of Mothers Union came in Sat. afternoon before this to have a talk and I was glad to see her. I found waiting [for] me when Adam went to the [High] Commissioner's office, letters from her and from Mrs. Malden & instructions about the Cathedral service which I was to attend on the 6th Aug [*sic*], the day after I had arrived instead of going to hospital. Well, in talking to Mrs. Maud, who is chubby & stout & good hearted & good headed, I found her ideas of the Mothers' Union were liberal as mine almost & instead of their seeming at all dictatorial, that phase of it seemed more on the other foot. She read me Mrs. Campbell's letter from Toronto which gave me that [dictatorial] impression & I've no doubt my own would have had much the same ring.[39]

A Letter from Elizabeth to "Mother & Sister"[40]

You see I can write a bit again, tho. I must only do a little yet. I wrote to the children yesterday, my first writing since the day before I left the steamer. God only knows what all I have been through but thanks to Him for his mercy in bringing me to a specialist in time. I think truly the Lord led me across devious ways & all wonderful to get to this surgeon to save my sight.

If it had struck me in mid ocean there would have been no chance of saving my sight.

[Elizabeth then re-examines the onset of her illness and the subsequent corrective operation.]

My left eye just escaped & he [Dr. Flemming] says having the tendency I will have to put a drop of eserine in it every morning for the rest of my life. That is the left eye. The right will never have it again. It is a wonderful operation & I was fortunate to have one of London's best men to do it, tho. it nearly cleaned me out. I do not know what he would charge anyone not an M.D., but he charged me 50 guineas—about 210 dollars & the hospital for ten days (a private one) was $80, and the anesthetic was another 15 dollars. Dr. Percy Flem[m]ing was the optical surgeon & he is very nice. He charges so much & is so much in demand he will seldom go to a private house. The patients go to these private hospitals near the surgeons.

He [Dr. Flemming] let me out last Mon. at my strong urging & he came here to see me Thurs. & now lets me out with goggles sometime every day. I expect to be able to go without goggles in another week & be able to go a little more every day. For days he did not want my head moved & my eye was tightly bandaged up for ten days. I never put in such a lonesome ten days since I first went away to school. All my faculties & nothing I could do & no one to come in & read to me. Adam always came once a day & stayed awhile, but I slept so little at night [that] the hours seemed very long. I was in London two weeks going through this before I was allowed out to see so much as the embankment [on the Thames].

I was so glad to get or hear Adam read a letter from Ernest and Christina [Smith][41] sent to 17 Victoria St., Colonial Office where all our mail goes. The children seem to be getting on well except for [the] heat & I do not know how you are not prostrated. I must not write more now. The heat is unheard of here, but not what you are suffering.

Sunday, 23 July

Adam's Diary[42]
Slept late. To St. Paul's, good music, but wretched sermon. Met the Richardson's [sic] of Kingston. Took stroll through publishing section. Lunch at Adelphi. Read for [a] time then to Sir H. Jost's [sic][43] for tea. Desborough there. Read and looked at old books, 1st editions of Dickens.

Elizabeth's Diary

Adam & I went to St. Paul's to morning service. Then we poked about that district—Cheapside, Paternoster Row, Amen corner & saw odd corners & shops & the Stationers Guild Hall &c.. Coming out of St. Paul's we ran across Mrs. Richardson & George & Eva (& her friend) of Kingston. They expected to return Aug 6th on *Royal George*. After poking around there, we took a bus to the Adelphi & had dinner then back to rest abit & at five went to Sir & Lady Just's for tea. The Desboroughs were there & we had a nice hour.

A Letter from Elizabeth to "Muriel"[44]

I will not be able to write the letter I would like to but I will write a short one. Papa thinks you had better keep on sending the letters to the High Commissioner's Office 17 Victoria St. & they can forward them to us wherever we are. Do you hear by this time that Sir Frederick Borden[45] is to succeed Lord Strathcona [as Canadian high commissioner to Great Britain]. It seems settled & they are talking very discouragingly about the suitability [of Borden] &c.. One thing I always say is that Lady Borden can do her part of it all right—anyway so far as money permits but their income & Lord Strathcona's differ very greatly.

We were [at] Capt. Desborough's for dinner last evg. & I peered about so much with my left eye coming home that I rather strained it & so I must be good to it & go to bed very early & not use it to write all the letters to you children that I would like. I still have to put a patch over my right eye under the goggles when I am on the street but I do not in the house. This means that on the street I have to rely on my left eye & that was why I overstrained it a bit yesterday.

This is Sunday & we went to St. Paul's to morning service & who should we run into after service but first Miss Boyd (who said she was with Mrs. Hentig & two others) & then outside of St. Paul's we met Mrs. & George & Eva Richardson & a Mrs. [illegible] who visited at the Gordons. We had quite a chat. They will be here till 6th Aug.. We wandered about awhile looking at quaint places such as Paternoster Row & Amen Corner & such queer old courts & places. Then we took the bus back to the Strand near us & had dinner at one of the swell Hotels, "The Adelphi." There are a bunch of swell hotels just here—The Savoy, the Cecil, The Adelphi & Charing Cross.

Last evg. we were so late in getting started for the Desboroughs that we took a taxi cab & we had a very interesting ride past the new Victoria memorial statue & Buckingham Palace & Hyde Park &c.. This afternoon we had tea, afternoon tea, at Sir Hoffmann [*sic*] Just's. You remember our friend, "Just" whom Dr. Doughty mimicked? He is now Sir Hoffman [*sic*] & Lady Just is quite interesting too.

Dear Muriel I want to reply to so many interesting things in your letters. I hope with all my heart you are relieved from your sufferings from the heat. How I have thought of you & pitied you those long days of heat. It is beating all records here but I don't think it has gone above 85 or so.

I do hope Norman Lyle is all right again without going to the hospital. I am glad you like him & glad D. A. is friends with him. You never mention Katherine Foster. Is she home? Did you not go to see her? I must make a start at some shopping tomorrow, for I have only ten days [left in England] I think now, not quite 2 wks. anyway. The Peacocks sailed for home yesterday. Principal Gordon called this afternoon, when we were out. Papa sees him often.

Monday, 24 July

Adam's Diary[46]
Spent forenoon with Beth shopping. Saw some officials and got some more old books and a picture.

Elizabeth's Diary
Adam went with me uptown & we went to a few shops to look at suits & dresses, to Debhan's where I was told things were a great fit & was much disappointed—nothing I wanted & high in price. We went various places & felt I was not likely to get things ready made that I wanted.

Tuesday, 25 July

Adam's Diary
To see Mr. ——— Askwith [*sic*][47] at 3.30. Hon. J. Burns[48] at 10.45 a.m. Saw ——— of Engineers and had good talk on appointments. Confirmed my views. Also Dr. ———. Gave same view. Long talk with Askwith [*sic*]. Doubtful of compulsory features of any kind.

Elizabeth's Diary
Next morning early I went out with Adam to South Kensington to Mrs. Peacock's dressmaker & was disappointed again—too high [in price].

So Adam put me down on Oxford [Street] & he went after men he had to see & I went to Peter Robinson's to look at dresses & then to Dales opposite on Oxford Circus. At Dales I saw a light suit which I tried on & bargained to take after some alterations were made & also arranged to have them make up my tunic dress over black satin for (2½ guineas $12.50). I was so tired— so hopeless of getting any better that I felt I must do something. I went back to Savoy Mansions quite tired out & to rest till evg., when the Doughtys & we were to go to the Desboroughs again to dinner which we did.

That evg. they had a Mr. and Mrs. Petto[49] to dinner too. He wanted to meet Adam. We had a very nice time tho. Mrs. D. did not seem to enjoy herself. She was not very well & [yet] she smoked a cigarette. I hope it will keep on making her sick. She is so delicate & certainly it will not do her any good.

Mrs. Desborough told me of her dressmaker, Mrs. S. E. Brown, 33 Kingslilobridge [sic] near Hyde Park (next beyond the Alexandra Hotel). Although that is the name, the person in charge is Mrs. Singer & it was she with whom I contracted for a very pretty grey ninon over pink satin [dress] & a good black serge street coat & skirt with a pretty waist of ninon over black but with a rich red trimming across front & sleeves underneath. They turned out [to cost a] very fine 8 pounds for the satin & ninon & 6 guineas for the st. dress. I went twice to be measured & arrange[d] & 2nd [time] to be fitted & then to try on for Adam to see & to pay up. Mrs. Doughty got her[self] a prune tunic made up here also.

Wednesday, July 26

Adam's Diary
Explored Covent Garden market and got some cherries. Adventure with old character re books which he did not have. Saw some interesting sections of London and got a few books. Doughty on hunt also.

A Letter from Elizabeth to Muriel[50]
We received a second newspaper last evg. with accounts of the fires in Porcupine and thereabouts. I hope the accounts are exaggerated & the loss of life not so great. I hope Willie & Ted have been heard from & Stewart Dobbs too. It will entail a lot of anxiety to those outside & awful suffering & death to so many on the spot. We only see odd snatches of news [from Canada] in the London papers—a bit saying that an election is soon to be held or something about Reciprocity &c..[51] Thanks for the papers & clippings. You would have been pleased to see Dr. & Mrs. Doughty & I all

reading over each other—some heading that caught the eye. Mrs. Doughty was the one I gave it to as we were all here to read the news but we all filed in and as Dr. Doughty said it was like getting a "packet" in the old days and made quite an excitement.

We received a letter from Lorraine last evg., being written the Sun. after she was at Marjorie's & of course she was very happy. By the time this reaches you she will be with you again and my three dear ones will be keeping house & home till I get back. It seems a long time since I came away & a long time till I get back.

My eye is getting better slowly now because I do not keep it entirely at rest. I go shopping for half days at a stretch & the Dr. says he never had anyone do that under three weeks. It seemed an awful waste of time to be in London & not able to do anything. I've despaired of getting anything ready made. Things were never so dear here Mrs. Desborough says. I suppose they put them up for the Coronation[52] & got in their goods for that purpose. I do not think one can do much better here than in Canada (Ontario I mean) except that there is a greater supply to choose from & they have perfectly lovely things. Men's clothes are cheaper & gloves are cheaper, but I have been quite disappointed in dresses and am just having some made by Mrs. Desborough's dressmaker. I've spent all the money I had intended to on clothes & still have no waterproof [coat] & not enough gloves. Mrs. Doughty has bought a lot of things too & she had a lot of new pretty things already.

It seems so queer—your letters keep up the story but it is always so far behind. Your letter e.g. Mon. 24th [July] showed you had yet no letter from us. I received a letter from Aunt Gertie written immediately after rec. word about my calamity. I was up to see Dr. Flem[m]ing yesterday & he tried some glasses on me which showed me that I could read again when I get through [the convalescence]. I am still to wear the goggles and bathe my eye three or four times a day. I hope it is cooler with you & that you can sleep & get on in comfort. There was a thunderstorm early this morning but it did not make it much cooler. We were at dinner again at the Desboroughs last evg., all four of us [the Doughtys and the Shortts] & we had a nice time.

The hansom cabs are cab with rubber tires (not a car [automobile] cab) [and they] have to have a bell on the horse so people can hear it coming. It sounds like sleigh bells in the night. I am hoping to have a letter from George soon & from each of you. Dr. Doughty is going to post these, so dear ones good night.

Papa is busy all the time & sends love to each.

Thursday, 27 July

Adam's Diary[53]
Went to Bank, explored that part of London. Got some more books and prints of people connected with Canada.

Elizabeth's Diary
Mrs. D. & I were up town looking at shops & things & that evg Mr. Biggar came in & then later Adam & the Doughtys went to the big reception at Claridges (the swellest hotel in London)[54] given by Mrs. Elmer Black[55] a vice.-Pres. of the Races Congress, for which Congress it was given. I did not feel quite up to it for it did not begin till 10 o'clock in the evg. & my hair was a difficulty.

Friday, 28 July

Adam's Diary
Went to Oxford in morning, Bell[56] and Adams[57] met us. Lunch with Grant and wife,[58] saw some colleges, All Souls, Christ Church &c. dinner with Adams, Bells [*sic*] and Gildart, successor to Dicey.[59] Very lively and interesting talk on Imperial problems. Enjoyed meeting very much.

Elizabeth's Diary
Adam & I went up to Oxford on the 10 something train. One day in the previous wk. Mr. Adams (who was once a lecturer at Belfast but who is on the financial Com. of the Govt. now, about Irish affairs) [and] Prof. & Mrs. Bell called to see us. Principal Gordon too had been to see us the afternoon we were at Sir [Hartmann] Just's,[60] but Adam saw the Principal often these days about new men [for Queen's University faculty]. We had a telegram before starting to come to lunch with W. L. & Mrs. Grant who were staying in rooms in Oxford.

We were met at the train at Oxford by both Prof. Bell & Mr. Adams & they advised our going to the East Gale hotel which we did. After washing up Prof. Bell conducted us over to W. L. Grant's & showed us Queen's Coll. & All Souls & Oriel & Radcliff [Camera] & Exeter & the Bodleian Library on the way. We had a very nice time at W. L.'s & I like Mrs. Grant nee Maude Parkin[61] as well as any woman I know, as a type after my own heart, about as near a complete woman as I know of. She & Kate Gordon Nickle will I expect be good friends. I could wish I were fifteen years younger to be in the same running with Mrs. Grant. They seem to have the promise of many happy interesting useful years ahead. I think W. L. was indeed lucky.

We had a good talk after lunch & then W. L. having to go to Rugby[62] for the night she [Mrs. Grant] went over to Prof. Bell's at All Soul's & left us there for tea.. Then we went to see Christ Church College. The dining room here is filled (the walls) by portraits of famous men, a Romney two Gainsboroughs & a Reynolds being of [*sic*] them. I was interested in seeing a good one of Lewis Carole [*sic*][63] & also of Mr. Riddell, father of his Alice in Wonderland, but on asking for further information about Alice I heard she had become a bit spoiled by the famous story of her & had married & become not even interesting above the usual. We went also to see the kitchen where they can broil 70 chickens at once &c. but it was in an awful upset for they were lowering the kitchen floor some fourteen inches. The steward was also lamenting their inability to make jam &c. The finest thing tho. about Christ Church College is the chapel which is famous for its arches & stained glass &c. & is very rich & old.

From there we went to the hotel to was[h] & get ready to go to dinner with Prof. Adams who had the dinner in All Souls "Common Room." He had Prof. Gilder [*sic*] & Prof. & Mrs. Bell to dinner & it was a big talking spree—especially did Adam shine & it was very interesting to hear him too. Adam[s] gave him leading questions & he talked on and on till after eleven when we returned to our comfortable beds at the hotel.

Saturday, 29 July

Adam's Diary
Out on river with Grant and wife. Lunch with Bell and wife at All Souls. Long and wife and Robertson[64] Bursar &c.. Visited Bodlean [*sic*] Library.[65] Left for London. Sorry could not stay for Dinner in commons with Dicey, Auson and Holland. Rain at London and dismal evening. Read papers re Lords situation.[66]

Elizabeth's Diary
Next forenoon W. L. & Mrs. Grant called for us & drove to the River Cherwell, a branch or tributary, of Thames & went for a lovely row up the winding willow "shaded" river. I had another good talk with Mrs. Grant & enjoyed it. We went back to the hotel & then to lunch with Prof. & Mrs. Bell. They had [at lunch] a Mr. & Mrs. Long (I think he was Leo) & Prof. Robertson who is lecturer in Magdalen & Bursar of All Souls & a

young man—I forget him [i.e., his name]. Prof. Robertson was lots of fun & we had a merry lunch. Afterward we talked with the Bells & went from there to the train & back to London in time for dinner Sat. evg..

It is odd to think that in the 20 or 21 Colleges at Oxford that they still have no baths, actually have never had bath tubs. Their daily bath or whatever must be carried there & carried off again & the bath is taken in what we would call a baby's bath tub! It is only three years since All Souls got electric light & they have no telephones at all in Oxford & a horse car system that is not very frequent or expert. They try to keep it free from the modern hustle of life & yet they say it is growing. [English] People in India [are] sending their boys home to boys schools which have recently increased round Oxford & then later people coming to live there & so more schools, more people, more shops. Some nice new houses are building [sic] in the outskirts. It is certainly Oxford as you read of it.

It had a very unusual appearance for all the quadrangles were dry & parched, the grass would crumble in your fingers. It was so dry & it in great spots looked quite dead, but they said it would revive when rain came. So unusual was the "condition" of no rain that only one Coll. was provided with hose sprinkler.

Often on the way we saw the Thames which is not a very big river, but pretty in its windings & its willows which they pollard every [year] or every 2nd year & keep in in [sic] order. Maidenhead is between London & Oxford & is on the River. We passed just out of London or beyond Slengh the Scott's [illegible] factory & further on the Horlick's Malted Milk factory which is greatly advertised here in Eng..

When we were going up to Oxford, some middle aged & elderly people put three children in our compartment—a boy of 11, a girl of 9 or 10 & a boy next younger. They went to travel to Shrewsbury to meet an uncle. They were nice clean looking children & well brought up. Their relatives had brought them some books to read & put them up a nice lunch & gave them many parting injunctions about not putting their heads out of the window & not to be troublesome &c.. It was so like children that in spite of their relatives kindly talk & repeated nice sayings they could not restrain themselves from undoing the books & taking a running look thro. them which of course brought upon them the remark "you will have your books used up before you get started." Soon after we started the youngest boy wanted something to eat and they had done up [consumed] most everything before we left. The elder boy asked if it would disturb us if he read aloud!

One of the characters around Oxford University that they tell stories about is Chadwick, Master of Oriel. They tell one of him that happened when he visited Harvard, viz that Principal Elliott [*sic*],[67] hearing he was coming hustled up & got up a lunch & invited some interested people to come & lunch with him. When luncheon time & Chadwick came, Chadwick, arriving from the station to Elliott's [*sic*], C. said "I'm tired, I'm going to bed," & to bed he went, visitor or no, luncheon or no, & left Principal Elliott [*sic*] to make explanations.

It reminds me of what an Englishman is reported to have said when asked his opinion of a joke. It was the remark that there was a difference between the Englishman's & American's idea of a joke & the Englishman protesting not—that humor was the same everywhere. The man, to illustrate, said: "Now I want you to tell me ten minutes later what view you take of this. A man met another on the st. who was heading toward the post office who asked if he could tell him where the P.O. was. 'Yes' he said 'I can' but passed on without further remark. Before he had gone very far he repented & hurried after the other man to tell him. Catching up to him, he said 'Did you want to know the way to the Post Office?' to which the other man said 'no' & passed on." The Englishman, when asked later what he thought, said he thought they were "both damned rude!" So Chadwick.

Sunday, 30 July

Adam's Diary
Went to Windsor after reading all morning. Heard even song service in St. George's. Walked round the terraces &c. Had tea, Mr. O'Halloran[68] being with us. Got home late and read and talked until bed time. Before that heard talkers at Hyde Park corner, large crowds.

Elizabeth's Diary
After we had dinner at the Adelphi & returned to the Savoy [Mansions] for Mr. O'Halloran, we five [the Shortts, the Doughtys, and O'Halloran] went to Windsor. By straining every bit of will & muscle I had we made the tube for Paddington station & by hurrying all I could to the far end of the platform with Adam's help & my umbrella as a cane, I got into the compartment with the rest, Doughty having run for the tickets. Of course I was used up, but when we reached Windsor, we sat in the chapel—St. George's chapel—& heard the boys sing at afternoon service. It was the best boys singing I suppose there is & it was most satisfying. The chapel is not so very large

but very handsome. The royal boxes are just over head at the left of the altar looking from the front enterance [*sic*]. There were quite a number at service. Among them Adam noticed Cordville a man he and Principal Gordon had just decided on as assistant in English for Queen's.

After service we walked about the terraces & looked over the bank at the beautiful view toward Eton. Then we went to a quaint tea room Dr. Doughty knew of & had tea & jam & bread & butter the staple breakfast & tea of the English. Later we went back to London & took in some of the crank talk at Hyde Park corner. All the faddists & freaks in London may hold forth in Hyde Park if they like on Sun. evg., if they can get anyone to listen & they generally, if not always, can. We listened to some scoffing at religion & others preaching. Sometimes one offering so many pounds in money if any of his listeners can prove the existence of God when his next neighbour is appealing to his listeners to come & be saved & comforted [by religion]. Another may be a single tax man or a man talking socialism & down with the Lords &c. or a women asking [for] an interest in some philanthrophy [*sic*]. Sometimes an altercation gets up & that creates special interest.

There were goodly listening crowds around each. It was like a huge talking "fair" where instead of going from one booth of things for sale [to another] one went from one crank to another to test their wares. It was not especially interesting more than once, but it is a new sight to Canadians & to anyone I fancy outside of London. It is the freedom of speech for which England is famous. Now in the crisis & altercation about the powers of the Lords & the lively state of English politics there is room for a lot of talk certainly.

It was 9:30 when we got home or later & the bus left us at Trafalgar Sq. & I was really walked [*sic*] home from there. I was so tired I could not speak but I made one remark before going to bed as soon as we reached our door & that was that if I was able to walk the next day I would thank God & take courage, for I had not done so much walking in years as I had that day & been exhausted by the run at the start. I really had a bad time in the night with my heart & was done up next morning. So stayed at home to rest.

A Letter from Elizabeth to Muriel[69]
There has been no letter from you now for some days & none since you heard of my calamity. I am afraid that you or George are ill, that the heat is too much. I will continue to keep up hope of things being all right anyway till tomorrow or Tues. because that is the day your letters most often come. It rained here last night & now is cooler.

We went up to Oxford Friday morning.... [Here Elizabeth largely repeats her diary entries for 28 July.] We ... then went to dinner with Mr. [sic] Adams & Prof. & Mrs. Bell & a Prof. Gildart & after dinner we spent the evg. listening to your father talk & it was talk worthwhile too. Adams kept asking him questions whenever he came to a stop which meant that the others of us only occasionally did anything more than listen. The men ate & smoked & drank coffee & smoked again & then again & then had lemon & soda & then smoked again, so it was beautifully arranged— your father not smoking did all the talking while the others did as above mentioned.

Next morning (Sat.) yesterday [29 July] W. L. & Mrs. Grant gave us a drive across Oxford & than took us up the River Cherwell which is the river the Oxford men do their skulling on mostly, since it is at their door & is broader than if they went down the Cherwell toward & on the Thames which also has a good many locks. It was blindingly hot, but the river was beautiful—it is narrow but has well trimmed willows & primroses along the shore. I liked Mrs. Grant quite as well as I expected too [sic]. It is just fine that she is going to Kingston but I do not know of anyone in K. who will be quite as delightful a woman, up to date & cosmopolitan. I told her all about the residence scheme[70] and gave her all the pointers I could think were desirable. They have taken the McGrassie house for the winter, the house just behind where we lived on West St. i.e. the corner of Union and Wellington. The[y] sail a few days earlier than we do & will be back by the middle of Sept. I think.

I had a nice letter from Mrs. Glover[71] asking us to visit them at Cambridge after the 8th & I think I told you I had a most cordial invitation from Miss Morrison [sic] to visit them at Innellen.[72] I do not know yet how I can arrange [these visits]. We expect to stay here this week & after that the deluge [i.e., the trip to the continent].

Mr. O'Halleron [sic] the Deputy Min. of Agriculture,[73] is here just now, going out with the Doughtys to church. I think I will get your father out pretty soon to the Temple church[74] where they say the music is fine. How fortunate it was Muriel that you made me that dressing jacket. What would I have done in the hospital without it. The things I forgot, the little things like nail brush & sponge &c., I have not had a chance to get as yet. Principal Gordon went up to Scotland a few days ago &, tho. he was here at these rooms to see us three times, I did not see him & your father was here once [to see him] when I was in the hospital. However, your father saw him a number of times by appointment & helped him about selecting some men [for the Queen's faculty]. Dr. Herridge[75] had lunch with the Principal too one day with father. Your father runs off occasionally to old book stores & we will have to buy another trunk or case to ship them all home. It fills me with despair to see so many more going into the house.

I wonder how you are getting on with the fly question. Keep a saucer of formaldahyde [sic] in the kitchen & in the upstairs attic any way & you can get a bottle of crude carbolic & burn a tablespoonful on shavings in a pan or old kettle from the laundry & fumigate any of the rooms or all of the rooms where the flies are. They will not stay I believe where you burn carbolic acid & that will do you no harm at all. I have never heard of formaldahyde doing any harm, but I do not like to inhale it all the time. How are the moths too— in my closet & in the parlour, sofa? I do hope that things are all right. If I were home I would undo the bags in the top drawer in my closet, especially my fur coat & mink muff.

My eye is not getting on quite as fast, as if I stayed in all the time but still it is going on [improving]. I was at Dr. Flem[m]ing's last Mon. & he tried glasses on it & I will be able to read all right, as well as ever when I get fitted, but you will be sorry to know that I will have to wear glasses all the time— one kind to read & sew & another all the rest of the time. I dread them, but if others do it, I can. I wrote my mother & Aunt Gertie & told them [how] I was getting on but I have not written anyone else. In the evg. I do not feel that I can use my eyes fairly & write more than a card nor can I really use them to read but *very* little till I get my proper glasses.

I suppose George is going every day to the Archives & I hope getting some excellent work done. Prof. Grant was asking when he was going up to Queen's? I suppose you will know the results in a few weeks now, if the examiners survive the papers & the heat. Yesterday the dear baby [Lorraine] was fourteen. That is an amazing thing. It was just the other day that Muriel was 14. How did this strange thing come about?

Mr. Wilfrid Campbell[76] called one day, but being out, I did not see him. Prof. Flux,[77] who used to be in Montreal, called, tho. your father has seen him officially too. We did not see Minnie Gordon[78] in Oxford, but she is coming up to London tomorrow. Mrs. W. L. Grant knew R. Hewitt well & was asking about him. Evidently he [sic] has suspicion of love affairs before. She also knows Mrs. Slopes-Sale, the wonder that we met at Mr. Fisher's.

Some man has got your father [in conversation] & as I am only in dressing gown I cannot go & rout him out. The Doughtys still think they will go home next week. If there was anything seriously wrong with you or George, you would call (or Lorraine either of course, but today she is still in Kingston) & I would then go back as soon as I could, but I hope nothing at all is wrong. You have written very faithfully so far & I know letters sometimes get much belated coming over here. I will stop now & hoping Heaven blesses you everyday. With love from your father and mother to our dearest ones.

Notes

1 Juliet Nicolson, *The Perfect Summer: Dancing into Shadow in 1911* (Toronto: McArthur, 2007), 1.

2 Alexander Reford, "Donald Alexander Smith, 1st Baron Strathcona and Mount Royal," in *Dictionary of Canadian Biography*, vol. XIV (Toronto: University of Toronto Press, 1998), 945.

3 Cecilia Morgan, *"A Happy Holiday": English Canadians and Transatlantic Tourism, 1870–1930* (Toronto: University of Toronto Press, 2008), 195.

4 Morton N. Cohen, *Lewis Carroll: A Biography* (New York: Alfred A. Knopf, 1995), 518; and Karoline Leach, *In the Shadow of the Dreamchild: A New Understanding of Lewis Carroll* (London: Peter Owen, 1999), 175.

5 Queen's University Archives, Adam Shortt Papers (hereafter cited as ASP), box 11, Adam Shortt Diary, 17 July 1911.

6 Note the incorrect spelling of Lord Strathcona's country residence in the transcription of Adam's diary. It should read "Debden" Hall.

7 University of Waterloo, Elizabeth Smith Shortt Papers (hereafter cited as ESSP), WA10, file 1772, Smith Shortt Diary, 17 July 1911.

8 Mrs. Hester Fielding was the wife of William Stevens Fielding, finance minister in Laurier's government, which was fighting an ultimately unsuccessful electoral campaign back in Canada while the Shortts visited Europe; *Canadian Who's Who, 1910* (London: Times Publishing Company, 1910), 78.

9 ESSP, WA10, file 1245, Adam Shortt to Muriel Clarke, 18 July 1911.

10 Senator Lawrence Geoffrey Power was a prominent lawyer and alderman in Halifax, Nova Scotia, before being called to the Senate in 1877, where in 1901 he was appointed speaker; *Canadian Who's Who, 1910* (London: Times Publishing Company, 1910), 186.

11 Senator Robert Watson was a millwright in Manitoba who became a member of the Liberal caucus in Ottawa in the 1880s, and then, after 1892, provincial minister of public works in Manitoba's Greenway administration until that government's defeat in 1899. In 1900, Watson was appointed to the Canadian senate by the Laurier ministry; *Canadian Who's Who, 1910*, 233.

12 George Eulas Foster was a high school and then university teacher in New Brunswick who was elected to the House of Commons as a Conservative member for Kings County in 1882. In 1888, he became finance minister in the Macdonald government and then in several Tory administrations that followed the passing of the "Old Chieftain" in 1891. By 1911, Foster still held influence in the Conservative federal caucus, and when Robert Borden formed a Tory ministry later that year, Foster was made minister of trade and commerce; *Canadian Who's Who, 1910*, 83; and David J. Bercuson and J. L. Granatstein, *The*

Collins Dictionary of Canadian History, 1867 to the Present (Toronto: Collins, 1988), 76.

13 John Morrison Gibson was an Ontario lawyer who had served Liberal premiers as the head of several provincial ministries from 1889 to 1905. In 1908, he was appointed lieutenant governor of Ontario by the Conservative Whitney government, a post he still held in 1911; *Canadian Who's Who, 1910*, 90.

14 See ch. 1, n. 57.

15 William Wilfrid Campbell was an Anglican clergyman from Ontario who became a clerk in several federal ministries while writing poems, novels, and various other works. By 1911, Campbell was known for his patriotic and pro-imperialist literary expressions; Laurel Boone, "William Wilfrid Campbell," in *Dictionary of Canadian Biography*, vol. XIV (Toronto: University of Toronto Press, 1998), 180–82.

16 See ch. 2, n. 8.

17 John Lyle Morison was a professor of history at Queen's University in Kingston, Ontario, after having studied and taught in Glasgow, Scotland. He maintained a residence in Argyllshire, Scotland, as well as Kingston, Canada; *Who's Who, 1915* (London: A. & C. Black, 1915), 1536.

18 ESSP, WA10, file 1772, Smith Shortt Diary, 18 July 1911.

19 Penberthy's was a women's clothier, established in 1883, which was one of the most distinguished stores on Oxford Street, a prominent shopping area in London; Ben Weinreb and Christopher Hibbert, eds., *The London Encyclopedia* (London: Macmillan, 1983), 570–71.

20 Philip Henry Kerr was a British aristocrat who had been a colonial official in South Africa and the editor of the journal *The State* from 1908 to 1909. By 1911, he was residing in London; *Who's Who, 1915*, 1193.

21 See ch. 1, n. 60.

22 See ch. 1, n. 61.

23 The Hon. Neil Primrose was the youngest son of the 5th Earl of Roseberry. Since 1910 he had represented the riding of Wisbech Division, Cambridge, for the Liberal Party; *Who's Who, 1915*, 1754.

24 Sir (Charles) Edward Troup was a career civil servant who had served in the British Home Office since 1880. In 1911, he was the permanent under-secretary of state for that ministry, a position he had first assumed in 1908; *Who's Who, 1915*, 2156–57.

25 A. W. Flux became the director of the census of production at the British Board of Trade following a teaching career that included a stint, from 1901 to 1908, at McGill University in Montreal as William Dow Professor of Political Economy; *Who's Who, 1915*, 747.

26 Note the incorrect spelling in the transcription of Adam's diary. It should read "Desboroughs." See "Frequently Mentioned Names" on p. xx.

27 See ch. 1, n. 80.

28 Sir Hubert Llewellyn Smith was the permanent secretary to the Board of Trade, having first entered this department as a full-time employee in 1903. Like Adam, he had written several publications on economic and educational subjects; *Who's Who, 1915,* 1991–92.

29 Robert John Lister was the librarian at the Board of Trade; *Who's Who, 1915,* 1299.

30 George Stapylton Barnes had worked at the Board of Trade since 1886, and from 1904 to 1911 served as comptroller of the companies department within this ministry; *Who's Who, 1915,* 110.

31 The King's Room was one of several private dining rooms at the Holborn Restaurant, which was considered among the most prestigeous eating establishments in London; *The London Encyclopedia,* 385.

32 ESSP, WA10, file 493, Smith Shortt to Muriel Clarke, 21 July 1911.

33 ASP, box 11, Adam Shortt Diary, 22 July 1911.

34 See ch. 1, n. 80.

35 This misspelling apparently refers to the Hon. John Burns; see ch. 1, n. 70.

36 Note Flux's incorrect initials in the transcription of Adam's diary, which should read "A. W."; see ch. 2, n. 25.

37 Sir Peregrine Maitland fought at the Battle of Waterloo in 1815, and shortly afterward attained a knighthood. From 1818 to 1828, he served as the lieutenant governor of Upper Canada, where he was closely identified with the ruling family compact. From 1828 to 1834, he held a similar post in Nova Scotia, but Maitland never became the "Gov.-Gen. of Canada"; *Canadian Encyclopedia,* 2nd ed., vol. 11, 1287.

38 Henry James Morgan, ed., *Types of Canadian Women* (Toronto: William Briggs, 1903), 228.

39 Mrs. Maud, Mrs. Malden, and Mrs. Campbell are not identified in publications like the British *Who's Who, 1915* and *Canadian Who's Who, 1919,* indicating the sexist bias of these works.

40 ESSP, WA10, file 1035, Smith Shortt to Damaris I. McGee Smith, 22 July 1911.

41 See "Frequently Mentioned Names" on p. xx.

42 ASP, box 11, Adam Shortt Diary, 23 July 1911.

43 See ch. 1, n. 80.

44 ESSP, WA10, file 493, Smith Shortt to Muriel Clarke, n.d. Although this letter is not dated, its context related to events taking place on 23 July, as revealed in both Adam's and Elizabeth's diaries for this day.

45 Sir Frederick William Borden was the minister of militia and defence, a department which, by 1911, he had managed for a record-breaking fifteen years in Sir Wilfrid Laurier's government. In June 1911, the prime minister announced at a London banquet that Borden would succeed Lord Strathcona as Canada's high commissioner in the imperial capital, but Laurier's government was defeated before the appointment was finalized; Carman Miller, "Sir Frederick William Borden," in *Dictionary of Canadian Biography*, vol. XIV, 97–100.

46 ASP, box 11, Adam Shortt Diary, 24 July 1911.

47 In 1911, H. H. Asquith (note the incorrect spelling in the transcription of Adam's diary) was the prime minister of the Liberal minority government, which he had initially formed in 1908, and three years later was immersed in the constitutional crisis caused by the Parliament Act of 1910. Indeed, Nicolson points out that Asquith, "On Monday 24 July [the day before the meeting with Shortt] went to the House to announce that to force the Bill through he had been promised the King's cooperation in creating four hundred extra Liberal peers"; Nicolson, *The Perfect Summer*, 172.

48 See ch. 1, n. 70.

49 Despite the misspelling, this could be Mr. Basil and Mary Peto of London. Basil was a building contractor and mining expert in the British capital, and, since 1910, a Conservative MP who had made three trips to Canada; *Who's Who, 1915*, 1703.

50 ESSP, WA10, file 493, Smith Shortt to Muriel Clarke, 26 July 1911.

51 The Laurier government's negotiation of a tentative reciprocal trade agreement with the United States was a major issue in the 1911 federal election and a leading cause of the Liberal administration's ultimate rejection by the voters; J. L. Finlay and D. N. Sprague, *The Structure of Canadian History*, 6th ed. (Toronto: Prentice Hall Allyn and Bacon, 2000), 320–22.

52 See ch. 1, n. 20.

53 ASP, box 11, Adam Shortt Diary, 27 July 1911.

54 Claridge's on Brook Street in London was established in the early nineteenth century and rebuilt during the 1890s as the hotel "most appropriately equipped to house the rich and the royal" in the British capital; *The London Encyclopedia*, 180.

55 Mrs. (Madeleine) Elmer Black was married to a wealthy American banker and used the considerable capital at her disposal to foster various liberal causes, such as the First Universal Races Congress held in London during the summer of 1911; *Who's Who, 1915*, 193–94.

56 Charles Francis Bell was the keeper of the fine-art department at the Ashmolean Museum at Oxford University and an authority on the works of J. M. W. Turner and English portraiture; *Who's Who, 1915*, 150.

57 Prof. William Adams was a teacher of political theory and institutions at All Souls College, Oxford, though he is not credited with any publications on these subjects; *Who's Who, 1915*, 12.

58 See "Frequently Mentioned Names" on p. xxi.

59 Albert Venn Dicey taught law at All Souls College from 1882 to 1909, when he became the principal of the Working Men's College in London. His *Lectures Introductory to the Study of the Law of the Constitution*, first published in 1885, was so highly credited that it was generally accepted as an integral part of the British Constitution; *Encyclopaedia Britannica*, vol. 4, 74.

60 See ch. 1, n. 80.

61 See "Frequently Mentioned Names" on p. xxi.

62 Rugby was the site of Rugby School, which counted many famous Englishmen among its graduates, including the poet Matthew Arnold, son of the institution's most eminent headmaster, Dr. Thomas Arnold (1828–42).

63 Although she misspelled Lewis Carroll's pen name here, Mrs. Shortt displayed a keen interest in the *Alice in Wonderland* tale that had infatuated so many readers throughout the English-speaking world. Its author, Charles Dodgson, entered Christ Church College in 1850 and remained there as a student, teacher, writer, and resident until his death in 1898. See ch. 2, n. 4.

64 Charles Grant Robertson was a fellow, since 1893, and domestic bursar, since 1897, of All Souls College, and tutor in modern history, since 1905, at Magdalen College. He was also the author of many works, including *A Historical and Modern Atlas of the British Empire*; *Who's Who, 1915*, 1828–29.

65 The Bodleian (note the incorrect spelling in the transcription of Adam's diary) Library was in 1911 and remains "the chief among the University's libraries" at Oxford, where it retains "a special place" for scholars at this institution; see http://www.bodleian.ox.ac.uk/bodley/about-us.

66 See ch. 2, n. 47.

67 Charles William Eliot (note the incorrect spelling in Elizabeth's diary) taught mathematics and chemistry at Harvard University from 1854 to 1863 after receiving his degree there, and then in 1869 became the institution's president, an office he retained until his retirement in 1909. Eliot was responsible for instituting many reforms at Harvard, such as the creation of the elective system for students and sabbatical leaves for faculty; Richard B. Morris, ed., *Encyclopedia of American History* (New York: Harper and Row, 1965), 703.

68 See ch. 1, n. 57.

69 ESSP, WA10, file 493, Smith Shortt to Muriel Clarke, 30 July 1911.

70 See ch. 1, n. 18.

71 Mrs. Alice Glover was the wife of Terrot Glover, a fellow and classical lecturer at St. John's College, Cambridge, who from 1896 to 1901 had been a professor of Latin at Queen's University in Kingston, Ontario; *Who's Who*, 1915, 840.

72 Innellan was the Morisons' (note the incorrect spellings in Elizabeth's letter) estate in Scotland; see ch. 2, n. 17.

73 Note the incorrect spelling of O'Halloran's name in Elizabeth's letter, and see ch. 1, n. 57.

74 The Temple Church was originally constructed by the order of the Knights Templar, a powerful secret society in the twelfth century. By 1911, the appointment of the chaplain, or master, of this church had become the prerogative of the monarch rather than the bishop of London.

75 The Rev. William Thomas Herridge was the pastor of St. Andrew's Presbyterian Church in Ottawa, a senator at the University of Toronto, and a trustee of Queen's University; *Canadian Who's Who*, 1910, 105.

76 See ch. 2, n. 15.

77 See ch. 2, n. 25.

78 See ch. 1, n. 66.

Chapter 3

Two Canadian Travellers in a "Stupendous" London

During this second phase of the Shortts' visit to England, Adam had fewer official commitments, as he sought guidance on potential reforms in Ottawa's bureaucracy. Only one day and one evening (3 August) were devoted to these consultations. Meanwhile, Elizabeth pursued her feminist agenda by discussing matters of mutual interest with Lady Chichester. This aristocrat, who led the Mothers' Union in Great Britain, pointed out that its members had decided not to duplicate activities that other feminist bodies had initiated. Shortt, the president of the Mothers' Union in Canada, proudly reported that the Dominion group had reached the same conclusion. Thus, for example, it left to the National Council of Women (NCWC) "many phases that might be considered as bolstering our objects of the Mothers' Union." Chichester and Shortt were clearly on the same page when it came to this central issue confronting feminists in the two countries (31 July).

Elizabeth also intently listened to the Countess Dowager's remarks on the importance of the national insurance bill, which the Asquith government had introduced but not passed because of resistance to such welfare legislation in the House of Lords.[1] For Chichester, the measure constituted "one of the things which the women suffragists can use well to show the legitimate interests of women in politics." Women were affected "in so many ways" by the proposed act, which Chichester was helping to shape by serving "on a Board or committee which is getting some amendments arranged to the Insurance Bill." For example, both earnings and maternity/sick benefits would be substantially improved by the legislation. Beth listened sympathetically to Chichester's remarks on this subject, but refused to endorse her call for women's suffrage. As we have seen, a conservative Mrs. Shortt was in 1911 not quite ready to endorse this contentious measure

(31 July), and was determined to maintain her personal independence even when dealing with a powerful figure like Lady Chichester.

When Chichester indicated that most of the male doctors were against the insurance bill because of the fear that it would encourage lady doctors to take over a significant portion of their work, the two women returned to common ground. Dr. Shortt had fought against such gender prejudice in the medical profession since her trying days at the Royal College of Medicine in Kingston. Later that same day, in a discussion with Dr. Fleming's wife, who was also a practising physician, she learned that the situation had improved somewhat for female doctors in England. In contemporary London, women physicians "did very well"; however, "they were not fashionable" and sexist discrimination still persisted (31 July). The battle for full equality had yet to be won in the medical field, and both Chichester and Shortt were intent on achieving that goal. On another occasion, Mrs. Shortt fulfilled a practical need confronting many middle-class housewives in Canada,[2] when she visited the Imperial Institute to secure able female servants, about to emigrate to the Dominion, for herself and her sister-in-law, Christina Smith (3 August).

However, once these practical obligations were met, the Shortts became typical tourists in a "stupendous" London (7 August) and the surrounding countryside. They were excited about a day trip to the Festival of Empire, which had emerged as "the most ambitious event held at the [Crystal] Palace since its inception" in the mid-nineteenth century.[3] Mrs. Shortt was impressed with the grand historical pageants mounted at the fair and noted in particular the dazzling costumes worn by many of the actors. Next the couple visited the Canadian exhibit, which Adam considered "very good," while it made Elizabeth "feel proud" (1 August). In their patriotism, the Shortts were able to accommodate loyalties to both native land and mother country. Two days later, Elizabeth informed the children that she had decided to accompany her husband to the continent on the second part of his European trip. Mrs. Shortt calculated that staying behind in England would save "not ... much if any over fifty [dollars] & ten years from now that will not make much difference" (3 August). In the days that followed, she would be more than pleased with the results of this decision.

Meanwhile, Elizabeth and Adam found time for excursions into the hinterland near the imperial capital. The former gave a vivid description of the journey through Surrey, which they encountered on a visit to Box Hill, while the latter concurred with a characteristically terse reference to the area's "beautiful scenery" (5 August). They were further pleased with what

Mrs. Shortt called the "lovely view of the rolling lands and estates" in Middlesex county near London, a perspective seconded by Adam (6 August).

These days in London and its environs culminated in a farewell supper for the Shortts, Doughtys, and Desboroughs in the main dining room of the renowned Savoy Hotel. To Elizabeth, it represented "the grandest hotel of extravagance I ever ate in & the supper was an expensive but tasty affair," while her more restrained husband viewed the meal as "swell but expensive and uninteresting." Nevertheless, it did result in another fine exchange at the dinner table (6 August). There were few things that Adam relished more than eating with friends who provided good conversation. As the Shortts prepared to leave for the continent, they were generally content with their initial sojourn in Great Britain.

Monday, 31 July

Adam's Diary[4]
Went to Bank. Visited some of the old part of London. Got some books and pictures re Canada. Beth had visit from Lady Chichester. Went to dressmakers and Dr. Flemming's. Biggar[5] in for tea. Had long talk on Books &c.

Elizabeth's Diary[6]
Afternoon early Countess Dowager of Chichester called & we had a real good talk. She is a staunch English woman without much claims to looks but of much strength of character. She told me her daughter had taken the C.M.B. certificate—certificate of Midwifery Board—which was of much service in her philanthropy work particularly if nurses were scarce &c.. She [Lady Chichester] too is most liberal & limits the work of the Mothers' Union to the theoretical, to that of influence in its main objects, because other organizations are in the field doing practical work better than they could do it. For instance they had a hygiene lecturer for a time in two places but finding so many organizations doing that & larger work, they thought it unnecessary to go on with it generally. I explained to her that we too had the same thing [in Canada]. The Woman's National Council was in the field with committees covering many phases that might be considered as bolstering our objects of the Mothers' Union.

Lady Chichester is on a Board or committee which is getting some amendments arranged to the Insurance Bill[7] which is of very great interest at present in England. The Insurance Bill interests women very much & it is one of the things which the women suffragists can use well to show the legitimate interest of women in politics. It affects women in so many ways, both in their earnings and in their maternity—sick benefit &c.. Oddly in [a] way, & yet not, the doctors are against the insurance bill because of the old fear that lady doctors would cut into their practice.

The profession of surgery & practice of med. has a sort of special condition in London. It interested me much. Surgeons are surgeons, anesthetists are anesthetists, physicians are physicians. The surgeons are called Mr. & the physicians doctors. This is London, not especially English [in general]. Dr. F. [Flemming] tells me the big specialists who charge some $5.00 for appendicitis & all sorts of fancy charges, need big fees & cases because living in Harley or Wigmore St., they have to pay high rents, enormous rents, like Miss Lancaster. Then a patient being wealthy enough to go to a nursing home pays a high price for the privilege—say 10 to 14 guineas a wk. or more. Then in major cases they have to have extra nurse or nurses about 3 guineas more each. Then [there is] their attending doctor or family doctor beside the anesthetist & other extras.

I asked what the other people did. The poorer go to the general hospitals to the general wards & get often if not generally good operations, but in a general ward! Miss Lancaster said if they could pay something they were expected to donate £20 or £40 to the hospital but no direct charge was made. I found out afterwards that general practitioners do things—operate—as do ours, on those who do not go to the big specialists & that there were private hospitals, not in the expensive neighborhood who took patients for four guineas a week.

It seemed to me that life on Harley St. & similar [places] had become an unnatural & artificial business & they had a bare street, with just an area stair & some steps to the front door & a square of ground behind, about the size of their house, which is mostly in a terrace. Dr. Flem[m]ing prides himself on the possession of a tree but looking down the back of the row in which Miss Lancaster lived 27 Wigmore I could only see one yard with any green & it was ivy on the wall & a shrub within. Think of the hurry & strain to make enough to pay expenses under such conditions & what have they for it?

In Canada all the expenses are less, even if there is worry to make both ends meet, we live, we have a chance to have ground enough to have something green & our view is not confined to bare stone or brick in walls & pavements. I don't think they can possibly visualize our conditions, even the best informed, unless they come to see. I don't know why it is that there is so very, very little in English papers about Canadian affairs & yet there is such a lot of talk about Canada. It seems as if it were mostly the immigration agents who give the English their impressions of Canada & a few other things.

After Lady Chichester left (Adam just came in before she left) I went to the dressmaker for final pay &c. & from there we took a taxi to Dr. Flem[m]ing's & he had a good look at my eyes & came to a conclusion about my glasses. That I would have to wear them all the time, one kind for reading & another generally & to continue the goggles for a few weeks yet over the others. Dr. F. was leaving for his holiday & he looked in need of it. His wife is a woman doctor. She is not as interesting on my one conversation with her this afternoon, but I had not a good chance [to observe her], as their boy was just home for his holidays, having just taken an entrance scholarship into Rugby—a fine looking chap of 14. He was unpacking and she was trying to pack & get ready for going away for a month's holidays. She told me that women doctors did very well, but they were not fashionable & that was the best description.

Tuesday, 1 August

Adam's Diary

Got Beth's glasses. Went to Festival of Empire all day, saw pictures, heard music, saw Pageant of London &c. Canadian exhibit very good. Many fakes and money making devices. Not large attendance.

Elizabeth's Diary

Adam & I went out to the Festival of Empire at the Crystal Palace. They had written us & sent us honorary tickets. We went out by train. It took about 20 minutes. It seemed a good way out & certainly we stopped at a number of suburbs & places. The Crystal Palace is an immense building of itself & the whole surrounding or acres of frontage was laid out in walks, exhibits, arcades, avenues & all sorts. It was a very bewildering panorama & beyond it all was Sydenham. I've never climbed so many steps in a day unless it was the Campanile at Venice[8] or the tower of the Parliament buildings at Ottawa.

We walked & climbed looking for things & then out again. One couldn't turn round without paying 2D. We took the "scenic railway" which must have been built at great cost. It went round a sort of semi under circle which had a high sort of wall on which was painted colonial special features & between the painting & the railway realistic representations of work (outdoor work) in Canada, grain farming, Australia, sheep shearing &c. &c., South Africa, mining & negroes doing this & that & New Zealanders doing something else.

There was a band concert of Coldstream Bank which we took in before the Scenic Railway & then we went up two stories in the lift (as they call elevators in England & the continent) after having climbed up a very great lot of steps. We had dinner here at a Leyous restaurant, which was advertised as widely & effectively as the most active American firm could do it.

After our luncheon we took a look at some of the exhibits. I was much interested in seeing the whole process of making silk hats—top hats. The frame is made of four layers of cotton & beeswax & shaped in blocks by hot flat irons. Then another man puts a good layer of I think beeswax & irons on the silk black plush business. Then a girl binds it & another finishes. It seems wonderful how a man could iron the silk stuff on so perfectly as it is done.

After seeing some very interesting & lovely things (the silver stamped in glass &c. &c.) we went to the Art gallery & looked at pictures most of the time till four o'clock. Here I saw an instance of why curators are put to take umbrellas & canes at the doors of galleries & museums for in the middle of a large picture was a hole that looked exactly as tho. someone had put the point of a parasol through it. I say we looked at pictures—well Adam did & I did sometimes. I was not suppose to use my eyes much (as the glasses had not yet come to me) & so I would take a running glance & settle on what I liked but for a look & then sit down & rest awhile. There was quite a gallery of paintings & Adam was quite interested.

Then we went down stairs, a flight, & listened to an organ recital in the main hall of the Crystal Palace. After that we went to see the day nursery & some of the booths & then had tea or dinner & by this time it was time to go to see the pageants at their special part of the grounds where a very large amphitheatre was built with a great space in front of green sward in the foreground, a hill & a pond in the background, with roads leading from the far corners of an old English house on either side &c. &c.

The program consisted of three pageants: Henry v returning after Agincourt [when] Henry v received the crown, the Jack Cade rebellion[9] & Merrie England. The first had companies of soldiers & archers, on horse & on foot: King Henry in royal accoutrements & his followers gorgeous in trappings. The queen & her retinue emerged from the house on the extreme other side & came down in stately procession of royal robes & pages and ladies in waiting to meet the King in the centre of the great open space.

There was a throne in the next pageant & a lot of gorgeous apparel of King & Queen & Archbishops & soldiers & peoples & ladies—such a lot. There must have been 150 or 200 taking part, perhaps more. In the second part where the throne occurred, it took about an army of the men taking part to unroll & spread a heavy plush affair which served for the carpet. There had been a wet shower while we were in the palace & that had made it heavier than usual. There was after this pageant the work of rolling the huge thing back again under shadow of the amphitheatre seats.

The next the rebellion or small plot of some dissatisfied [Englishmen] to try to raise a party to unthrone the King, was one also of parties on foot & on horse & a lot of going about & talking but which ended in their carrying off the head rebel & chucking him in the pond. The last part—Merrie England—had a swarm of people taking part: booths, maypoles, drinking places, dances, games, a clown, a man on stilts &c. &c., with a great variety of costumes of the time, all very pretty & telling of no end of expense & trouble. The amount expended on this Festival which was running for several months, must have been immense. People in London & many near places took part & it must have been a great strain on time & pocket money to go there many nights during these months. The pageants differed [in personnel] & I do not know how many kept on at each or anything about that part.

After we saw the end of this about 9:30 we went to see the Canadian Exhibit & it was one to be proud of. The exhibit was placed in a duplicate representation of the main Parliament building at Ottawa, about 2/3 its size I heard some one say. It looked very well indeed & the exhibit within was really most excellent. Samples of animals of Canada from Buffalo & beaver to every other one, spread out on prairie & woodland. There was the most perfect, the most wonderful, display of apples, considering that it was near to the end of July & they were apples of the previous winter. There were exhibits of grain, of Montreal arts & crafts &c., of canned fruit, cheese &c., & such a remarkable display of butter. It represented the yard before the stable door which a boy was about to open. In the space before the door were a girl, another boy, a hen & some small chicks, three cows & a calf, all every bit of it was done in butter in the most remarkable life like way. One could scarcely believe it possible.

There was a very large exhibit of minerals and a large one of the fish which are in Canadian rivers & lakes. I could have stayed much longer here but it was getting late & we were tired with the day of it. It was eleven or after when we reached Savoy Mansions but it was satisfactory to feel proud of [the] Canadian exhibit. Yet there only seems to be a bi-weekly mail [between England and Canada] & the English seem to take no interest in Canadian affairs unless it be cabinet changes—or the north west harvest—which is entirely a money interest. Anything that has a real bearing on the big imports or investments may get a few lines of notice.

Wednesday, 2 August

Adam's Diary
At Bank and round by City Road.[10] Wesley's Chapel[11] &c. Saw some old books. Had official interviews. To Desborough's to dinner. Talk on old books, customs &c., miscellaneous subjects. Lady Chichester visited Beth.

Elizabeth's Diary
We went first to see about my glasses & as that made us to [*sic*] late for our Wed. appointment (he took so long), we went along to Walker's & bought a macintosh for me which I had expected to do the day after we landed, but this is different from all summers that anyone remembers in London—no rain, no fog, no mist; glaring hot sun every day.[12] It rained & hailed with a vengeance for a short time in London the day we were in Oxford, but it seemed to have been a myth by the time we came back.

Then we went to the House of Lords, as Lord Percy had kindly procured a note from his father the Duke of Northumberland which he had enclosed to Adam, procuring us a thorough sight of the famous Houses of Parliament. Minnie Gordon who wished to go with us came down from Oxford that A.M. & met us at the entrance under the tower. A few minutes before this we met Mr. Tyrell of Toronto, brother-in-law to Mrs. D. Gibson. He was only in London for a short time & was full of things to do. We invited him to go in with us. There was a lot of red tape, even with the passport of the noble Duke, but we did see it very thoroughly.

It was the more interesting because of the strenuous debating going on afternoons & evgs. on the Veto Bill or Parliament Bill, which was to remove the power of the Lords to veto entirely a bill of the Commons.[13] It was very interesting to see the rooms where the pros & the antis are divided & let in one by one & counted or rather let out one by one [and counted], when a division or vote is taken. The rooms & corridors for this did not seem so very large, but were large enough I suppose. It has [created] a more vivid picture in my mind of the last passionate & notable debate between the last ditchers [the "no" voters], the non-voting [members] & the pros for the bill which took place last Friday & ended in the division which will be a notable epock [*sic*] for all time in the history of the House of Lords. I wonder how much of the long list of conflicts & reforms which will grow out of this I shall see. I was interested to see in this morning's *London Post* which had backed Lord Halsbury & the "last-ditchers" a letter from the duchess of Somerset which had indeed an ultra "last ditchers" sound.

The House of Lords & the House of Commons are very stately & rich & somewhat dim too, but have such an appearance of richness & stability that one is quite satisfied with it as the home of English History. We parted with Minnie Gordon who seemed changed in appearance, seeming thinner & more loveable. She went back to Oxford after some work &c. she wanted to do in the British Museum. Adam went with me to see my new dresses tried on & pay for them & then we went to luncheon & I home & he to seeing [government] men.

I went back to the Mansions to rest & in the evg. we went out to Capt. Desborough's again to dinner. A Mr. Young, a bookseller, was there & Mrs. D's brother who had come from Vancouver on a visit. I did not care for either of the men. Mr. B. her brother was hard to talk to. He has stores on the West [side] of Vancouver. Had seen & met Rev. Mr. Kidd there but did not know his name? I had a nice talk with Mrs. D. who is an odd mixture. She talks & talks to men & smokes & smokes cigarettes but she does a lot of good work among the poor, especially the babies & mothers of babies among the poor. She has none of her own. She was awfully good & invited me to stay a week with her before I would go to Scotland. It was very kind of her to do so much for us & for me in many ways.

They live in a very historic neighborhood—20 Cheyne Court. Everything is Cheyne around there, named after Lady & other Cheynes hundreds of years ago,[14] but made most famous by Carlyle's residence on Cheyne Row nearby & which we saw. We went by taxi cab & came home by no. 11 bus.

A Letter from Elizabeth to Muriel[15]

We received your letter on Mon. & today, [in] the evg. found a couple of copies of the [Toronto] *Globe* which I think Mr. Foran [*sic*][16] sent. Things move on & time takes no account of us. It is four weeks today (tonight) since my calamity came and today I was able to have my new glasses, one pair to wear on the street & another to read & write with, tho. for two or three weeks yet, I will have to wear the goggles over them [on the street]. I will enjoy things much more now. I have not visited any galleries yet except yesterday the picture [gallery] & other parts of the Festival of Empire & it was trying just to take a glimpse & not look more than half the time.

FIG. 5 Muriel Shortt. Courtesy of University of Waterloo Library, Special Collections & Archives, Elizabeth Smith Shortt fonds (WA10, file 2302, Muriel Shortt).

Dr. Flem[m]ing is very nice indeed & has been most kind. I find him an interesting friend too. He said one day just before I came out of the hospital that he had never had such a cheerful glaucoma case. He said a few days ago that he had never had a glaucoma case go off & do as I've done: go out of hospital at ten days & go shopping in about two weeks. I wouldn't have chosen to go out shopping so soon, only that I could forsee [*sic*] I would have to begin or I would fail to get it done.

I've bought all I intended to & more & have paid a bit more than I intended but I think you will like everything I have. I am often tempted to buy you an afternoon gown but it would be too risky. I think you had better right away keep your eye on silk sales or whatever you would like for a dress to supply the place of the old green one which you will have to put pretty much in the background for a time anyway. I don't know what you have in mind yourself, but you will probably have thought it all out.

Quite a few here have girdles—cord & tassels—on afternoon gowns. I think I told you I could not find gowns that suited me & so had three made, at least a suit & two gowns & I bought a white with black stripe flannel to wear here & now—coat & shirt, but it is tighter than I would wish it to be. Tho. it has not rained yet I bought today a thinnish waterproof so as to be ready.

As I say I have my glasses this afternoon & now gradually I will get your letters all read & be able to tell you of details in them & as to the numbers. I feel quite sure we have received all you have sent. The story has kept up & we always look so keenly for them. What a nice lot of young people you have now.

We are going to the Desboroughs to dinner tonight & tomorrow evg.. Mr. Biggar[17] invited us, the Doughtys & W. L. Grant & wife[18] who are in town. Your father however is to dine with Mr. Kerr the heir to the Marquis of Midlothian[19] and Sir Henry [sic] Primrose[20] asked your father to lunch or tea with him, so he has gone today. The Countess of Chichester called on me Tues. & we had a most interesting conversation of which more anon.

I will write soon again. With much love to my dear, faithful Muriel

Thursday, 3 August

Adam's Diary[21]
Saw people at Foreign and Colonial offices. Obtained letter re facilities from Brit. Embassies on Continent. Dinner with Philip Kerr. Talked Irish Home rule, Imperialism, Immigration &c till midnight. Very interesting evening. At Reform Club[22] Writing letters.

Elizabeth's Diary
Mrs. Doughty was due at Mrs. Singer's to get her wisteria tunic gown fitted, so I went with her to 33 Knightsbridge & from there we took a "bus" to South Kensington where I went to see Miss Lefroy[23] of the Imperial Inst.[24] about getting a Scotch girl out for myself in the party sailing 31th of Aug. Miss Lefroy was away on her holiday but I saw a substitute & had quite a talk about immigration. Miss Lefroy was to be back very soon—Aug. 15—& I was to see her when I returned. The red tape is always the uppermost thing & people will get to doing things in a perfunctory, mechanical sort of way. I wonder if people doing the same thing for years in other places get so much of the nature of this, as they do in England.

From here we went to the Albert & Victoria or South Kensington Museum which would take a week to [do] justice to at all. After we had lunch there we did all we could stand of the paintings & some of the price-less [illegible], inlaid Louis xiv tables, cabinets &c. & many wonderful things. I was not supposed to do this sort of thing, so could not do it as well as I would, but I enjoyed a good bit.

We went home very tired & we had tea (afternoon) in our sitting room & rested until it was time to dress to go to Mr. Biggar's dinner which he was having in his suite in the Oxford mansions. His niece Miss Casey who is beginning or has begun her career as an actress presided, as there is no Mrs. B.. Adam could not go as he had previously accepted an engagement for dinner with an [sic] Philip Kerr with whom he lunched last wk. & whose acquaintance he made in Ottawa when Mr. Kerr was out [there]. Mr. Kerr is heir presumptive to the Marquis of Lothian[25] [sic] & nephew of the Duke of Norfolk (the present Marquis being a bachelor). Adam had a very long tete a tete dinner with Kerr. I think Adam must have exhausted himself for he did not come till after midnight.

At Mr. Biggar's there were Dr. & Mrs. D., W. L. (Prof.) & Mrs. Grant, a Mr. Wallace (friend of Peacock's) & a pianist whose name I forget & Miss Robinson or Robertson, daughter of Christopher R. of Toronto[26] (cousin of Mrs. Stewart Houston)[27] whom I had known in Toronto at the [NCWC] Congress as assistant to Mrs. Willoughby Cumming.[28] We had a very pleasant enjoyable dinner. I sat at Mr. B's right hand & Mrs. D. at his left. After dinner I had a good talk with Mrs. Grant & liked her much. I also had a talk with W. L. & altogether had a very pleasant evg.. I wore blk. sequins.

A Letter from Elizabeth to Muriel, George, and Lorraine[29]

I've just received Muriel's letter written July 27th & am so glad to receive it & hear of you all. I am sorry about Lorraine's not being quite well. She did not tell me about it at all. I suppose she thought it too far away for me to tell her about it. She should have had a dose of castor oil when it first began & then it would have stopped. I am glad you are having so nice a time with Katherine Foster & Alice McLean & Jean Addington & those three nice boys. I think they are indeed three very nice chaps. I am always glad to know fine men & women. The world needs them all—everyone. Papa wrote George yesterday, so you will have heard of him.

At last after many pros & cons I have decided to go to the continent with Papa. We will be gone about three weeks, but your letters will be forwarded from 17 Victoria St. to us at different places. I thought perhaps I would stay here & save up some of the big expense my eyes incurred, but in the end the difference would not be much if any over fifty [dollars] & ten years from now that will not make much difference, for:

> she who spent her coin on flannels red
> and she who took pneumonia instead
> will both be underground in fifty years
> and prudence pays no premium to the dead

I believe tho. that I am going to live awhile. God brought me through devious ways & saved my sight for some further use in the world I think. Give my love to Mrs. Acland & Mrs. Haydon & Mrs. McLean & the others. I might have sent them a card if I had my usual sight.

I got my glasses yesterday & my courage is reviving. It is very nerve straining to go about these streets of bedlam without good sight & good walking ability. I have astonished myself tho. as to the walking. Of course I cannot do as much as most people but I do five times the amt. I can do at home.

If you looked in my hand bag you would think I had looted an oculist's shop. I have the two pair [of glasses] I brought with me (which I can put away now) and I have the goggles which [I] will hang on [to] for a few wks. still & I have glasses to wear & glasses to read with. Later, when my eyes have settled down to be what they will continue to be, Dr. F. says the two glasses can be made in one & I shall not have the continual changing. He thinks I will have to wear them all the time unless I specially want not at some reception but he thinks I will not want to leave them off. He is very nice indeed. He knows Dr. Minnes & thinks if I ever had to have anything done he would be quite equal to it.

I must not forget to say that I rec. the photo of me that you sent, but I fear I forgot to acknowledge it. I was abit disappointed in it—it looked so staringly [sic] white like a dead person. There does not seem to be any shade anywhere. Otherwise, it wasn't bad. Were you satisfied or did you say anything to him about it?

About Georgina, you had better speak to her. I don't think she would stay without the child and probably she would not be content anyway in the winter after her easy summer. I went yesterday to see the Sec. of the British Immig. Assoc. about sending me a Scotch girl in the party sailing Aug. 31st. She would get there ahead of me if she goes. I will I expect be back here before the 31st & will know in time to write ahead about it. I also interviewed them about two [servants] for Aunt Christina to go there & if she is already arranged, she (Aunt C.) is to write Miss FitzGibbon. I have had two letters lately from Helderleigh.[30] She [Christina Smith] spoke about Lorraine [meeting them at Kingston] but I left it to you, for I thought Lorraine would be home some time before they would be going home via Kingston & it would not be possible in that way.

Dear little Lorraine she bravely kept all but joy out of her letters to me. I am glad George is enjoying his work [at the Canadian Archives]. I can't see tho. that that keeps him from writing to mother. He used to write me faithfully every week when he was at school & I never failed [writing] him. I expect he thinks I get it all from Muriel but then I like to have [news] from you both & Lorraine too, who writes every week anyway.

We are going from London to Paris (just there overnight) to Berne & Geneva, to Vienna, to Berlin, to Amsterdam the Hague & sail from Flushing to London. Your father could be got anytime of urgency through the English Embassy at Berne, Vienna or Berlin as he has letters to these & will be in touch. The letters however, we have still [coming] to H. Com. Office 17 Victoria St.

I am staying in this morning; we were so late getting to sleep last night & I have a number of things to do. I have just written Aunt Chrissie and must close this as it is time to dress & go out to lunch. When we come back to London we will go up to Cambridge for a couple of days to visit the Glovers.[31] I will be glad to see them again.

We were at dinner last night at Mr. Biggar's & among others there were W. L. & Mrs. Grant. They are in London till tomorrow & then go on to Scotland. They will sail early in Sept.. I like Mrs. G. quite as well as I expected. She is fine, one of the complete people that you do not wish were a "little more this or that."

Later—I had to leave off & go out to lunch. When I came in there was George's letter & a journal & clippings. So you had a snow storm! Will write to George again—soon—so glad to hear from him. I was thinking Muriel that perhaps a gown made on the black & gold combination would be nice—a gold silk slip under & a gold cord & tassel girdle. I am sending in a paper or letter a black & gold net collar that if you should plan a gold & black dress might work in. If it is not useful in that way you can keep it till I find what I have to give my sisters as souvenirs when I come home. Tell me when you write next if you have decided & if you want the cord & tassel girdle. I can probably get it cheaper here than there.

Shopping is a weary work here too. The lovely thing about getting a dress by a good dressmaker here is that they buy everything & all I had to do was to say what I wanted & be fitted twice or three times. There are lovely trimmings too.

We are getting to the stage of packing & sorting a bit as the books have to be got off out of the way. Papa is sending them to the Civil Service Commission I think or to the Archives. So glad all is going well. My eyes hurt a bit, but I've used them more last night & today. I mean [I] have not had the goggles on all the time—must take a rest. With so much love to each & hoping all is well. Kindest regards to Miss Gibson.

Friday, 4 August

Adam's Diary[32]
Went to Bank to get money for tickets. Spent part of afternoon looking over books at barrows of street vendors. Got several interesting things in books, pamphlets and pictures, very cheap. In during evening reading and packing up books. Imperial Service Museum.

Elizabeth's Diary
We dalleyed [sic] round in the early morning. It was the difficult thing to get anyone to start mornings. I think they must have got into bad ways while I was in the hospital. Adam was able to get underway long before the Doughtys & she was the most indulged & was often miserable & he nearly always took her breakfast to her about nine. Breakfast in England is a small matter: bread & butter, toast, jam & tea. On the continent it is slimmer still for it is two small rolls & tea & frequently honey or jam & the tea is very poor indeed. I was so disappointed in having milk instead of cream in the tea in England & most everywhere since I left home.

Adam & Dr. D. had to go away along past St. Paul's to the Bank so Mrs. D. & I undertook to do some of the shops round St. Paul's & Cheapside,[33] but it was a failure mostly. Nothing seemed bargains & nothing especially attractive. We all had luncheon together & after Mrs. D. & I did more casting about we went home by 4:30. She went out again with Dr. D. but I was waiting for Mrs. Grant who came in late but as they were near on the Strand she could do it even late & I was very glad to see her & have another chat. They went on to Scotland next day. I hope I shall see them again in Can..

Prof. Morrison [sic][34] & his sister both wrote me rich kind letters inviting me to come & spend a fortnight with them & recuperate. It seemed so dreadful to me to get out of London & go to Glasgow & from there to Greenock & from there to Innellan [in Argyllshire, Scotland] alone that I could not face it & had to forego it. Anyway I could not go & plant myself on them for two weeks, kind & dear as they are. I know what an incubus a semi-strange woman might be to a domestic menage & particularly when the only son was going off on the 19th again to Canada. So much as I would have liked to have spent a week with them I had to forgo it. My eyes were getting a bit better tho. I tried them more than I would have done under the usual circumstances of life. They always needed care every day tho..

Saturday, 5 August

Adam's Diary
Took coach to Boxhill [*sic*]³⁵ and return. Very fine day and beautiful scenery and villages &c. Had lunch there and came back by coach. Spent evening at rooms. Obtained tickets for trip to Continent. People leaving city for Bank holiday.

Elizabeth's Diary
After a scuttling about, we four got of[f] on a coach trip to Box Hill in Surrey. The coach was to start about eleven or 10:30 (I forget which) from Hotel Victoria. We could only make it in a taxi & Dr. D. was away & not back when we started, so we left word for him to follow & his taxi drove up about a minute behind ours at the Hotel. The coach is owned by a millionaire named Chapman, same sort of thing as Vanderbilts.

The coach is high, has the seats on top & bags &c. are put inside. There were four fine horses & a guard who blew many times on his horn as we trotted off in style. One gets to the top of the coach by a short ladder of steps which the guard holds to the coach & there are straps hanging to hold by as you go up. We were off on time & we went miles & miles before we came to the outskirts of London. The horses were then changed—the whole four—for four other fine steeds at the Dog & Fox. Then on & on past Putney & Wimbledon Common & some more suburban places through quaint English towns & villages thro. Epsom of racing renown & on again changing horses again at the King's Head & on again till we reached Box Hill about 1:30 & there was a fine luncheon set out for the fourteen who had come by coach. It was not so very expensive either.

In this tavern was a room which the maid showed me which Keats had occupied and another which Nelson had used. There was a lovely big garden with flower beds & shrubs & shaded by trees where we had coffee after luncheon & rested abit. Then all hands to the coach again & with winding horn we were off. We changed horses again at the same places &

drank our afternoon tea sitting on the top of the coach at the Dog & Fox, the men getting down & getting it for us.

There was a mixed lot on the coach. One old duck, or perhaps he was more of an old reprobate member of some Poor Law Board &c talking about what they did when they thought a man could work & wouldn't, said they set him up in a suit of clothes & gave him 10 shillings & turned him over to the Salvation Army for them to secure him work & keep an eye on him. If he ran away & came back to them, they fined him for stealing [and] running away with the clothes they lent him & this kept them from coming back on them. "It's wonderful what the S. Army can do for some of them—for instance one man who was a good worker but who persisted in drinking, they sent out to Canada & as he couldn't get drunk there (!?!?), he remained sober & was now a rich man!!" It was a horsey crowd, or would be horsey.

We got back soon after six & had dinner & thus Dr. D. & Adam, feeling in for a "toot," we all went to Pertland Sq. to see & hear the wonderful "expert slight of hand or something" that Lord Grey[36] had spoken to them about, but the place was closed till Mon., so went home & to bed tired but much pleased with our day.

A Letter from Elizabeth to Muriel[37]

We have been off today on a coaching trip into Surrey. We four started off about 10:30 & went to the coach to [sic] Hotel Victoria where the people (fourteen in all) collected. There were four fine horses & we all had seats on top. The guard had a long, thin horn & he tootletooted on it frequently. He had a buff coat, or rather gray, & white top hat & high boots & the wealthy, horsey man who owned the horses & coach had a top hat & drove.

In the outskirts of London at the Dog & Fox the horses were changed & then we started off fresh. We went through beautiful Surrey & through such quaint old English villages as Malden & Merton[38] & Epsom (& saw the Epsom downs) & Wimbledon Heath & Putney Common & saw numerous cricket teams at work & Lord Chas. Bereford's house[39] & a number of other Estates. We stopped again at the King's Head & changed horses (next to the King's Head was Nell Givin's house). We arrived at Box Hill the end of our journey before two & dinner was waiting for fourteen. Behind the hotel there was a beautiful garden & tables & chairs & we had our coffee out there. We started back about 3:15 & arrived here before seven having changed horses at the same places coming back. In the hotel at Box Hill there was a bedroom which had been used by Keats & another by Nelson.

I had a letter from Auntie Vie [Violet] & another from Aunt Martha[40] (both together) this evg.. Aunt Vie seems very well & in good spirits. Aunt Martha's house is building [sic] all right & plaster is being finished & the really interesting part of [it is] coming on. She expects to be in it in September. Yes, I think you had better ask Georgina if she would be willing to put the boy [her child] somewhere & I'm pretty certain that she won't & so a change will come about. You will need to speak [to her] two weeks before her month is up or arrange for her to stay two weeks after her month is up at the same wages.

The Doughtys are sailing for home next Tues. or Weds. & will be there about ten days afterward I think. They have had a nice time & have been over to Paris in the hot time. I expect it will be hot & very dirty travelling on the continent, but there were many reasons why I decided to go.

I am glad George is getting on so well both in the work & the golf. I gave the scores to your father & he seemed pleased. How are the balls holding out? I suppose dear Lorraine is home now & consorting with Mary & Marion. I sent Mrs. Haydon a card tonight & must write a lot of letters as soon as I can. My poor diary began on the first part of my trip but came to an untimely end. Perhaps I will begin now when we are more to ourselves.

Will the dressmaker who made your pink dress be good enough to make the afternoon dress or will you to to [sic] Miss Brisbois? If you go to Miss B., see at the first if she will make it for ten [dollars] as it is so early in the season. I find I cannot get much shopping done now. The streets & shops are bewildering tho. I am getting my courage back again with my glasses. It certainly does not help one's courage not to have one's sight. I wore the goggles all day today & my eyes do not feel tired tonight as yet.

We saw all sorts of outfits today: ponies pretty & ponies sad & donkey carts & all sorts. The English people seem to take life good humoredly & are pleased with very simple fun. Mrs. Desborough asked me to stay a week with her if I stayed here but I just couldn't make up my mind to visit here & with the Morrisons [sic] & give up the continent. With dear love to each of you & feeling such happiness in your individual faithfulness & goodness. Papa & I send all sorts of loving greetings to you each. Send regards to Miss Gibson & I hope she is enjoying herself.

Sunday, 6 August

Adam's Diary[41]
Remained in house all morning. After lunch to Finchley and Barnet.[42] Fine views over the country in Middlesex.[43] Home by bus and train. Desborough's [sic] to supper at Savoy Restaurant.[44] Doughty also, very swell but expensive and uninteresting. Pleasant chat.

Elizabeth's Diary
We Adam & I wrote letters & sorted up. I had hoped to go to the Temple Church on the Strand (named originally from the Knights Templar) where Mrs. Desborough says they have beautiful singing. We (Adam & I) went after we had dinner at the Adelphi by tube to Highgate (where George Elliot [sic] is buried)[45] & then took a train out through Finchley to Barnet, quite a run into the country & with a lovely view of the rolling farming lands & estates in that part of Middlesex. We came back another way from Highgate, taking busses till we arrived home about 8 o'clock.

We Dr. & Mrs. D & Adam & I took Capt. & Mrs. Desborough to supper at the Grand Savoy. It is the grandest hotel of extravagance I ever ate in & the supper was an expensive but tasty affair. The flunkies & waiters, in plush & others in the usual waiter style, & the plush ones & the band giving quite an air of over rich. We went back to our apartments after & talked for some time.

Monday, 7 August

Adam's Diary
Bank holiday, everything shut up. Packed up all forenoon. Simpson's for dinner, excellent meals there.[46] To see old Chelsea Church where Sir. Thos. Moore [sic] is buried.[47] Carlyle's house, George Eliot's house, also Swinchern [sic], Wm. Morris and Roselti's [sic] place.[48] Completed packing &c.

Elizabeth's Diary
We (Adam & I) put in a busy morning packing & then out to the Café Cecil to dinner & packed & fixed up till we went out to the Desboroughs about 3 o'clock. They met us a little way from the house & we went up to see Chelsea Church [built in] 1291. It is well worth seeing. Some of monuments were very old of an ancient flavor. That to Lord & Lady Dacre was of two recumbent figures on the usual ——— [slab] but beside the tomb about a foot

lower down, was a recumbent marble figure about the size of a large doll which I suppose was a baby Dacre, but [about] which the guidebook said nothing.

It was Lady Cheyne however whose name is still most in evidence, as their [sic] is Cheyne Row, famed from Carlyle's residence there (& where the house he lived in is being kept by the city for a museum of Carlyle's belongings & life) Cheyne Walk, fronting a small park & the River has the Queen's House, no.7, so named from Chas. II['s] deserted wife Catherine who lived here.[49] Later [sic][50] the young Elizabeth, who was to be the famous Queen Bess, came to spend her summers in this house, Chelsea being a fashionable suburb. In this row too at one time lived Sir Meredith Swinburne[51] & [William] Morris[52] George Elliot [sic], when Mrs. Cross came here to live but having caught cold, died after only 3 wks. of occupancy & was buried at Highgate. Near this corner too is a physics garden, begun as an herb garden & being endowed to go on became a sort of botanical experimental garden as well as one of domestic drugs.

London is full of history, saturated with it & I think one of the guide books has 14 pages of names & biographies of famous people. London is stupendous 6,000,000 people swarmed together a weltering mass of humanity of all sorts & kinds—clever & stupid, ill born & well born, rich & poor all struggling for something except [to be] the "shirtless" man. The church[e]s such as that Chelsea [one] where families have died out makes one think of the transitoriness of it all: *sic transit gloria mundi* [so passes the glory of the world].

One is much struck with the success of British organization &c., in seeing how well regulated everything is & one is amazed when one thinks of the bigness & the success of the water supply for these teeming millions, a good & sufficient water supply & many Canadian cities, who [sic] had nothing much to do but keep the supply clean, are indicted with the loss of lives of hundreds of people because they didn't keep their nature given supply clean. Then again the sanitary conditions! I was in London a month & seldom saw a fly—only twice while I was in the hospital & only a very few times did I see a fly where we had our meals [at the] Cecil & Adelphi or other [restaurants]. I don't think at any time I saw two at the same time & no screens: no screen doors, no window screens any where. I found that there were bylaws about manure bits &c. & the regulations were carried out & the streets washed up at night. The spitting bylaw seemed to be well enforced too, for steps to subways & tubes, & all sorts & kinds of steps were kept clean. It is a truly wonderful thing when one thinks of it.

There are things of many kinds of difference between England & Canada & yet the diff. is due partly to the oldness of the one & the newness & briskness of the other. The old taverns with their peculiar names, many of them famous in Dickens & other writers, such as The White Hart, The Green Man (from archery days), The Bunch of Grapes, The Saddle of Mutton & Cauliflower, The King's Head, The Dog & Fox, the Black Bull, Ye Olde Pied Bull, The King's Head [sic], The Crown & Sceptre, The White Hart [sic] &c. &c. I was interested to see the Chelsea Barracks for so many years the retiring home for old soldiers where they have freedom of going about the streets or grounds, as they can, & where they recount past exploits play checkers & put in their evg. of life. Not far away is the school for soldiers' sons which does credit to one civilization that must have its soldiers.

A Letter from Elizabeth to Mother and Gertrude[53]
This is another sort of goodbye letter but I hope no further calamity will come to me. We leave in the morning for Paris to stay over night & then on to Geneva the next morning & after a couple of days to Berne & then after a few days to Vienna & a few days [later] to Dresden & Berlin & home to Eng. in about three wks. by Amsterdam, sailing from Flushing to London. I want to be back by [August] 30th if possible as a party of servants sail on the 30th & I want one of them & am trying to look after two for Christina. I had a letter from Violet & from Martha & it was good to hear that Violet was so well. Christina also enclosed a letter of Cecil's[54] which said he would likely be in Hamilton for a few hours to see you & mother.

[Elizabeth then recounts her travels to Box Hill, Middlesex, Chelsea Church, and the homes in the Cheyne area.]

Well, I am getting better & I hope to be rid of my goggles in a couple of weeks unless I use them in the sun or wind. I will be so glad to get rid of them. I am supposed to be using my general glasses under them, but they are too big. So I am changing about among the three kinds but wear the goggles on the street all the time.

The Doughtys are leaving for home on Wed., if they can secure a stateroom which they think they can. When we come back we will stop here [the Savoy Mansions] the few nights we will be here [London]. We are storing three trunks here and only taking valise & two hand bags &c.. because baggage is such a bother on the continent.

Muriel & George seem to be all right & now I suppose Lorraine is with them again. I hope you will not experience such heat again. You poor dear girl, how you must have suffered during those two dreadful weeks. The going up & down must have been bad enough but hot nights exhaust one & wear you out. It has been a record here, never has there been such continuous heat, clear sky & lack of rain. We were here a month yesterday & only once have seen any sort of shower & no fog at all. It did storm the day we were in Oxford here, but not there. I did not buy a mackintosh till a few days ago & have had no need of it. It is wonderful here. Londoners have never seen so much sky in a whole summer they say as this month. It has been over 90 they say some days. It is very warm today.

They say we will be warmer in Paris & travelling. I don't mind that so much as the dirt of the trains. We will be about 7 hours tomorrow to Paris & about 10 or more next day to Geneva. I think I must not write more now than to send my love to you each & hope you will write to me care of H.C. office 17 Victoria St. & they will forward to me. With so much love, as month from now we will be ou[t] there [in Canada] &c..

Notes

1 The National Insurance bill, which provided health and unemployment benefits for Great Britain's entire working population, had been introduced by the chancellor of the exchequer, Lloyd George, in the Commons, but its passage had to await the resolution of the constitutional crisis that arose upon the Lords' refusal to approve the measure; Juliet Nicolson, *The Perfect Summer: Dancing into Shadow in 1911* (Toronto: McArthur, 2007), 31–32, 173–75.

2 Marilyn Barber points out that "[t]he constant scarcity of servants in Canada facilitated immigration, but especially in the twentieth century, channelled many immigrant women into a low status occupation shunned by Canadians." In the years between 1904 and 1914, "over three quarters of female domestics arriving from overseas were of British origin"; Marilyn Barber, *Immigrant Domestic Servants in Canada* (Ottawa: Canadian Historical Association, 1991), 3, 8.

3 J. R. Piggott, *Palace of the People: The Crystal Palace at Sydenham 1854–1936* (Madison: University of Wisconsin Press, 2004), 174; see also Cecilia Morgan, *"A Happy Holiday": English Canadians and Transatlantic Tourism, 1870–1930* (Toronto: University of Toronto Press, 2008), 181–83.

4 Queen's University Archives, Adam Shortt Papers (hereafter cited as ASP), box 11, Adam Shortt Diary, 31 July 1911.

5 See ch. 1, n. 47.

6 University of Waterloo, Elizabeth Smith Shortt Papers (hereafter cited as ESSP), WA10, file 1772, Smith Shortt Diary, 31 July 1911.

7 See ch. 3, n. 1.

8 The Campanile of San Marco is a huge tower, over 98.5 metres high, construction of which was initiated c. 888–912 and completed c. 1156–73.

9 Jack Cade was the leader of a major rebellion against King Henry VI in 1450, whose victory at Sevenoaks, Kent, led to his forces temporarily occupying London. He was eventually expelled from the English capital, and, after being captured in Sussex, died while being returned to London.

10 This famous street, built in London in 1761, extends in a long westerly curve from Finsbury Square across Old Street to Islington High Street, and, besides Wesley's Chapel, includes other significant buildings, such as Moorfield's Eve Hospital.

11 This chapel opened, by John Wesley in 1778, had become the mother church of international Methodism. Wesley's remains are found in a grave behind the church, not far from the home he used when residing in London.

12 See ch. 1, n. 64.

13 As David Brooks put it, "the bill proposed to do away with the upper House's veto entirely in respect of finance, & to make it suspensory rather than absolute in regard to other categories of legislation, with an effective power of delay lasting up to two years"; David Brooks, *The Age of Upheaval: Edwardian Politics, 1899–1914* (Manchester: Manchester University Press, 1995), 136.

14 Cheyne Court, like Cheyne Gardens, Mews, Place, Row, and Walk in this part of London, is named after the Cheyne family, who were lords of the manor of Chelsea from 1660 to 1712, and the proprietors of much of the land in this distinguished section of the British capital.

15 ESSP, WA10, file 493, Smith Shortt to Muriel Clarke, 2 August 1911.

16 Despite her misspelling of his name, Elizabeth is apparently referring to Mr. Forin, the secretary to the Civil Service Commission headed by Michel Larochelle and her husband.

17 See ch. 1, n. 47.

18 See "Frequently Mentioned Names" on p. xxi.

19 See ch. 2, n. 20.

20 See ch. 2, n. 23.

21 ASP, box 11, Adam Shortt Diary, 3 August 1911.

22 The Reform Club was founded in 1832 to serve British radicals, and by 1911 mainly accommodated members of the Liberal Party after having become renowned for its rich interior.

23 See ch. 2, n. 39.

24 The Imperial Institute was founded to celebrate Queen Victoria's Golden Jubilee in 1887. By 1911, the Institute continued to promote many aspects of the contemporary British Empire, including immigration from the mother country to the colonies.

25 Here Elizabeth has mistakenly identified the heir apparent to the Marquis of Midlothian; see ch. 2, n. 20.

26 Miss Robinson was one of Christopher Robinson's five children. Mr. Robinson was the editor and proprietor of *The Dominion Presbyterian*, a religious newspaper published in Ottawa since 1900; *Canadian Who's Who, 1910* (London: Times Publishing Company, 1910), 195.

27 Mrs. Stewart Houston was the daughter of John Beverly Robinson, a former member of the family compact and later a lieutenant governor of Ontario. Mrs. Houston had performed as a singer on the concert stage in both Europe and North America, and upon her retirement from this career became active in various reform causes, such as the National Council of Women of Canada and the Society for Prevention of Cruelty to Animals; *Canadian Who's Who, 1910*, 110.

28 See ch. 2, n. 39.

29 ESSP, WA10, file 493, Smith Shortt to Muriel Clarke, "August 5." This letter, along with a second one, is dated 5 August, but the context, as defined by the diaries of Adam and Elizabeth, mainly relates to events occurring on or near 3 August.

30 Helderleigh was the name E. D. and Christina Smith gave to their mansion and estate in Winona, Ontario, which had just been completed earlier in 1911; *Silas Smith, U.E.L., and His Descendants*, compiled by R. Janet Powell from history collected by Miss Gertrude Smith and other descendants (n.p., n.d.), 24. See "Frequently Mentioned Names" on p. xix.

31 See ch. 2, n. 71.

32 ASP, Box 11, Adam Shortt Diary, 4 August 1911.

33 Cheapside was the main market location in medieval London, and by 1900 was famous for its upscale offices, warehouses, and shops.

34 See ch. 2, n. 17.

35 Box Hill presents a spectacular view of down and woodland, and is especially honoured for its many beautiful box trees, which give the town its name.

36 Albert Henry George Grey, the 4th Earl Grey, was governor general of Canada from 1904 to 1911. In this capacity, he encouraged closer ties to the mother country through, for example, the Laurier government's creation of a Canadian navy, a move denounced in French-speaking Quebec as "Grey's Bill"; Carman Miller, "Albert Henry George, 4th Earl Grey," in *Dictionary of Canadian Biography*, vol. XIV, 439.

37 ESSP, WA10, file 493, Smith Shortt to Muriel Clarke, 5 August 1911.

38 The town of Merton dates back to the twelfth century, when an Augustinian priory was established there. Later the town became well known as a garden suburb of London.

39 Admiral Lord Charles William de la Poer Bereford had been a leading naval officer until his retirement in 1911, serving, for example, as the commander-in-chief of the Mediterranean Fleet from 1905 to 1907 and the Channel Fleet from 1907 to 1909; *Who's Who, 1915* (London: A. & C. Black, 1915), 166–67.

40 See "Frequently Mentioned Names" on p. xx.

41 ASP, box 11, Adam Shortt Diary, 6 August 1911.

42 These are the names of two suburbs located about six miles from the centre of London. Barnet was the site, in 1471, of one of the most important battles of the Wars of the Roses, while Finchley was famous for the Finchley Manor House, built by Thomas Allen in 1723.

43 In 1911, the ancient county of Middlesex surrounded London, from the Thames, at Staines, to the Lea, near Waltham Cross, and furnished those who worked in the British capital with housing, services such as schools, and some outstanding and accessible country scenery.

44 The main restaurant at the Savoy Hotel was opened in 1889, and by 1911 was well known for its accommodation of the rich and famous, which on one occasion led to the flooding of an adjacent courtyard with champagne at the behest of millionaire patrons during the Edwardian era.

45 Note the incorrect spelling of George Eliot's last name in Elizabeth's diary.

46 Simpson's-in-the-Strand was a famous dining room in London that also catered to the well-to-do (though on a less extravagant scale than the Savoy) and was a traditional place for prominent Englishmen to luncheon, while women were served a similar meal in segregated facilities.

47 A Norman church was built on the site of Chelsea Old Church in 1157, and in 1290 it was named All Saints Church. Sir Thomas More (note the incorrect spelling in the transcription of Adam's diary) rebuilt the south chapel in 1528, and used it often for his private worship. Most of his body is interred here, though More's head was buried in Canterbury after his execution for treason in 1535.

48 Here Adam is apparently confusing William Morris with George Meredith, the Victorian poet and novelist, who in 1862 rented a house on Cheyne Walk jointly with Algernon Swinburne, the poet and critic, and Dante Gabriel Rossetti, the painter (note the incorrect spelling of Swinburne's and Rossetti's surnames in the transcription of Shortt's diary). Their home became a prominent gathering place for many artists and writers in the London area, particularly in the years between 1871 and 1881.

49 Catherine of Braganza was the Portuguese, Roman Catholic wife of King Charles II of England, and she came to live at 16 Cheyne Walk (note the incorrect number in Elizabeth's diary) after it became evident that he preferred the charms of his many mistresses to those of the Queen.

50 Elizabeth is confusing the historical sequence, here: Elizabeth I (Queen Bess) reigned from 1558 to 1603, while Charles II, Catherine's husband, ruled from 1660 to 1685.

51 At this point, Elizabeth is apparently creating a single false identity out of George Meredith and Algernon Swinburne; see ch. 3, n. 48.

52 See ch. 3, n. 48.

53 ESSP, WA10, file 1035, Smith Shortt to Damaris I. McGee Smith, 7 August 1911. The finding aid for the Smith Shortt Papers lists this letter from London as "August 2," but the context of the material relates to events on and around 7 August. The date at the beginning of the document is clearly a "7" rather than a "2."

54 See "Frequently Mentioned Names" on p. xx.

Chapter 4

A "Just Perfect" Switzerland

The Shortts' visit to the continent did not begin well. After a hot and wretched train ride from Boulogne to Paris, the Canadian couple were taken to their hotel in the French capital by what Adam described as a "most reckless" cab driver. For Elizabeth, the episode "spelt civilization gone mad." Mrs. Shortt did not leave her lodgings that evening, while her husband noticed little of interest during a walk along the Seine except some "good fights" there (8 August). As Beth curtly acknowledged in a letter to her eldest daughter, Muriel, "I don't like Paris" (11 August).

The journey to Switzerland on the next day represented an improvement, and the Shortts' arrival in Geneva became a liberating experience. After a pleasant evening at the city's Hotel Victoria, Mrs. Shortt "awoke in beautiful Geneva." Some shopping and tourist stops occupied the two Canadian visitors in the morning, and following lunch they left on a vessel bound for Montreux via Lake Geneva. As Adam put it, the trip was a "delightful sail up lake all afternoon" (10 August). Thus began one of the key features of the couple's stay in Switzerland: their deep and abiding fascination with the country's splendid terrain.

Meanwhile, during their overnight stay in Montreux, the Shortts visited the Protestant shrine at the castle of Chillon (10 August). Here the Protestant reformer Francois Bonivard was imprisoned under deplorable conditions from 1530 to 1536 by the Catholic Duke of Savoy. Bonivard's sufferings were immortalized in Byron's poem "The Prisoner of Chillon" (1816), which made the castle into a great attraction for anglophone, Protestant travellers like Elizabeth and Adam.[1] Upon leaving Montreux, Mr. and Mrs. Shortt found themselves in the Alpine region of the Swiss Republic. Elizabeth was almost overwhelmed by the beauty of the mountains there, which by the end of the visit she was describing in rapturous terms: "there is a feeling of exhilaration from the air & the grandeur & one feels one has never known the world or the wonders thereof till one has been among the mountains of Switzerland" (16 August).

The Shortts also had a high opinion of the values that they encountered within the Swiss nation. As Beth put it, the country contained "a wonderful people," as well as a superb landscape. "I admire them immensely" (11 August). In more specific terms, she praised Swiss industry (11 and 16 August), thrift (11 and 15 August), and cleanliness (15 August). Moreover, for Mrs. Shortt, both the homes and clothes were charming and they further enhanced the attractiveness of Switzerland (11 and 15 August). Despite the hardships posed by their rugged environment, the Swiss appeared healthy and content (16 August). After only two days in the republic, Elizabeth concluded that "I have enjoyed Switzerland more than all the rest since I left home…. Switzerland is just perfect" (11 August). This positive analysis of the Swiss identity was further developed as the Shortts journeyed to the republic's capital, Berne. Here Adam resumed the business side of his trip. Lengthy and revealing talks at the country's state department on Swiss government appointments proved quite productive. Once his professional responsibilities were fulfilled, Adam rejoined his wife in their common pursuit of tourist destinations. Both reached the same judgment that Berne was "quaint and interesting." A city market, native costumes, the town clock, some shops, a local museum, and a stop at Berne's celebrated bear pit were all beguiling to Mrs. Shortt (14–15 August). She happily concluded that "we enjoyed Berne very much" (16 August).

On 16 August, the Shortts were again travelling through Switzerland's impressive mountains on their way to Zurich, where they rested for one evening. Understandably tired, the middle-aged couple ventured beyond their hotel only for a brief night-time stroll, which allowed them to view a few public buildings, old homes, and a street procession accompanied by a band that was marching through the area. But if Elizabeth and Adam were a bit fatigued by their trip to Switzerland, they were elated with its results. As the former put it: "We could both be content to stay in Switzerland summer after summer & going to Vienna is rather a trial to Adam than a pleasure after Switzerland" (16 August).

Tuesday, 8 August

Adam's Diary[2]
Left for Paris via Folkstone and Boulogne, very warm, country burned up. Not very interesting trip on French side. Through Paris in Taxi, most reckless driver. Walked up Seine in evening. Fights on river good. Much drinking but little drunkenness. Mostly English at hotel.

Elizabeth's Diary[3]
Up good & early to do all last things & store & pack & pay &c.. We started from the station about 10 o'clock by train for Folkstone & passed through some lovely English country places. But here & everywhere was evidence of the great drought. England has not been the normal England this year & many other places could say the same. The train trip down was very dirty. I kept a newspaper on my lap & shook it occasionally, depositing the soot on the floor with lots that were there & on the seats & bags. Folkstone is much like the other south coast shipping places—the centre of activity being the wharves.

The boat was ready & lots of porters, so we were soon on board & it was a lovely day for crossing. We had dinner on board & as soon as we reached Boulogne porters swarmed on board & we were entrained for Paris after passing the customs which did not amount to much in our case but marking the bags. Then came a long hot miserable run to Paris. There were two young dandies with the various impediments including smelling salts & a fussy English clergyman & his wife in our compartment. It was fearfully hot & all I could do to hold on to the end of it in Paris.

Arrived in P.—we took a taxicab & had quite a run about & ended up at Hotel Lyons opposite the big station from which we were to depart next day. I had no desire to spend any of our short time in Paris [doing something else]. That drive in the taxi spelt civilization gone mad. It was a modern miricle [*sic*]. There was no order observable like in the London traffic & people, taxis, street cars, bicycles & cabs just dodged about & escaped one another when they could. We did not see anyone killed, but many escaped by a miracle. It was the maddest whirl of humans all going or coming in the most cheerful disregard of their lives, but seeming to be moving by some wonderful device in which they mostly escaped.

Wednesday, 9 August

Adam's Diary
Left for Geneva at 8:30. Fiercely hot all day. Americans (Porter) in car got drinks and fruit at stations and sweltered. Interesting villages and no farm houses till last of journey and amongst mountains. Cooler at Geneva. Walked in evening. [Stayed at] Victoria Hotel.

Elizabeth's Diary
We were off by nine o'clock & this time we had a pater [father] & mater [mother] & son of America (New Jersey) named Porter I think, for our travelling companions. This was one of the hottest days known in France & in the corridor of our compartments it was 102+ [degrees Fahrenheit]. This was the longest hottest journey we had & yet I stood it better than the previous one.

It was over ten hours from Paris to Geneva. Often there were interesting things to see & observe. We passed the forests of Fontainbleau, such a lot of forest in the vicinity of Paris & Lyons no doubt was due to the estates where the trees had been preserved. The farming was diff. from Can. too: hundreds of acres & no fences & no houses till one saw a cluster or village of them. We arrived in Geneva very tired hot & dirty & went to Hotel Victoria & were very comfortable. After we had washed & dressed & dined it was after eight so we just took a walk over to the gardens nearby & heard the fountains playing & the band across the river & then to a good bed.

Thursday, 10 August

Adam's Diary
Tramped round quaint old hillside streets of Geneva. Saw site of Calvin house &c.. Got watches for Muriel and George. After lunch left on Boat for Montreux.[4] Delightful sail up lake all afternoon. Cool on water but very hot on shore. Took car ride in evening to Castle of Chilton [*sic*].[5]

Elizabeth's Diary
Awoke in beautiful Geneva. I could have been content to stay on & on here. The Rhone divides the city in two & there is a small island which makes a Plaza & has the statue of Rousseau & is a part almost of the "English Gardens." In the forenoon we set out again to see something of the city. We went up & down queer narrow streets & saw on one a tablet saying there

was where Calvin had lived. We bought watches here for Muriel (gold) & George (gun metal) at a reputable looking shop on a main st..

We left after lunch on the Evian, one of the nice boats on Lake Geneva or as they call it (Gen-nave). I never saw anything more lovely than the whole vista as one sails from Geneva up the Lake (called Leman & by us Geneva): the sloping shores & many villas & the towering mountains beyond, getting our first sight of snow capped Mont Blanc. It was a beautiful afternoon & everything so perfect. I felt glad I had come & that it would do me good. We reached the other end of the Lake about six, passing several inviting looking places like Lausanne[6] on the shores till we came to Vevry [sic][7] & Montreux where we stayed. It was here rising from the shores of the Lake on the slop-ing terraced hillsides that we saw how every available inch of room could be taken advantage of in growing grapes &c..

How should I describe the beauty of Montreux & Vevry [sic]? We stayed at Hotel Richmont & after dinner we took a trip in the st. car to the Castle of Chillon & I must say that a near view of it inclines one to have the blues. The side next the shore which is much more exclusive than one would imagine from the pictures, have [sic] only very small windows, too small except to let in a slit of daylight. The awfulness of being shut out of the light of day must be great & beyond imagination.

Friday, 11 August

Adam's Diary
Forenoon went up to Caux on elevated road very fine views. Left on Elec-tric for Zwisummen [sic] and Spitz [sic].[8] Most interesting trip climbing mountains and going through mountain valleys on other side. Fine views of snow-capped peaks. Arrived in Spitz in time for dinner. Beds in parlour, fine music. Very warm.

Elizabeth's Diary
In the morning we took the cog railway up the mt. & had a tense feeling of getting up above things. We had a very beautiful panorama spread out before us of mountains & Lake & River (Rhone branch which empties here). After we returned & had luncheon we took the train for Spiez in Switzerland on the shore of Lake Thun. I think the trip from Montreux to Spiez over the mountains one of the finest things I've ever seen. Oh Geneva & Montreux & the mountains to Spiez are so beyond everything lovely & magnificent. I would like to go back & do it again.

It is amazing—the industry & thrift of the Swiss people. Through their mountains they cultivate almost to what one would believe inaccessible places & their picturesque dwellings add only beauty to the scene. Almost never does one see an outbuilding or cattle or anything but the house & the divided fields, divided not by fences or hedges, but by plots of grain (very little) or hay or grass. If one inspects their dwellings nearer they will find the animals under the same roof as the people. In some cases they are under the house proper; in others they occupy sections [of the house]. I wonder, if a child born over [an animal section] & growing up from childhood in a constant smell of manure would find it disagreeable or would he find something lacking in a house where there was none. It is something like the constant odor & near acquaintance with cow manure in India.

The eaves of the houses extend several feet over & under these the fire-wood down to the small twigs are neatly piled for winter use. Through the mountains when there is a heavy winter of snow there are slides which carry down a corner or section of wood on a mountain side. This wood is then used up & gradually a new growth takes its place. The forests on the mountains are of [sic] mainly of spruce & are so thick that the trees grow very tall & straight & only have branches on the tops. Where a section is swept down by snow & every one cleaned off, it leaves the trunks of the others open to view and suggests the simile of fur being torn or worn off a spot on an animal so sharply is the difference defined & the bareness compared with the clothed hill.

A Letter from Elizabeth to Muriel, George, and Lorraine[9]
[In Montreux, 10 August.] We can scarcely keep track of the day of the week or date. We stay a night in each place till we get to Berne. I hope to write a letter to you there. We left London, Tues. 8th [August] about 10 o'clock & went down to Folkstone & sailed over to Boulogne & from there by train to Paris which we reached about seven. It was terribly warm & dirty. Really I could not tell you how miserable a long journey with the temp. in the corridor of the car up to 102 & the place & yourself just black dirty & yet I'm glad I came.

Spiez, later [11 August]—Yes here we are at Lake Thun at Spiez at Hotel Erica and we have had the most gorgeous day you can ever imagine among the Swiss Alps. The Swiss are a wonderful people. I admire them immensely. You just cannot imagine the beauty of Switzerland. I thought everything was perfected in Geneva & the Lake up to Montreux, but today has been grand, magnificent. You must each one come sometime & see the wonders of the world & the beauty thereof. They pronounce Geneva, Gennave, so softly & it is a delight. I could have stayed on & on there or here or Montreux.

I know it will seem long since my last letter sent off last Sun. or Mon.—& this is Friday—but this has farther to go & there will be a gap of a week I'm afraid. Papa sent each of you a post card but probably they will reach you same time as this. I almost hope so for he did not write anything [else] & you will think I am disabled somewhere. My eyes are quite a trouble to me for I save them when I can & I have to hold the goggles over the glasses all the time the sun shines to keep from straining my eyes.

The sun shines every day too & no rain. The only cloudy day was the one we went [on] the coach trip in Eng. & that made it perfect. We are in a world of no rain too, since we left home. I bought a raincoat in London after a month of fine weather being sure it would soon rain & we are now carrying the two raincoats everywhere & yet no rain. Of course it is a record year of heat & drought & I'm sure the country people must feel it very much. Here in Switzerland the grass or hay is so *very, very short*. I could talk & talk to you tonight about Switzerland.

We expect to get to Berne tomorrow & I am hoping to have letters from you forwarded from Eng.. You would be amused we are to sleep in the parlour tonight; the hotels are so full here. We have had fine rooms on the 2nd floor so far which is fortunate for me, since elevators are not so much in use as in Canada & America. We are never out of the sound of the English language; there are so many Americans and English on the go. At the hotel in Paris everyone at table d'hote dinner that night spoke English & at Montreux most of them in the dining room & everywhere the same.

I don't see why the wealthy are not here in greater numbers than they are. It is a long way from home & I felt as if I were saying another goodbye to you all when I left England, but still once I'm home again the distance will have made no difference. I have enjoyed Switzerland more than all the rest since I left home & it has only been a few days. This is a beautiful place too—just tourists & hotels & scenery.

I expect we will be in Berne three days so I will write again on Sun.. I hope all is well with you each dear one. Just think a month from now & we will be on the ocean nearing Canada & home. I will be so glad to get a letter from home at Berne. Well Muriel we bought it [a watch] in Geneva & I hope it will be satisfactory. It is good. There is the supper bell!

Would you believe it we are doing this continental trip on three bags & left the trunks behind in London? I thought if the matter became impossible we could get shawl straps or something. It has been enough to look after anyway: three bags my small bag, coats & umbrellas. We were both glad to hear George liked his work.

Yah! Yah. [In German, *jah*, pronounced *yah*, means *yes*.] We are now in German Switzerland & our French language which has been paramount since we left England is left behind & it is now *Manner* & *Frauen* [German: *men* and *women*] &c. &c.. There now, if there aren't Americans, we thought this was German entirely [*sic*]. Well good night; your father would join me in sending love to each of our dear, dear children. That is right dear Lorraine, that's a prayer for all. God bless Papa & Mama & bring them safe home again.

P.S. I had no English stamp just as we were leaving & I have carried this letter to Paris & then Geneva & here [Spiez], but hope I will get it started [in the mail]. We will be in Berne over Sunday I expect & then go on to Vienna stopping over probably at Innsbruck. Oh, Geneva is perfect. We came up the Lake yesterday from Geneva at the other end to this place of hotels on the mountain side, at the other end [Montreux]. Geneva or as they call it Gen-nave is a beautiful place & the Lake & environment [are as well].

We expect to go tonight to Spiez & then to Berne & then to Interlaken & then to Lucerne. Switzerland is just perfect. I don't like Paris. It's mad. I didn't go about the streets except for one taxi drive & they [French drivers] look just crazy—all going madly every which way. I hope it is not so hot with you. Coming from Paris to Geneva it was over 100 in the corridor of the [railway] car sometimes & a ten hour trip & everything dirty with dust is tiring, but I'm glad I am [of] good use now. By the time this reaches you, we will be making for London & [just] about there. Love to each.

Saturday, 12 August

Adam's Diary[10]
Went to Frutigen by Electric, thence by carriage to Kanderstey [*sic*].[11] Saw construction of new line and switch tunnels. Two Germans with me. Walked up to [Lake] Deschiner.[12] See over 5,000 feet. Good view of snow and water falls. Got back in time for dinner. Had strenuous day but felt well. Very hot.

Elizabeth's Diary
Spiez—We stayed at [the] Hotel Pensura Erica and as Adam became so desirous of climbing & being nearer the snow line, he suggested that we

stay here over Sat. & we did. I had the first chance owing to my eyes & the hurried time after to write up [my diary] & mend a few things that were needing it. I had a very good day Sat. for there was plenty of garden & tables & daises so I wrote till five & then after a walk & getting some different views I had time to write more. Adam came back about 8 just as I was finishing dinner. He had gone by rail to ——— & there fell in with two Germans who climbed every year. They were hiring a conveyance to go up some 7 to 9 miles where the climb began & Adam chipped in with them & went too. Then they climbed till they got high enough to see one of those still blue lakes formed in mountain basins by the snows from the glaciers. When he came to return he found he could not make connection without hiring again [at] the last stage an old man who had a horse &c.

A Letter from Elizabeth to Muriel
Spiez, August 10th [*sic*]¹³—I believe I am dating this right but I am guessing by going reckoning from dates past. A calendar is one thing I forgot which would have been very handy—just put that item down for making up a list for your transp. abroad. It is so lovely here & the mountains yesterday, having taken such a hold of your father, he thought we might stay over tonight again here & go out to Berne tomorrow. He went off at 10 hrs. A.M. to take a train, cog electric branch, up the mountain with a view to walking down.

I have had a delightful restful day writing up my diary which I did from ten till five. Since then I've taken a walk, read some from our guidebook, fixed my hair & washed & just now the dinner bell has rung at 7:30 & Papa is not here yet.

Sunday, 13 August

Adam's Diary¹⁴
Went for walk to old castle of Spitz [*sic*]. Read papers re Final debate on Veto Bill in Lords. London food strike and terrible records of heat in Britain, France &c. Left on 2 p.m. boat for Thun¹⁵ thence to Berne after bad connection. Went for walk in Berne in evening. Concert on Plaza by Cathedral. Still very warm.

Elizabeth's Diary
Sun. morning we took a walk to the castle but there was no admission. After luncheon we made a very hurried rush to the boat which left for Berne or rather sailed up Lake Thun as far as Thun & there we had to change again.

We had an amusing experience. For some reason the boat instead of landing us at the usual connecting wharf—left us in Thun. There was no train & no porters & no conveyances apparently. However Adam persuaded a man to go in search of a cab. The town of Thun is not big & was having its Sun. peace. In the stillness as I sat waiting on a bench I heard a terrible clatter of wheels on stones & said to A. "something is coming anyway." And it truly did come & it was only a one horse drosky[16] or cab with heavy wheels & brake. He understood we wanted to catch a train & he went at a good rate. I felt like John Gilpin,[17] for everyone who was abroad looked to see what was doing & heads appeared in the open windows & doors. When we reached the station after this excitement we found there was no 2:15 train but one at 3:15. We reached Berne before dark but not in time to get washed & fed & be in time for the Cathedral [service].

Monday, 14 August

Adam's Diary
Called on British Embassy, Mr. Howard[18] not there but to return tomorrow. Went to see officials of Dept of Agriculture, referred me to Baumgartner of Agricultural College at Ruti.[19] Also head of Dairy School. Went out on train, Saw Mr. ——— also recommended Baumgartner highly. Saw him at College, long talk. He will let me know.

Elizabeth's Diary
Next morning, Aug. 14 while Adam went to see the Ambassador I took a trip about on my own account & saw something of queer interesting Berne. It is like no other place. The numerous arcades of stone running along the face of the stores through street after street make it interesting & unusual. Berne was quite attractive to me and I was more than glad here to receive some home news. Lorraine's letter came but evidently Muriel's had gone astray or been sent to Vienna. Several [Toronto] *Globes* came & we read some interesting items of news. Adam had to go out of town to Un Ober— something to see a man for Mr. Fisher[20] &, tho. he expected to be back in time for the organ recital he was not able to be. That afternoon I wrote letters &c. & got some catching up with things done.

A Letter from Elizabeth to Muriel
Mon, 13 Aug.. [sic][21] No letter from you now for a long time—I think two weeks. You see Mon., 7th of Aug., was a Bank holiday in London, which

seems to be like our civic holiday, & everyone goes away. So the usual Canadian mail did not get distributed, nor did it come before nine [a.m.]. It probably came just after we left & we charged the Doughtys (who are equally irresponsible) to forward it if it did. We also left orders with the head of the establishment & also in the office, but whatever you or anybody else sent then seems to have not come on. Papa wrote the [High] Commissioner's office but it would not reach him that day in time to prevent that mail having gone out, I'm afraid.

We may get a letter from you tomorrow before we go to Vienna, for we sometimes got letters from you on Friday & in that case it will likely get here by tomorrow. I felt so very disappointed at not hearing from you & George. There was one from Lorraine which had the London stamp Aug. 9th, & which she had written on July 30th in Kingston. I left your letters in London so I cannot give you the date of the last, but I think it was no. 6. I read them all over before I came away & read all the clippings & put all letters of yours in the trunk. We stored them with Mrs. Rose of the Savoy Mansions near the Strand. If Dr. & Mrs. Doughty are home you can ask them if any mail came for us the morning we left & if so what &c.?

I wonder if you went up to the Corys?[22] If you did no doubt you had a good time. It was too bad Armand could not be there. I had a letter from Mrs. Acland[23] this A.M. too and it was good of her to write. She said you had helped her a lot with Mary's picnic at Rockcliffe.[24] I am sort of getting caught up here. I had a day at Spiez & am taking a half day today & have washed my head & hairbrush (which gets quite black), & a pair of stockings & sorted up & got a clean frill in [them] &c. &c..

You see, I could not write my diary after the blow fell & could only just write to you people & glance at the clippings & the headlines. Sat. & today I am doing more & writing in my diary—a long back write up—not near finished yet & getting these letters written too. Your father has gone to Un-Ober something or other to look after a man for Mr. Fisher this afternoon, & while he went to see the Br. Ambassador &c. this morning I went to see the shops. It [Berne] is like no place else & is very quaint & interesting. Most of the shops are under long stone arcades. The fronts of shops, as seen from the other side, look like long stone corridors divided into arches.

I'm sure this Switzerland trip is doing me lots of good. I astonish myself by the amount of walking I have done some days—more than I ever expected to do. One day when I had over done the thing & we reached home 9:30 P.M. I said after I arrived at the door: "well if I can walk tomorrow I will thank God & take courage for I never expected to walk so far again." Well that time was the only time I've been knocked out, but I took next half-day off.

I will I hope write again soon, but after we leave here, prob. day after tomorrow. It will likely only be post cards till we reach Vienna which we hope to do by Sat.. Love to Miss Gibson & I [sic]. Have you seen that there never has been such heat in Paris or London or Germany? There must be something quite upset in the planetary system: a spot in the sun or something—no really glaring sun, but then I wear goggles.

Dear Muriel I think of you with love & confidence & hope you are growing in patience & ability to detach yourself! With much, much love.

Tuesday, 15 August

Adam's Diary[25]
Saw Ambassador Howard who came with me to [the Swiss] State Dept.. Had very satisfactory talk on appointments. All highly advertised but few exams. All appointed by council. Viewed the city in afternoon. Very quaint and interesting. Got an old map of America, Munster's 1596.

Elizabeth's Diary
Aug. 15th, Berne, Tues.. Adam went to see Mr. Howard the English Ambassador in the morning & I went on a toot of my own. Saw the most wonderful market scene I ever expect to see. When market day comes the surrounding country comes to town—not only is the central plaza for the market full, but it extends down street after street, sometimes oxen [tied] to the carts & such odd carts. Pigs for sale are covered down & fastened securely by what is like a heavy fish net so Mr. Pig has a chance of air & of being seen both.

Quite a large number come in their native dress & it is sometimes picturesque & sometimes thriftily odd. I noticed one woman who had pigs for sale (the market being nearly over) take off her check apron (which was soiled) & put it in the waggon under the seat & fetch out a clean one of the same kind which was neatly folded & tied. All through Switzerland & Austria they take pride in folding down the bedclothes in very particular fashion & in laying out the night dress in quite taking fashion.

One of the prettiest of costumes is that with brocade dress, at any rate the front of it, full lawn sleeves, but short with a peculiar velvet bodice cut so as to leave the bosom free. Over this is the most elegant chain & brooch affair: a brooch on each shoulder blade & one on each side in front & five chains draped from back brooches forward & across in very ornamental fashion. We priced a good silver set of it & it was about £5. The velvet bodice is silver laced in shape of [a] V with [the] top of [the] V at the bosum. It gives a picturesque effect.

The men through Switzerland & Austria are fond of green, particularly of bronze green & look quite dandified. They are of course climbers & glory in it. The Alpine stick & cane with prod & iron shod boots & shoulderbag are in evidence everywhere. A characteristic heavy woollen stocking & knee breeches are common.

After seeing the market I went to look at their clock tower where when the clock strikes 7—11—& 4 father time hits the gong, a cock crows & a small bear or a procession of small bears pass around below the dial. The bear is the mascot of the Bernese & is carried everywhere on everything. We bring a small wood one home. I went from there to see the Parliament Blds. & the terrace where a splendid view is had of the river & the mountains in beautiful panorama. Then I took in the "world monument" a large affair of figures holding the world on a high natural rock.

I also took a look in at the R.C. Cathedral which is Rococo in style but not specially interesting. I got in by 12:30 & was very thankful I could walk so far. Adam came in later & we had luncheon & then set out again. He went to the bank & I waited for him by the shops, which nearly finished me, being so tired before [starting again]. We bought a souvenir spoon for Lorraine & then took car for the Museum, which is very good & especially interesting because the native dress of diff. cantons is there kept.

From here we took train to the Schangli where there was a concert & where we had tea. Later I did the most wonderful thing for me. I walked round & down one of the splendid avenues & saw the famous Berne bearpit which was only five bears in a bearpit which many came to see & feed. Then we walked to the Eng. Cathedral where we supposed acc. to guide book that there was to be a concert but alas there was not & there was no cab or a [street]car very near. So we started in the direction of a car when Adam was taken with the morbid desire to spend an hour or more in a 2nd hand book store looking for things he did not have.

After this we took car for the hotel but like other failures I can observe, the cars do not stop at each street or where you want to get off, but at some special stopping places. So I was taken past where we wanted off. I was near dead & had to have strychnine then & again in the night & even after a cold sponge & two cups coffee I was tired enough to be glad of sitting in the train for hours while we could.

Wednesday, 16 August

Adam's Diary

Left Berne early, transferred to Boat at Thun,[26] fine sail up lake to Interlaken,[27] every hotel crowded, did not stay over. Up Lake Brienz. Climb mountain, very fine, also descent towards L. Lucerne. Tea at Lucerne.[28] Zurich at night, walk about.

Elizabeth's Diary

We started early & took train for Thun & then to boat & sailed again the length of Lake Thun to the beautiful spot, Interlaken, where we could see the Jungfrau with its snowy, uneven top. It was very difficult for Adam to pass Interlaken. He had the most yearning desire to go up the mountains near the Jungfrau & have a near view of it, but our time is so very limited, we have to get on. We took the train across to Lake Brienz & then sailed the length of it & then took train over the mountains & through the valleys to Zurich.

The ascending road over mountains sometimes gives one a tense feeling of anx. of consequences if anything went wrong & of using one's nervous energy to help push the train up, but, on the other hand there is a feeling of exhilaration from the air & the grandeur & one feels one has never known the world or the wonders thereof till one has been among the mountains of Switzerland. We saw a number of snow capped peaks, but we noticed so many streams dry & others very low to their normal conditions. We reached Zurich & found a good hotel in Schwartz & we had a room looking out of [*sic*] the [Limmat] River as it entered the Lake Constance or Bodensee.[29] After dinner we set out to find the park & concert but did not. However, we saw some of the principal buildings & came on a band & procession. We saw some quaint very old houses too.

A Letter from Elizabeth to the Children[30]

I have this small chance to send a word to you, since we have two hours to wait till our train goes out to Zurich. Yesterday in Berne I did such wonderful stunts of walking that I am too tired today to go wandering. I surely did surprise myself, but I did too much, partly, chiefly due to there being a mistake about the evening organ recital in the evg. [*sic*] at which we were to wind up & I [to] get a rest, & as there was no concert & [*sic*] I did not get a rest.

We enjoyed Berne very much. It is the oldest & oddest of the big places. In population it is about the size of Ottawa but seemed much more quiet. The bear is the fetish or patron saint or whatever of Berne & they forever keep a bear pit. It is endowed. We went to see it of course of which more anon, when I see you. In the morning Papa went seeing [government] men & I did a big stunt all by myself[,] went out with him about 10:30 & went about the place on foot till 12:30, with two rests on benches while consulting the maps & changing my glasses.

We received four *Globes* from Mr. Foran [*sic*] & in one I saw the account of the mishap to Jim & Eleanor & May & their visitor & Norman Wornsmith. It was a very narrow escape & how fortunate they didn't have the baby. I wonder if Eleanor was any the worse after it. We did not receive anything from you at Berne. The Consul at Berne (the Ambassador I mean) said he had written Papa to [*sic*] London, but he never received it either. I expect it came about the same time as yours & got lost because of the bank holiday. I will hope much to get letters at Vienna on Sat. & will write you again from there.

We stop at some place near Innsbruck tomorrow night I think & Friday night at Salzberg [*sic*]. So after tomorrow it will be Austria & German & marks & fenigs [*sic*] & no more francs and centimes.[31] I am sending three cards to Mrs. Hare & I want to write a note to Aunt Christina just now, if I can. I'm afraid we will not be in London in time to see the servants going on 21 [August], so I may not succeed in getting one. There's lots I want to know & to say. With dear love to each of our dear ones.

A Letter from Elizabeth to Mother and Sister (Gertrude)[32]

I have a few minutes & will write a note to say we are on our way to Vienna & hope to reach there Sat. & receive more news from home. Somehow, owing, I suppose to the big Monday holiday (the Bank holiday) the day before we left London, some of our mail due that day has gone astray. We received some newspapers at Berne & have in that way a few interesting items of Canada & home. We hope to get back to London by 1st of Sept., but we have a lot of travelling to do before then. I cannot keep track of dates & I feel as if it had [*sic*] been months & months since I left home. It is hardly to be conceived that it is only ten days since we left London.

I have lived a lot since then & enjoyed a lot. The Switzerland part of the time has been of most good & most enjoyed. I think being in bed with my eyes [resting] must have done my eyes good, for I have done wonderful stunts for me in going about. Twice I've overdone it & had to take a few doses of strychnia but I am pleased to be able to do so much.

Sometime, Gertie I hope you will come & see Switzerland. There is no place like it & no people like the Swiss for hard industry. Their ways are not our ways but then they have so hard a time to make a living & seem both hardy & happy. The beauty of Lake & mountain scenery is beyond description & can only be enjoyed sufficiently when seen. I do not get much time to write & having such a lot of back writing to do I have never yet caught up but hope to in Vienna. We could both be content to stay in Switzerland summer after summer & going to Vienna is rather a trial to Adam than a pleasure after Switzerland.

I wear goggles during the sunshine, & when I want to see better I put another pair [of glasses] under it. I have another to read & write with, so you can think they are a nuisance to one who never carried around such an extensive collection of spectacles &c. Just now Adam is doing a walk, but I was too tired & have just sent a note to the children & to Christina while we are waiting for the Zurich train. I do hope you have both stood the heat without wearing you out too much. I often think of mother & wonder if she is standing the heat pretty well. I hope Cecil[33] did get to see you for a few hours anyway.

I think the trip is doing me good. It ought to. It seems selfish sometimes to be enjoying so much & you sweltering in Hamilton in the heat. We hear news of politics a little, but will [hear] more when we get home. We sail [back to Canada] Sept. 6th & hope to be in Lon. by 1st. With much, much love.

Notes

1 Cecilia Morgan, *"A Happy Holiday": English Canadians and Transatlantic Tourism, 1870–1930* (Toronto: University of Toronto Press, 2008), 244–45.

2 Queen's University Archives, Adam Shortt Papers (hereafter cited as ASP), box 11, Adam Shortt Diary, 8 August 1911.

3 University of Waterloo, Elizabeth Smith Shortt Papers (hereafter cited as ESSP), WA10, file 1772, Smith Shortt Diary, 8 August 1911.

4 Montreux is a highly popular resort centre well known for its beautiful site and environs on the east end of Lake Geneva.

5 Note the incorrect spelling for the castle of Chillon in the transcription of Adam's diary.

6 Lausanne, found on the north shore of Lake Geneva, is well known for its university and cosmopolitan way of life, which complement the city's beautiful views of the lake and the Alps.

7 Vevey (note the incorrect spelling in Elizabeth's diary) provides another magnificent view of the Alps and Lake Geneva, while serving as the main urban centre for the Lavaux vineyards.

8 Spiez (note the incorrect spelling in the transcription of Adam's diary), a small town on Lake Thun, at the foot of the Niesen, a mountain of the Bernese Alps, is widely regarded as a pleasant summer resort area.

9 ESSP, WA10, file 493, Smith Shortt to Muriel Clarke, 10 and 11 August 1911.

10 ASP, box 11, Adam Shortt Diary, 12 August 1911.

11 Kandersteg (note the incorrect spelling in the transcription of Adam's diary) became famous among mountain climbers in the Swiss Alps as a connecting link between the Oberland and Valais ranges, and, in the summer months, as a place to visit the Oeschinensee, a picturesque lake.

12 Note the incorrect spelling in the transcription of Adam's diary, which should read [Lake] Oeschinen. See previous note.

13 This letter is dated 10 August, but the context of the material in the first part relates to events taking place on 12 August; ESSP, WA10, file 493, Smith Shortt to Muriel Clarke, "August 10," 1911.

14 ASP, box 11, Adam Shortt Diary, 13 August 1911.

15 Thun is a town on the Aar River, where the river flows out of Lake Thun, providing a beautiful panorama of the Bernese Alps as well as some unique features, such as the flower-laden terraces on its main street, which supply footpaths for the visitor.

16 A drosky is a light, open four-wheeled carriage originally created in Russia.

17 John Gilpin was the central figure in William Cowper's comical poem "The Diverting History of John Gilpin," originally published in 1782, which

eventually became one of England's most popular ballads; *Compton's Pictured Encyclopedia*, vol. 3 (Chicago: F. E. Compton, 1956), 502–3.

18 Esme William Howard was Great Britain's ambassador in Switzerland from 1911 to 1913 after serving in the diplomatic corps from 1885; *Who's Who, 1915* (London: A. & C. Black, 1915), 1075.

19 The historic field of Rutli (note the incorrect spelling in the transcription of Adam's diary) was where the representatives of three Swiss cantons formed an alliance in the late thirteenth century, which led to the expulsion of the country's Austrian occupiers and the beginning of Switzerland's independence.

20 Sydney Arthur Fisher was minister of agriculture in the Laurier government (1896–1911) and introduced the legislation creating the Civil Service Commission, which Adam Shortt and Michel G. Larochelle headed; Anne Drummond, "Sydney Arthur Fisher," in *Dictionary of Canadian Biography*, vol. xv (Toronto: University of Toronto Press, 2005), 351–55. Unfortunately no mention is made here about the specifics of Adam's mission, for Fisher and the Laurier government, while the civil service commissioner was visiting Switzerland.

21 As this correspondence progresses, it becomes apparent that the letter, previously cited in n. 13, contains material relating to 14 August, as well as 12 August.

22 This probably refers to Laura and William Cory and their family in Ottawa. In 1911, William Cory was deputy minister of the interior within the federal government, and, like Adam, a member of the Rideau Club; *Canadian Who's Who, 1910* (London: Times Publishing Company, 1910), 50.

23 See ch. 1, n. 24.

24 In 1911, Rockcliffe Park was a suburb to the northeast of Ottawa. This residential area had become famous for housing members of the national governing elite, including senior civil servants.

25 ASP, box 11, Adam Shortt Diary, 15 August 1911.

26 See ch. 4, n. 15.

27 Interlaken lies between Lakes Thun and Brienz, and has become famous as the tourist centre of the Bernese Oberland region, furnishing, for example, a fine perspective on the illustrious Jungfrau mountain.

28 Lucerne is another tourist town, located on the edge of Lake Lucerne, providing exceptional vistas of the Alps, a highly regarded fine-arts museum, and some interesting churches. Lucerne was the centre of Catholic resistance to the Reformation in Switzerland.

29 The Bodensee (Lake Constance) runs for forty miles, and, though a little smaller than Lake Geneva, often seems to travellers as immense as a sea.

30 ESSP, WA10, file 493, Smith Shortt to Muriel Clarke, "August 16," 1911. Although no date is affixed to this letter, its context indicates it was written on 16 August.

31 Note the incorrect spelling of the Austrian coin, the pfennig, in Elizabeth's diary. The pfennig was roughly equal in value to a North American penny; Peter Csendes, *Historical Dictionary of Vienna* (Lanham, MD: Scarecrow Press, 1999), 49.

32 ESSP, WA10, file 1035, Smith Shortt to Damaris I. McGee Smith, 16 August 1911.

33 See "Frequently Mentioned Names" on p. xx.

Chapter 5

The Ambiguity of Austria

The Shortts found much to admire in Austria. After arriving in Vienna, capital of the multicultural Hapsburg Empire, Adam enjoyed talks with Austrian officials over the operations of their federal bureaucracy, which extended for two days "in a full, interesting, and instructive manner" (22 August; see also 23 August). The stay in Austria was a professional success for Canada's civil service commissioner.

But the Canadian couple's positive interest in Austria did not end there. Both Elizabeth and Adam were attracted by the country's captivating landscape, fine parks, beautiful public buildings, and one exceptional church. Certainly the beautiful scenery of the Tyrol region was comparable to that of Austria's Swiss neighbours (17–18 August). Later, Mr. Shortt observed that the Hohensalzburg Fortress atop Salzburg's Mönchberg cliffs was "very picturesque" (19 August). As they cruised down the Danube to Vienna, Mrs. Shortt was struck with the stunning castles and monasteries they frequently encountered (20–21 August). She touchingly recalled in a letter to her daughter, Muriel, a song that a youthful Beth had sung about a similar experience on this fabled river, which at the time she had not thought would ever become a reality for her. (21 August). Austria's large, well-kept parks constituted another enticement for her. The Mirabell grounds in Salzburg were captivating (18 August) while the Prater in Vienna was beautiful (23 August). For this Canadian social reformer, such public facilities served an important collective as well as individual purpose. "In summer it is such a blessing for the people to have so much of the peace & beauty of nature accessible" (23 August).

Many public buildings within Austria also evoked considerable praise from the Shortts. On three separate occasions, Elizabeth used the superlative term "magnificence" to describe these pieces of architecture (21, 22, and

23 August). She wrote in her diary that, "the carvings and the monuments and the fountains are truly beyond imagination till one has gone about and really seen them" (22 August). The churches in Austria were generally appealing, but St. Stephen's in Vienna constituted "one of the noblest gothic structures in Europe" (21 August).

Austria, then, had impressive credentials as a land of grandeur and culture, but these significant achievements belonged to the past rather than the present. Here Mrs. Shortt echoed the sentiments of numerous Canadians visitors to the continent who thought that, "so many European cultural treasures were produced by lost or vanished civilizations."[1] For her contemporary Austrians no longer possessed the creative energy of their ancestors, as they had fallen prey to an overindulgent lifestyle that had stifled their ingenious tendencies. For example, Elizabeth noted, when discussing Vienna's elegant public image: "nor do I think there would be any chance now, if all were starting over again, that it would excell [sic] any other place, for the people seem to indulge in eating and drinking to such an extent that they would not aspire beyond the common" (23 August). Unlike many English Canadians in 1911, Mr. and Mrs. Shortt were not prohibitionists. Indeed, when they lunched at a historic restaurant in Salzburg, they drank some excellent Prelate wine (19 August). However, Elizabeth and Adam did believe in self-disciplined moderation, and they thought that the Austrians' failure to pursue the same course was leading the nation into decline and decay.

Some signs of this cultural deterioration were evident in Mrs. Shortt's analysis of daily life in early-twentieth-century Austria. The couple's accommodation in Salzburg was "not what I call clean," and it was "the one hotel I did not like" (18 August). She was further shocked to discover that their lodgings in Vienna offered no hot water (21 August). On the same day, Beth revealed that after boarding the vessel that carried them down the Danube from Salzburg to Vienna, she had become dubious about the drinking water in Austria. Such health problems were deplorable to a physician from Canada who was intent on encouraging hygienic reforms wherever possible.

Elizabeth was further disturbed by the large number of beggars that she and her husband encountered in Austria. For her, "this is only second in my experience to Venice for beggars." Beggary was not an acceptable economic pursuit for Mrs. Shortt, who became particularly upset about "a healthy youth leading a blind man, supposedly his father, & asking alms because of him" (20 August). Here she reflected another common assumption of Protestant English Canadians travelling on the continent. In a similar fashion, they dismissed mendicants "based on middle-class notions of the importance of 'honest labour' and bolstered by a Protestantism that had little room for the holy mendicant."[2]

As this quotation indicates, religion furnished another key element in Mrs. Shortt's assessment of Austria's depreciated national identity. The introduction to this volume showed how the Shortts' progressive impulses originated in Protestant Christianity, and especially its zeal for implementing the principles of the Social Gospel movement. Beth's diaries and letters on her 1911 trip to Europe, however, also reveal a less pleasing anti-Catholicism, which she linked to Austria's decline. Anti-Catholicism represented the negative side of her positive devotion to Protestant values and institutions. Strong-Boag aptly stated that the "certainty" Shortt derived from her Anglican faith "did not always fall short of intolerance."[3]

This anti-Catholic position was quite common in English Canada during this era. As J. R. Miller has pointed out, "between the British Conquest and the Great War ... anti-Catholicism was a constant and influential force in Canadian life."[4] Many anglophone visitors to Europe at this time expressed the same perspective prominently. Morgan states that "Protestant English-speaking Canadians [travelling in Europe] were not free of anti-Catholicism ... these Canadians were dubious about the 'ordinary' priests and monks and the rituals they presided over [sic] churches and cathedrals."[5] Thus, Catholicism was associated in Mrs. Shortt's mind with the mistreatment of Protestant dissenters (19 and 21 August) and aggressive and manipulative priests (20 August). Even more contentious was Elizabeth's assertion that the Church's monasteries were hopelessly outdated institutions in the early twentieth century (20 and 21 August).

This assertion could be used to document Miller's summary of anti-Catholic attitudes in this period: "Poverty was the lot of both individual Catholics and Catholic countries.... 'Not that they are wasteful, indolent and incapable, but their energies are paralyzed and their resources gradually absorbed by the Church.' The same was true of countries. 'Look at Austria, Spain, Portugal and Italy.'"[6] Elizabeth essentially supported this outlook when she wrote in her diary: "The immense monasteries do surprise me in this age & time & the simple fervor & reverence of the people.... I wonder if a peasant or farmer acquire merit by erecting one [a wayside shrine] ... or does the church put them there? I fancy the priests get them to do it somehow" (20 August). Austria was the only thoroughly Catholic nation visited by the Shortts in 1911, and for Beth this religious identity provided another reason for its unfortunate atrophy.

Thursday, 17 August

Adam's Diary[7]
Taxi round Zurich, some shopping. Train for Innsbruck[8] up lake and up river then over height and down into valley. Picturesque in upper regions. Innsbruck in evening, round town a bit and saw some of old haunts but many changes in places and houses.

Elizabeth's Diary[9]
In the morning [in Zurich] we wandered about looking at quaint narrow streets & odd shops & then hired a taxi & had him show us some of the parks & residences & public buildings. They were fine too. We went on before noon by train to Innsbruck. This was our last grand mountain day. We were up so high among the mountains that we came so much nearer the snow line & saw a number of snow glaciers which really seemed would be accessible in a three hours' good climb. This was a beautiful day thro. the Tyrol[10] until we came to Landeck[11] when we came to Lessening mts. & descended a good way in company with the River Inn.[12]

This is one of the joys of travelling through mountains: the following of streams up till they vanish into dry mountain streams or starting with the small streams & going on with them till they become rushing rivers. Adam said the scenery of the Inn (the lay of the mountains and the[ir] character) was more like the Fraser River and the Rockies than any we had seen. For my part I like the Swiss mountains best. They have so much more green wood.

We had dinner on the train as we have several times [on] boat or train. It is not much more expensive than the hotels & not as expensive as in Canada on the train. I've enjoyed my meals everywhere & have no fault to find with the cooking, but alas [for] me they can't make tea. I've only had one good cup of tea since I left the hospital & that was on the electric line between Montreux & Spiez. I would like to tell them so. The worst I've had anywhere was on the Paris-Vienna train. There is a unanimous scorn of drinking anything but coffee wine & beer. Being "mad English people" as far as they are concerned I persisted in tea, so-called, till that day on the Paris-Vienna train from Zurich to Innsbruck. Through Switzerland the drinking water was good but in Austria I'm not so sure at all.

One of our added expenses in this travelling about so much is the everlasting tipping. After each meal the porter to the hotel, out of the hotel, the chambermaid, boots &c. over & over & over again & then the porter on & off train or boat. Adam is continually handing out money. Innsbruck seemed bigger than when we were there before & no doubt it was very much. Adam went out for a walk after dark but I went to bed.

Friday, 18 August

Adam's Diary
Saw parade in morning for Empress' Birthday.[13] Left for Salzburg. Very fine through mountains and glaciers and up and down streams to old city of Salzburg. Out for stroll in evening.

Elizabeth's Diary
In the morning we went up to see the wonderful monument to Maximilian[14] with its 8 carved large sections on each side—carved marble & very beautiful it all is. I remember it as one of the wonderful things of our last trip. The 12 large bronze figures on each side, that seem more than human size as they stand up a bit, are very grand. The fine statue of Hofer[15] too is very fine on the side in the church. We went to a bookstore for maps & I went to the museum & went in & then soon came out & saw a big procession of military: 6 companys [sic] of foot in blue gray, a band & a company of infantry [sic] without their horses. We had struck the national birthday, I mean the birthday of Emperor Fra[n]z-Joseph, who is 81. It was analogous to our 24 May [Victoria Day]—the crowds & fireworks & bands & processions.

After looking about the shops a bit we took the st. car to the hotel & got off for Salzberg [sic] on the 10 something train. This trip would have seemed much more interesting if we had had it before the mountains. It was fine & we had a beautiful young stream & river to follow. Arrived in Salzberg & found the Golden Rose where we stayed for the night. This was the one hotel I did not like. We had a big room & comfortable beds, but the people were not what I call clean: not the kind that sweep under the mats. We had to choose from a long list of Golden Angels, Golden Roses & golden all sorts & just sort of happened on the Golden Roses [sic].

We had tea in the Garden & then we went out to see Mirabel [sic] Park[16] which is very handsome indeed with high statues & walks & fountains & shrubs & flowers galore. I saw five hedges of beech, which seemed a novel use of beech. Then we took in an outdoor concert & went home before it was done.

Saturday, 19 August

Adam's Diary
Visited old castle on rock in midst of city,[17] very picturesque and interesting. Had lunch in old Monastic cellar cut in rock. Visited churches &c and took train for Lintz[18] on Danube in evening. Hotel overlooking the Danube and lights on river.

Elizabeth's Diary
Next morning we took in some of the town & especially the old castle on the young [*sic*] mountain beside the city. We went by steam cable & cog railway. The first place the guide takes you after climbing a stair is a room at the foot of the tower where there is one small grated window, a trap door or grating, a stone floor & walls & a heavy stone, a foot sq., with heavy chain attached. This was the room where heretics were imprisoned & if refractory hung by the hands from the beam & the heavy stone attached to their feet. If they would not yield or for other reasons they dropped them down the trap door & let them die of starvation or other horror. On the other side of the landing before going up farther was a wee window & a stone low arch with door, like a dog kennel, & that was where they tortured heretics by putting them in a sitting position but where they could neither stand nor lie. I did not go any farther.

Adam went with the others & the guide up so[me] steps &c. & along corridors & many ups & downs seeing the rooms of former Princes & revelling rooms &c. &c.. After we went to the Stifs Kellar, the cellar of the old Benedictine monks, where Haydn & his friends used to resort. Like good sports we had our midday meal there with a crowd of other sightseers. We had some of their Prelate wine much like Sauterne & very good. We saw the old old chapel & the cemetery of St. Peter & the peculiar part of the old monastery stuck against the face of the cliff, & we went into St. Peter's & saw among other things a statue in memory of Haydn: around the base were tablets, each bearing the name of a composition of Haydn's.

There is a memorial to Mozart in Salzberg [*sic*] as he too was born here. Indeed, there is a statue to Mozart in the open plaza. Paracelsus[19] also died here. Salzberg is worth seeing & has fine buildings, very fine, a University & big schools, but it seems as if the Roman Catholic church had the whole say in things.

Well, I left off at Salzberg on Friday. We came down by train in the afternoon to Linz on the Danube, a good-sized city & beautifully situated on the two sides of the River. We had a very nice large room looking over the river & only about a stone's throw from where we were to go on board the *Danupshift* in the moyen [*sic*]. We had a very good night & had both tea & breakfast outside as most of the hotels & gardens are arranged that way. One would wonder in looking about, as to who went home for meals—the gardens are so pack full of people eating & drinking, drinking & smoking.

Sunday, 20 August

Adam's Diary
Left early on steamer and had fine day's sail down Danube to Vicuna [*sic*].[20] Broad low shores, old towns, castles, forts, monastries [*sic*] then high hills, almost mountains all well wooded. Swift river and great gravel beds. Reached Vienna with lights on river and city.

Elizabeth's Diary[21]
This is rather funny: to end the page, as it is last night, & this morning to have this peculiar experience—a priest here in my bedroom & I in my Kimono & it is not much after nine! He came begging for the Hospital here [Linz]. The chambermaid knocked & said something & then the priest appeared with a book & proceeded to talk about what he wanted & I to explain that as I gave to our own [Anglican] institutions I could not give here. He said he could not speak English & I proved clearly I couldn't speak German & he did not seem to know enough French to work on. He had a paragraph in English which explained what he wanted it for, but he couldn't understand why I couldn't understand that enough to give him money as requested.

This is only second[-worst] in my experience to Venice for beggars— beggars for this & that & because of age & infirmity & all sorts. You may be besought five times an hour in different ways. Last afternoon we went out & in two hours two had tried to sell matches, one bootlaces or something, two women in diff. places because of age, & worst of all a healthy youth leading a blind man, supposedly his father, & asking alms because of him. Strange that one could exhibit a blind man's infirmity for gain rather than work, but likely he gets more per day.

We went off in the steamer at nine Sun. morning and travelled 126 miles down the Danube. I used to sing with fervor a song which was strong on the lines "Can I forget that night in June before the Danube River, Can I forget that night in June before the Danube River." I scarcely hoped to get so

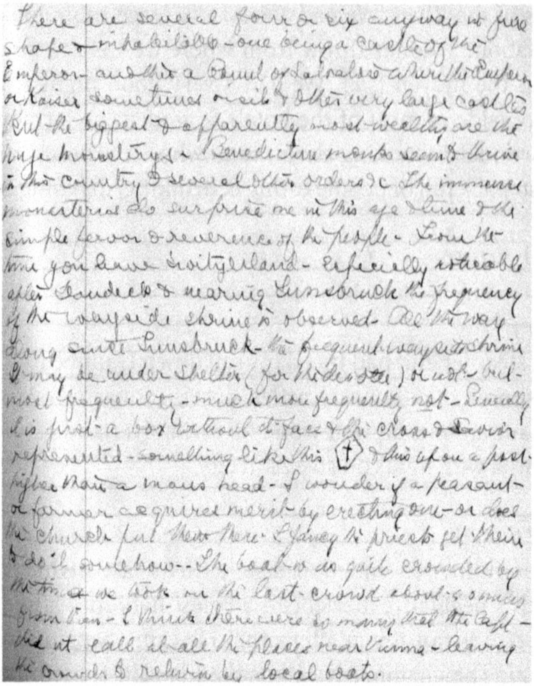

FIG. 6 Elizabeth's sketch of a typical wayside shrine in Austria. Courtesy of University of Waterloo Library, Special Collections & Archives, Elizabeth Smith Shortt fonds (WA 10, 1911, diary 13).

very far away as the Danube & yet we (Adam & I) had that lovely experience of this long trip on the Danube. The scenery is even finer than the Rhine [illegible]. The hills are higher & that makes the windings of the River more picturesque.

The old castles & monasterys [sic] on the banks, on hills or cliffs, make it very interesting & beautiful. There are several four or six anyway in fine shape & inhabitable, one being a castle of the Emperor, another [of] a Count of Salvatore where the Emperor or Kaiser sometimes visits & other very large castles. But the biggest & apparently most wealthy are the huge monasterys [sic]. Benedictine monks seem to thrive in this country & several other orders &c.

The immense monasteries do surprise me in this age & time & the simple fervor & reverence of the people. From the time you leave Switzerland, especially noticeable after Landeck & nearing Innsbruck, the frequency of the wayside shrine is observed. All the way along since Innsbruck the frequent wayside shrine. It may be under shelter (for the devotee) or not, but most frequently, much more frequently, *not*. Generally it is just a box without its face & the cross & Savior represented, something like this [see Fig. 6] & thus upon a post higher than a man's head. I wonder if a peasant or farmer acquires merit by erecting one—or does the church put them there? I fancy the priests get them to do it somehow.

The boat was quite crowded by the time we took on the last crowd about 40 miles from Vien.. I think there were so many that the Capt. didn't call at all the places near Vienna, leaving the crowds to return by local boats. Not being "up" on the German language nor in the holiday times of the Austrians we did not know till we reached Innsbruck & fell in with arriving crowds & bands that the Kaiser's birthday season was due. This was too, no doubt, the reason of the crowds going & coming here [Vienna], especially coming, & enjoying themselves.

Sun. evg., when we arrived. Things were lively eno. yesterday but there did not seem to be such a fearful going & coming. It was dark when we reached here. Indeed night seems to fall quickly as soon as the sun is down. It is quite dark by seven & night by eight o'clock, even now. We had in mind several hotels but came to the Hotel Kaiserin Elizabeth (who was the wife of Kaiser Franz Joseph & was assassinated in Paris, I think, some few years ago).[22] There must have been other Kaiserins of that name, but anyway, I've no doubt her tragic death appealed to people's imagination & they have used her name in many ways.

Monday, 21 August

Adam's Diary
Called at British embassy and found arrangements made for me to see rep's of Austrian Central Govt. Will see them tomorrow. Took round on Street Car and saw chief public buildings, very fine city. Saw interesting old shops with antiques &c.

Elizabeth's Diary
Yesterday morning I felt very seedy & took off while Adam was away seeing the ambassador whose name is Cartwright[23] & who was very useful & very friendly, but who is just going off on his holiday. I wrote letters & this diary &c. & went down to mittagessen [German: *lunch*] by myself. Later in the afternoon Adam came in and we then went to see St. Stephen's church

which is truly wonderful. I can't remember that Cologne was as fine as this, tho. Cologne Cathedral has two towers & this one. It is beyond description: the amount of beautiful work in stone. It seems quite impossible that stone could be carved so finely & so very beautifully & in such bewildering quantity of detail & amount. It is one of the noblest gothic structures in Europe, they say, & I could believe it is. It was begun away back in 1147 but was later burnt & rebuilt & the tower which is 449 ft. high finished in 1433. That seems a long way back, but these old castles & the old prisons & dungeons & moats take one's mind away back to a fierce but fanatically religious people, who did actually live move & have their being in this continent.

We also went round the Ring Strasses [sic] which is now a street but was once the wall that surrounded the old town or Stadt & which is now a sort of magnified circle to the more modern city which expands & enlarges round it. This of course makes the streets irregular because it was not planned to be a wheel at all. In this old city or Stadt, especially on the Ringstrasse, are the chief beautiful buildings: University, Bourse,[24] Royal Palace, City Hall, Museums, theatre & Houses of Parliament & other handsome more than handsome buildings.

There is such a wealth, such a prodigality almost, of magnificence & greatness in their buildings. Such a great number of fine monuments & such a truly tremendous amount of carving & of statuary on the buildings & on plazas. The musicians come in for a share too. For though there is a monument to Mozart in Salzberg [sic] there is another here also [and] fine monuments to Shubert, to Beethoven, Schiller, & Goethe, beside poets & royal persons galore.

This (& other continental towns) is a great place for toys & trinkets, windows full of them again & again. Small figures abound of cats, dogs, ducks, horses, pigeons but especially of small boys & girls & soldiers. Soldiers & officials are much in evidence & not infrequently we see scars representing young men as having belonged to the "corps" at college.

It is very warm & low barometer & I do not feel as able as before. Yesterday it had all the appearance of rain & actually rained a few drops not enough to wet the pavement & a rainbow formed, but that was all. The skies seem to have got so free of moisture that there was nothing to make rain of. I see the consequences of the almost universal drought is being felt already & in London vegetables are three times as dear as usual, except tomatoes which have had their innings & abound.

The event of yesterday was getting mail & anyone who is far from home knows what that means. It had seemed a long while since we had any. It seems impossible that we should be leaving England for home two weeks from tomorrow but so are we booked.

Until we reached here, or rather till the Danube boat, I've been drinking water fearlessly but I am suspicious now & it is trying. If you ask for wasser [German: *water*], they bring you Vichy or Mattonis, Geisshubler or some bottled stuff. I had the hardest time to get any on the boat on the Danube & only that [because] a German man felt some pride that foreigners should not think they had no drinking water & made the waiter bring some [or] I would not have had any. They only want people travelling or lodging to use it for external purposes; at any rate they want to sell beer & wine. I've no doubt they think of us as those mad English people who drink water instead of much beer. They can't make tea except by exception on this continent apparently. Only once in all my travels since I left home have I had tea with cream in it—unasked!

This is not what might be called a swell hotel, except that it is central & the prices are high. We have a nice big room, two beds, sofa, two easy & two other red upholstered chairs, a big mirror & drawers, a wardrobe, cloak stand, [illegible] desk & dressing table & other table, a high fine room on the front, hardwood floor & rugs & double waterstand &c. &c., & yet we have no hot water in the room, tho. we have electric light. We have good beds & the light "feather bed" for covering when it is cold enough. We have one blanket & sheet & then the "feather bed" is the extra. They are covered with white cases like the pillows & when they put that & three pillows on the bed it seems pretty well loaded. The maid calls the bed "open," when the "feather bed quilt" is not on top & the top lace covering on top of that again.

I noticed all the way that weeds are much the same: "yarrow" is everywhere in Eng., Switz., &c., &c., tho. here wild carraway seems to be as common as our mustard. There are funny differences in farming. In Switzerland everything seemed to be done by human labor. In Austria the ox is often seen, even on the wharf at Linz there was an ox cart. Once I saw a horse & ox unequally yoked together here in Austria & I see many of the horses here that are badly used & boney.

The wheat here when done up is put, not like our stacks, but on poles or sticks stuck in the ground in a row along the side of the field or patch where grown. On close inspection I think there are 3 small sheaves set up against the stake at the bottom & then these small sheaves are criscrossed up to the top & one put upside down on the top of the stake. The hay in Switzerland is dried much in the same way on these poles. They look a little way off, like a row of bears standing on their hind feet. It is quite novel & funny looking.

FIG. 7 Lorraine Shortt. Courtesy of University of Waterloo Library, Special Collections & Archives, Elizabeth Smith Shortt fonds (WA10, file 2310, Lorraine Shortt).

Since we came out of the Austrian mountains, farming has been on a more extensive scale, and from Salzberg [*sic*] here, it seems a rich farming country as houses and the big monasterys [*sic*] testify.

The houses are quite different from the Swiss, often are large with 2½ storys [*sic*] & with rows of small windows along the etapes or floors of the house. Here in Vienna (& in Salzberg) the buildings are fine: villa or residence or public. Only Florence & Munick [*sic*] stand out in my mind as having such fine ones & so many of them: Florence, more in the private mansion magnificence & Munick in its wealth of art & many public buildings of magnificence. This city [Vienna] reminds me more of Munich than any place.

One thing that seems common to the cities of this continent is fleas. I look sometimes as if I had smallpox on my legs—what I do suffer from them! It is not the quantity but the persistency. I don't suppose I ever had more than one at a time & then maybe not again for days, but I am never free of the evidence of them! I use [illegible] to keep them off & boracic acid solution to cure them when I suffer from them.

We have had the most remarkable record of no rain I ever experienced & that many places ever experienced. We left (the latter part of June) Ottawa bathed in heat & sunshine & hoping for rain. It did rain, a thunder shower as we went on board at Montreal, but since then we have not been rained on. When we were baking in Oxford they said they had a shower in London, but not when we saw it nor since we came to the continent: England, France, Switzerland, Austria all scorched & browned for lack of moisture & because of heat. All the time (except the day we went to Boxhill) glaring white sunlight like India & often temperatures that not only make the people swelter but spoil their cheerfulness. I've no doubt it had something to do with the unhappy times they have had over the "strikes" in England: they were so miserable that the conditions of living were harder to endure.

In the mountains & the mountain valleys it was not quite so brown; no doubt because of dews & later thawing, but many dry beds of large streams even up there bespoke the unusual conditions. It seemed very strange to see any snow at all on the mts.. We did not actually see many goats on the hills & mts. but often the very narrow path bespoke the kind of step that trod the way.

A Letter from Elizabeth to Muriel[25]
We received your two letters—Aug 1st & Aug. 6th which had been sent on to us here. I think we have likely received them all, but I forget whether there is a "1" [i.e., the first letter] at London. There is [an] 8 or 9. I also received one from Lorraine written from K. [Kingston] at Ontario Park when with Mrs. Platt. I'm going to write Mrs. P. & thank her for her great kindness to Lorraine. I'm afraid people think Lorraine is on the public [dole] so to speak. She should have gone home when Mrs. G. [Garnoley] went to Gananoque. However, it's all right, I suppose, & no doubt she is at Helderleigh[26] having a good time. How is she to get home I wonder?

I'm sure you are having a very good time by all accounts with all your nice young people. I am very sorry your eyes are troubling you. I am much concerned about them. Suppose [Dr.] Minnes says there is nothing wrong but rest needed. Well, there must be some condition somewhere that is producing these results.

I had a letter of sympathy from Cecil,[27] written en route to Portland [Oregon] from Hamilton. He is bringing the family back the first week in Oct. in time for school. He said both Arthur & Harold[28] were working for pay in Portland, Arthur assisting the field surveyor & Harold office boy in his office. He said it was only another year till Arthur would be at R.M.C. & then McGill I think.

I had a good letter from Gertrude too. She said Mother was much the same, but she (mother) thought she might drop any time & said she wanted the end to come. Be good to all old people dear child. It seems a sort of tragedy to live & grow old in body & mind. The irrevocableness of it gives my heart pain. I'll never forget seeing mother last June and from what Cecil says she has failed a lot since then. He said Alice [Coon][29] was improved by her failing & he thought it would do her real good. I hope it may. It was hard however.

We reached here [Vienna] last evg., being a day late in our itinerary because of coming over a hundred miles down the Danube River by boat instead of by rail. I used to sing with much fervor: "Can I forget that night in June before the Danube River. Can I forget &c." & I scarcely thought to sail so far on it all on its broad bosom. The Danube has as many I think & as beautiful, castles & monasterys [sic] as has the Rhine. Three or four of the castles are used & are immense; one is that of Franz Joseph, a summer place & another is a Duke of Salvatore's where the Emperor sometimes visits but some of the old ones, & particularly some of the ruins, were very picturesque topping a hill or rock by the river. Truly those old barons & monks knew a good view—a good position.

One thing impresses me here: the immense monasterys, the frequency of them, the amount of ascendancy they must have. After seeing some of the prison horrors at Salzberg to which they subjected the heretics I hope they will never get a hold over things again. Well I hope George came back in good time & after no accidents & that you are both going on in a normal way, as normal as you can under the circumstances. We arrived here last evg. & Papa got the mail this morning. I was feeling very much tired out & have been staying in all the morning while Papa has gone to find the English ambassador & investigate Civil Service. He hopes to come in late in the afternoon & then I will go out with him.

This beats everything unless it's Paris. I never saw such [a] sight in my life as in our drive across the city from the Quay to this Hotel Kaiserin Elizabeth last night. If you can think of the most illuminated, brilliant evg. fête you ever saw multiplied & magnified by twenty anyway, you can still have no idea of the extent of it nor the crowds & packs of people for place after place & street after street. It is a big gay city & the noise today is fairly deafening. I do not feel much desire to go out & wrestle with it.

We will get to Berlin by Friday I expect & probably leave for England via Amsterdam a week from today. Good bye just now my dear, dear Muriel.

[P.S.] Kind regards to Miss G. [Sarah Gibson]. I would like to write more but hope to soon again. Hope you had a very nice visit with Edith Cory[30] and had very pleasant remembrances of your visit. My eyes give me bother enough, and I hope when I have less to look at they may get much better.

Tuesday, 22 August

Adam's Diary[31]
Called on Vice Pres. Tis of Administrative Government of South Austria and Vienna. He transferred me to Count. ——— who went over Austrian system of Civil Service with me in very full, interesting, and instructive manner. To see another man tomorrow. Round some public buildings and Falks garten[32] in evening.

Elizabeth's Diary
Aug. 23rd, Vienna. Yesterday [22 August] afternoon we went to get a nearer view of the University, Hotel de Ville, Parliament Blds., Royal Palace, theatre &c. and these are all & each heavy in splendid carved stone & beautiful architecture. The carvings & the monuments & the fountains are truly beyond imagination till one has gone about & really seen them. Building after building, even on the shopping streets, have large carved stone caryatids[33] supporting the doorway or have rows of figures along the higher facade, bespeaking glory of other days—collonades [*sic*] [with] carved figures [in] gold or bronze or stone are multiplied in number & magnificence.

On each corner of the top of the sq. main building of the Parliament buildings are splendid bronze monuments of chariots & horsemen. I don't know what it represents. Again, on top of the Royal Palace & about the Royal Palace & at the gates of the palace, splendid monuments, not merely of one figure but groups, symbolical & mythological or historical. A very handsome one is between the two museums to Maria Thereasea [*sic*].[34] We went to see St. Peter's church[35] & also the Augustine[36] in which is Canova's beautiful marble design in memory of *uxori optissamae* [Latin: "the best wives"], Albertus Figuris, standing before the tomb with wreathes of bay &c.. It reminded me of the beautiful one of his in Venice. The churches are fine, but St. Stephen's is a wonder.

After this we went shopping a bit. The tricks of the trade are much the same in diff. countries. The aged one of in [*sic*] Canada [is] putting 0—&9, the "9" trick. In Eng. it is pennies tacked on in small figures even farthings often. In Berne the silk in a window had 1.30 marked on it &, of course one thought it was 1.30 a metre, but up above the silk in a quite inconspicuous place was put: "those by ½ metre." Here in Vienna it is the same. Krones, yes, but almost always it is 0. krones [or] 5.0 or 50 heller so that when one thinks one is getting something for say 4 krones nearly a dollar, it turns out to be nearly [$]1.25. The coinage is a bother. I can think quickly eno. in francs or krones or marks but it is the fraction that is a bother.

We bought a blouse & some lace collars & then I left them at the hotel & we went to the Volksgarten for our dinner & to hear the band concert which began at 7:30. The place did gradually get a good audience, but after every piece a little clapping produced an encore which was rather provoking for they only got half way thro. the concert by a quarter to 10 & then they retired to eat & drink & in despair & fatigue we left at 10:15 before they played "Norma" &c. & there was no sign of their return.

It is quite interesting to watch the people at such a place. They seem very demonstrative or gallant. Last night a middle aged man kissed his wife or sister when she came in, & several young men in saluting young or married women either, kissed their hand! One imagines a good many romances &c. as one looks.

Wednesday, 23 August

Adam's Diary
Another interesting talk with Count ——— another official on Austrian representative system &c and race and language problems. Round city on special car and saw much, including suburbs, monuments &c. Left in evening for Dresden by night train.

Elizabeth's Diary
We went out at about 2:30 & I did not have a rest till four. Then I was quite done up, but after sitting a time I went on & did the other things, taking one rest in the Augustine church, & did not come to anchor till nearly 7 which was beyond possibility of imagining for me. The consequence being that I am too tired to go out this morning [23 August].

August. 28th [*sic*] the afternoon of the day on which I left off here [23 August] we went up at three to take the seeing Vienna trip in the unusual way of a train of very special street cars which are given a sort of right of way over the lines. The cars (four of them) were mahogany with wide flat glass windows & we had chairs (each one) which could turn. Two men went with the cars as guides. Standing between two cars, he gave explanations as to places & things, as we went along. It was not as full of information for me as if it had been English & I bothered Adam a good deal, asking him what he said. But Adam had his difficulties too for when an uneducated native talks he is sometimes difficult to understand in any language. Of course the main buildings on the Ringstrasse were pointed out to us but we knew them already. We went a long way & saw much that was very interesting, the tour taking three hours.

One thing I always enjoy is the parks & gardens and these old world cities have beautiful parks & gardens. They nearly all have [a] Volksgarten which are parks in the city where bands play daily & beer & other liquors are freely disposed of & where people come to eat & listen. There are generally a number of smaller ones and also greater. The great park the Prater of Vien.[37] consists of over 4,000 acres along the Danube & is of big, natural wood, with drives & walks. It is splendid. I remember how much I was impressed with the Bois de Soulanges near Brussels, which had such splendid trees & drives & was so big. In summer it is such a blessing for the people to have so much of the peace & beauty of nature accessible.

In the course of our tour we found that their gas &c. is municipally owned which is not at all surprising in a country where there is so much of absolutism &c.. As one might expect, we stopped about 5 o'clock for everyone to go into a Restaurativo [sic] & drink & eat. We began to fear we would be too late for the P. Office & so left our party & went back as direct as we could. Adam & I packed up and then he went to the P. Office, & when he returned we went to the Bahnhof or [train] station.

Vienna, or as they call it *Wien* (vine), is very well worth seeing & one could have very well put in several wks. instead of days. The large museums were not open in the afternoon & mornings Adam was occupied & the one morning I could have gone I was too done up to try it. It seems odd now, when *Wien* is such a huge city, that it should have been named from the small stream which here joins the Danube. It is of course a very old city having been an important Roman military station in the long past & Marcus Aurelius died here so long ago as A.D. 180. It was only in 1857 tho.' that the old wall enclosing the old stadt [German: *town*] was torn down & the Ringstrasse, or Boulevard, between the old and new town made.

I don't believe there is any other city of such architectural magnificence nor do I think there would be any chance now, if all were starting over again, that it would excell [*sic*] any other place, for the people seem to indulge in eating & drinking to such an extent that they would not aspire beyond the common. In Austria apparently, at the hotels & other places, the number of rolls were counted which one consumed at breakfast, or other time, & charged extra. Cheese might be on the menu, & they bring cheese & butter, then when you eat a role [*sic*] with the butter & cheese, it is charged as an extra. We had good cream cheese here & in Switzerland.

Well, we thought we would have more time in Dresden if we travelled from Vienna to Dresden by night. As we could not get a sleeper for some days we concluded to try it in the usual compartment. We entrained at 8:30 & were due to leave in 10 min after but half hour & hour went by & no move. Then we discovered there had been an accident on the line & that was all they would tell. We did not start till after eleven & such a long miserable night as it was.

There were two (man & wife) Belgique [Belgians] in our compartment & pretty stout too. The woman promptly laid herself out on my side of the compartment & I had the smothered feeling of being factured [*sic*] in a corner, as I was. It was like sitting & sleeping in a bishop's chair with a small table in front of one. Morning came & still no Dresdren [*sic*]. We were going through Bohemia & the peculiar names, having the 2 & "tsch" combinations showed it clearly.

The conveniences on the continent are rather surprising to the English speaking. They are frequent especially for men & I think are improved in many respects since I was on the continent before. We passed from *homme & dame* [French: *man* and *woman,* as on lavatory doors] to *Mannen & Frauen* [German: *men* and *women*] to *Herren & Damen* [German: *gentlemen* and *ladies*] & in this Bohemia I noticed they called in "Eachbody abort" [i.e., aboard], but whether it was just a general injunction or limited to the males I do not know. It sounds so peculiar to English speaking people to see the injunction to "Abort." Often there are women in charge [of the convenience] & a fee is charged, but often not & generally then they are not clean.

I think if there is one region of the earth where they were a frequent necessity it was here with so constant drinking & drinking & eating. I don't think in all my life together I've seen so many stout women & men as this last six weeks. One would think that all women who got past 45 became more or less coarse & very much out of shape with stoutness, particularly abdomen and breast. The children are pretty & normal looking & often very often I see nice looking young men & women, but the middle aged women are not handsome to look at & only a few of the men. One thing I notice that seems to go with much wine & beer & that is the frequency of the [portraits of] nude women in galleries & the tendency to that sort of thing.

A Letter from Elizabeth to Mother and Gertrude[38]
Vienna. I received your twice welcome letter yesterday as it was forwarded with the others from London. We had mail at Berne & hope to again this week at Berlin & then not again till we reach England which we will probably do Sept. 1st or thereabouts. This is a wonderful city. It reminds me of Munich & Paris, but a sort of mixture of both. It's a marvel in its magnificent buildings & sculpture. I don't remember that even the cathedral at Cologne was anymore wonderful than St. Stephen's here.

With your letter I had one from Cecil[39] written on his trip west. I was glad to hear from him. He said you were anxious to hear from me again & I was glad you mentioned in your letter that you had just received one from me. I have not [had] much time to write being handicapped by [lack of] strength & sight & time. I have written more tho. than I would have if I were as strong as Miss Gibson, for when we reach a place where we are to stay a few days, I take a morning off & mend & wash & write. I started a diary which came to a sudden end but which I have been trying to write up in retrospect & only today have I succeeded in getting up to date even in a survey backward which is not quite like a diary.

I hope you have not had a return of the heat. It has been dry & hot everywhere. We have somehow got into a world of no rain & of constant glaring sun. The drought & heat is common to Eng., France, Switzerland & Austria so far & I hear it has been very hot in Berlin.

This is Aug. 23rd & we are intending to leave here tonight & travel all night to Dresden. We can not get a sleeper before the 25 so are going to try a night of sleeping in the coach. I hope it will not be too upsetting. I've proved a pretty good traveller, but I overdid it yesterday & am laying off this A.M.. We will only have a day in Dresden I'm afraid, & then we will have three I think in Berlin & then a whole night or day to Amsterdam from which we expect to sail for England by the 30th & from now on I will feel I am on the road home.

I expect you have seen Lorraine, for in Muriel's letter yesterday I find Aunt Christina[40] was taking her home with her. I am wondering how she is to get back, but they will arrange it all right I expect. I only intended for Lorraine to be away from home at most 3 wk., but I hope she will be all right.

I notice mother does not write any letters which makes me think she is not the same as she was a few months ago or the heat is really very trying.

Of course you write me so well I am not at all complaining but I wonder if mother is not well enough to write. I am very glad you are not having so hard a time. What a new order of things to have a new Post-M. Gen.. I do not know Dr. Beland.[41] What a big event the [1911 national] election will be. I do hope for is elected [*sic*] & the best of the Conservatives. I never realized what an important era in so many lives a change of Government made, but I see a lot of things that may happen [to] a lot of people, if there should be a change. I may not get time to write more this time, so goodbye with much love to you each if I don't.

Yes dear sister—"the prayers of the righteous availeth much." Truly the Lord led me in devious ways to that event in London & I feel that He means me to live for some further work that is for me to do. I never did realize what a calamity loss of sight would mean till I had my eye bandaged up after the operation & had the use of one only. I have to keep putting a drop in my left eye every alternate night so as to keep it from going off. There is no glaucoma in it now he says but it also might go off, under some conditions, if I didn't use the drops. It seems strange that more people don't go blind when so little is know[n] about symptoms of such serious importance.

I am going without the goggles now most of the time except when the sun is very glaring & when travelling all day. I've only just now begun to do so however. Dr. Flem[m]ing is to see my eyes when I get to London & he says I can later have both reading & seeing glasses ground in one & I asked about it in London & that would be 14 do. more, but it would be worth it. It is a great bother to be changing glasses all the time & forever having to carry an extra pair about. But any bother is small compared to being without the sight of one eye.

I suppose Alice[42] has gone west by this time & begun her professional career. Cecil seemed to think she was much improved. It was such a pity that she brought vicarious chastening on dear Myrtie[43] who I do not think needed any more, but it's past now. I am glad you liked Miss Gray. When you have a housekeeper, a congenial visitor would be rather good? With much love, goodbye again.

Notes

1 Cecilia Morgan, *"A Happy Holiday"*: *English Canadians and Transatlantic Tourism, 1870–1930* (Toronto: University of Toronto Press, 2008), 364.

2 Morgan, *"A Happy Holiday,"* 56.

3 Elizabeth Smith, *"A Woman with a Purpose"*: *The Diaries of Elizabeth Smith 1872–1884*, ed. Veronica Strong-Boag (Toronto: University of Toronto Press, 1980), xiii.

4 J. R. Miller, "Anti-Catholicism in Canada: From the British Conquest to the Great War," in *Creed and Cuture: The Place of English-Speaking Catholics in Canadian Society, 1750–1930*, ed. Terrence Murphy and Gerald Stortz (Montreal: McGill-Queen's University Press, 1993), 43.

5 Morgan, *"A Happy Holiday,"* 266.

6 Miller, "Anti-Catholicism in Canada," 35; the italics are mine.

7 Queen's University Archives, Adam Shortt Papers (hereafter cited as ASP), box 11, Adam Shortt Diary, 17 August 1911.

8 Innsbruck is the capital of Austria's Tyrol region, and in 1493 it was made the principal seat of the ruling Hapsburgs by Emperor Maximilian I, a status it retained until 1665.

9 University of Waterloo, Elizabeth Smith Shortt Papers (hereafter cited as ESSP), WA10, file 1772, Smith Shortt Diary, 17 August 1911.

10 The Tyrol region in western Austria is completely alpine in character and large portions of it are considered ideal for skiing and mountain climbing. It also provides a strategic link between Italy and Germany.

11 Landeck is the foremost town of Austria's upper Inn River valley and boasts a thirteenth-century fortress and some fine churches.

12 The Inn River is a major tributary of the Danube, and flows for 510 kilometres from Lake Lughino in Switzerland in a northeastern direction across western Austria and southern Germany.

13 18 August was not the birthday of Empress Elizabeth, who was assassinated in August 1898, but rather that of the reigning Hapsburg monarch, Emperor Franz Joseph, who celebrated his eighty-first birthday on this date; Jean-Paul Bled, *Franz Joseph*, trans. Teresa Bridgeman (Oxford, UK: Blackwell, 1992), 3, 258–60.

14 The Holkirch in Innsbruck was built by Emperor Ferdinand I in 1553–63 to house the tomb of his grandfather, Emperor Maximilian I, who ruled from 1493 to 1519. The resulting monument contains reliefs and bronze statues, which are stunning to behold.

15 Andreas Hofer was a Tyrolese military hero who led a popular local resistance against Bavarian and Napoleonic French rule from 1809 until his execution by

French authorities in 1810. His remains were brought to the Holkirch in 1823. Construction of the tomb by J. N. Schaller was initiated in 1834.

16 Mirabell (note the incorrect spelling in Elizabeth's diary) Park furnished the gardens for the Schloss Mirabell in Salzburg. The grounds are famous for their trees, terraces, and central fountain with several attractive sculptures.

17 The fortress of Hohensalzburg, or "old castle," dominates Salzburg's ancient town and contains state apartments and churches, including a Benedictine monastery originally built between 1464 and 1507.

18 Linz (note the incorrect spelling in the transcription of Adam's diary) is the capital of Upper Austria and the third-largest city in the country, with numerous commercial and industrial activities. Its position on the Danube, as well as the beauty of its surrounding countryside, make it a fashionable destination for tourists.

19 Paracelsus (1493–1541) was a German Swiss physician and alchemist who demonstrated the importance of chemistry in medicine and homeopathic treatments. After a lifetime of wandering throughout Europe, the British Isles, and the Middle East, he died mysteriously at Salzburg in 1541.

20 Note the incorrect spelling of Vienna in the transcription of Adam's diary.

21 The subsequent material in this diary entry explains that Elizabeth is discussing events that happened on 20 August, not 22 August, which she initially identifies as the date of the occurrences.

22 Elizabeth, the wife of Emperor (or Kaiser) Franz Joseph, was assassinated by an Italian anarchist in 1898, but the homicide took place in Geneva rather than Paris; Bled, *Franz Josef*, 259–60.

23 The Rt. Hon. Sir Fairfax Cartwright was appointed the British ambassador to the Austro-Hungarian Empire in 1908, and continued to hold the post in 1911 after a distinguished career in his country's foreign service; *Who's Who, 1915* (London: A. & C. Black, 1915), 368.

24 The Börse (note the incorrect spelling in Elizabeth's diary, where she employs the French term for this institution) was Vienna's stock exchange, opened in 1771 and reformed in 1875, Peter Csendes, *Historical Dictionary of Vienna* (Lanham, MD: Scarecrow Press, 1999), 190–91.

25 ESSP, WA10, file 493, Smith Shortt to Muriel Clarke, 21 August 1911.

26 This was the name of the estate in Winona, Ontario, where Elizabeth's older brother, E. D. Smith, resided. See "Frequently Mentioned Names" on p. xx.

27 See "Frequently Mentioned Names" on p. xx.

28 See "Frequently Mentioned Names" on p. xx.

29 See "Frequently Mentioned Names" on p. xx.

30 Edith Cory was the daughter of William and Laura Cory, who, like the Shortts, resided in Ottawa; see ch. 4, n. 22.

31 ASP, Box 11, Adam Shortt Diary, 22 August 1911.

32 The Volksgarten (note the incorrect spelling in the transcription of Adam's diary) was created between 1821 and 1824 to commemorate Austria's defeat of Napoleon at Leipzig in 1814. The gardens were extended on the northern side in 1862 and this area became a popular site for musical concerts; Csendes, *Historical Dictionary of Vienna*, 206.

33 Caryatids are supporting columns in the form of sculptured female figures.

34 Note the incorrect spelling of Maria Theresa's name. She ruled Austria, Bohemia, and Hungary from 1740 to 1780.

35 St. Peter's was the first Christian church built in Vienna over the Roman ruins. In the period from 1701 to 1753 it was reconstructed in the Baroque style, with many artists, such as Matthias Steinl and Johann Michael Rottmayr, assisting with the creation of the church's interior; Csendes, *Historical Dictionary of Vienna*, 153–54.

36 The St. Augustine church was erected in the years between 1330 and 1339. In its St. George's Chapel is a cenotaph fashioned in 1805 by Antonio Canova, which is considered one of the finest expressions of neoclassicism. Franz Joseph, the Hapsburg ruler in 1911, was married to Empress Elizabeth in this church in 1854.

37 The Prater, Vienna's main public park, was used by the emperors as a hunting ground until Empress Maria Theresa made it accessible to the general community in 1766. By 1911, it was a popular location for leisure activities, such as jogging, horse riding, and tennis; Csendes, *Historical Dictionary of Vienna*, 158–59.

38 ESSP, WA10, file 1035, Smith Shortt to Damaris I. McGee Smith, "August 22," 1911. This letter is dated 22 August, but the material within relates to 23 August, as the fourth paragraph reveals.

39 See "Frequently Mentioned Names" on p. xx.

40 See "Frequently Mentioned Names" on p. xx.

41 Dr. Henri Beland, a physician and member of Parliament from Quebec, was surprisingly appointed the Laurier government's postmaster general on 19 August 1911, only a little more than a month before the 21 September general election in which Laurier's administration was defeated by the Conservatives; Ernest J. Chambers, *The Canadian Parliamentary Guide 1912* (Ottawa: Mortimer, 1912), 124.

42 See "Frequently Mentioned Names" on p. xx, under "Mauritana Smith."

43 See "Frequently Mentioned Names" on p. xx, under "Mauritana Smith."

Beauty and Hostility in Germany and the Likeable Dutch in Amsterdam

As Adam and Elizabeth Shortt made their way through Germany and Amsterdam in the Netherlands, sharply divergent perspectives emerged. Dresden and Berlin possessed many fine attributes, such as interesting art exhibitions (24–26 August) and public parks (25 and 27 August). For example, Mrs. Shortt was enthralled with the porcelain collection at Dresden's Zwinger Museum, where a handsome arrangement of Chinese, Japanese, and Meissen ware from the host country, which she had not previously encountered, were presented. That same day, she was thrilled by a visit to the city's Royal Palace, where Beth discovered "one of the most wonderful collections of priceless things in one room I think I've ever seen … jewels in necklaces, in decorations, brooches, bands, crowns, swords & innumerable combinations" (25 August). Later Adam became excited over the choice exhibits at the Berlin Zoological Garden and Aquarium, where a variety of wildlife were displayed (27 August).

However, the Shortts also formulated negative images as they defined their impression of imperial Germany's identity. They were appalled by the large number of overweight seniors the couple encountered in Berlin (27 and 30 August). Elizabeth bluntly stated that it was "the exception to see fine looking people past middle life or even many shapely ones" (27 August). She also sarcastically identified the German capital as a city "gorgeous in its admiration of war & war gods & royalties" (28 August). David Clay Large has noted that when the city became the capital of a powerful German empire in 1871, the military aura was so pronounced that most Berliners treated the armed forces with a deference that endured there through the First World War. One observer, the Danish diplomat Georg Brandes, even claimed that troops in Berlin were "privileged beings next to whom civilians counted for nothing."[1] This militaristic orientation deeply troubled the Shortts. As we have seen in the introduction, Adam was one of the few academics in the dominion to become a member of the Canadian Peace and Arbitration society in order to ensure that "the European military curse" did not cross the Atlantic. Not long afterward, his wife joined Canada's fledgling peace movement. In 1917, when the First World War had fostered a martial spirit within English Canada, Beth opposed vigorously an NCWC resolution to make military training compulsory for schoolboys throughout the country. For her, a new emphasis on exercise and classes in physical education offered a more promising and nonviolent alternative. In the end, largely because of Mrs. Shortt's intervention, the leading feminist organization in Canada developed a compromise motion that "called for physical training of all school age children but with military drills for youth as long as the War lasted."[2]

Adam also hoped to cap his talks on reforming Canada's federal bureaucracy with further discussions in Berlin, where he sought to utilize German expertise. However, his overtures were rebuffed (26, 28, and 29 August). The Canadian civil service commissioner was forced to rely on public documents in libraries, which contained some valuable information. Nevertheless, the envoy from Ottawa remained annoyed, because the officials from the foreign office whom he was scheduled to meet never appeared (29 August). Earlier he had suggested that this rejection "seemed very suspicious" (26 August). Unfortunately, Shortt did not spell out the nature of these misgivings. In any event, Germany's was the only government that failed to accommodate this Canadian representative's quest for information on his business trip to the Old World.

In contrast with the mixed feelings that had emerged in Dresden and Berlin, Mr. and Mrs. Shortt embraced Dutch hospitality in Amsterdam without equivocation. Adam noted in an approving fashion that the Dutch were not usually overweight as the Austrians and Germans had been (30 August), an observation seconded by his wife the following day (31 August). Beth also valued highly the sense of curiosity she discovered in Amsterdam, as well as the Dutch dedication to public sanitation (31 August). Here Elizabeth expressed a popular opinion among English-Canadian travellers to the Old World in this period. While a majority of anglophone Canadians complained about the unsanitary conditions they encountered on many European streets, they felt that the spotless thoroughfares in Holland furnished a pleasant exception to this generalization.[3] Moreover, Amsterdam's zoo presented some previously unseen animals and a few hours later a pleased Mrs. Shortt left a band concert with "the Toreador swig in my ears" (30 August). There was no doubt that the Shortts enjoyed their brief visit to Amsterdam much more than their lengthy sojourn in Germany. As Beth wrote on her return voyage to Canada, we "could have enjoyed a longer stay [in Amsterdam] than we had" (ch. 7, 11 September).

Considerable confusion, however, emerged over another aspect of Elizabeth's diary entries in this phase of her travels. A strong characteristic of her reports is their general reliability. For example, in an intriguing encounter on 28 August with a fellow feminist from Germany, Dr. Alice Salomon, she delivered a characteristically sound description of the state of women's political, economic, and social rights in imperial Germany at this time. Nevertheless, the next topic discussed by these female activists—the nature of prostitution in contemporary Germany—appears riddled with inaccuracies. The first two sentences of Elizabeth's account dealing with this matter seem to suggest that prostitution in Germany in 1911 was generally licensed. But a British authority on German prostitution in the late nineteenth and early twentieth centuries, Richard J. Evans, has revealed that "registered prostitutes formed an increasingly small portion of the total number.... Well before the turn of the century, it seemed, the police regulation of prostitution had become a futile anachronism."[4]

The same source indicated via email that, in 1911, "there were 1.9 million live births in Germany, of which just under 10 per cent were illegitimate." This meant that there would be a little less than 190,000 illegitimate births in Germany, a far cry from the 400,000 recorded in Elizabeth's diary. Finally, Mrs. Shortt related that, "the houses of prostitution are mostly filled by girls from Roumania." This assertion was also spurious, as Evans writes that, "The vast majority of prostitutes in Germany were German. Indeed there were very, very few of other nationalities."[5] Young women from Romania were not the main source of sex-trade workers for the bordellos of imperial Germany in 1911.

Thus, all three principal assertions in the discussion on this subject were false. Without further information, it is impossible to know if Salomon, Shortt, or a combination of the two were responsible for the errors that ensued. It is also conceivable that extraneous circumstances, such as the fact that Dr. Salomon "was very busy getting ready to go on Friday [28 August] to Stockholm," muddled the discourse that followed. The historian is obliged to note the mistakes that one encounters in this passage, but she/he must also rejoice that such flaws are exceptionally rare in the Shortts' writings.

Wednesday, 23 August

Elizabeth's Diary[6] (for Adam's diary entry on this date, see chapter 5)
Well, we did arrive at last in beautiful Dresden after 14 hrs. on train. The
approach to Dresden along the Elbe river is fine: the hills slope down to the
river & the train runs along the valley winding around curves & thus giving
a good view. Some of these hills are just rocks of most fantastic shape at the
summit. Indeed one can hardly distinguish at times whether or not there is
a castle ruin on top or not.

After fourteen weary hours, I suppose the accident did disorganize the
running orders so that we were much longer than usual. We did not find out
what was the extent of the accident, but I see in an English paper an account
of one in the region at Kassa[7] where six people were killed & ten wounded
in the rear coach of the one into which the other ran. Thank God we were
not on that train. We might well wait patiently for things to be put in order
when we had no accident to ourselves.

Thursday, 24 August

Adam's Diary
Went about Dresden and saw best buildings. Spent afternoon in Art Gallery.[8] Very good; through some shops in evening. Very fine shops well
lighted. Many English and Americans in city.

Elizabeth's Diary
It was near eleven before we were washed, so we waited till we could have
lunch at twelve. I was near exhaustion for lack of food & sleep. I was foolish enough to take some wine (instead of getting tea) for luncheon. In
almost every hotel there is some compulsion put on one. In Vienna it was
that unless one took one['s] main meal at the hotel extra would be charged
for the room. In this one in Dresden it stated that extra would be charged
unless wine was taken at this particular meal which one had to take at the
hotel. In this hotel one must take breakfast or pay extra. Well I took wine, it
was very much like Sauterne & was very nice, but it did not stimulate me &
carry me on like tea. It made me more sleepy than I was.

We went to see the great Dresden Art Gallery. Dresden is called the
Florence of Germany & it has a great deal to be proud of in its galleries. We spent the afternoon looking mostly at old masters and it was well
worth seeing & refreshed my memory as to special features of Rubens, Van

Dyck, Rembrandt, Teniers,[9] Ruysdael,[10] Jan Steen,[11] Potter,[12] Holbein &c. The great *Sistine Madonna* of Raphael's is here & is given a room to itself & made a sort of altar piece of by being so set. I always liked the copies but of course they fail to really represent the original. The cherubs at the bottom of the picture are very fine too. I do not like it as well as the *Ascension* in the Academy at Venice, but it is so very fine anyway. The Holbein pictures were placed at the end of a room & made as an altar. The drawing from which Holbein's picture is made is there also on a side wall. It is I suppose natural that artists like accentuated things, but when portraying old age I wonder sometimes why so generally they choose such very wrinkled, unlovely faces.

We went out later & had tea & bought some fruit in the market which seemed so very odd, being held late in the afternoon & there was no sign of closing or of being near an end—fruit & vegetables & flowers abounded— we did not go into the meat-side. Vegetables & even fruit are much smaller than usual because of the drought. Pears & plums & grapes are reasonably cheap, but peaches are very dear. The chief grapes are pale, green-looking color of our [illegible] but [with] more body. There is a large kind & another as small as Delawares but better bunches in each case than Delawares. They are a pleasant sweet grape & the pears are like our communis one.[13] I enjoy them. I sat in the Park half an hour watching the children play & people meet & part &c. & Adam went to the post office to get my colored glasses which had had to be mended. We went to bed early both being tired & sleepy.

Friday, 25 August

Adam's Diary

Saw Dresden Park,[14] very fine, also porcelain museum &c..[15] Visited pictures again, especially modern ones. Saw some more book-shops but nothing of much interest to me. Took afternoon train to Berlin. Passed many square miles of Pine plantations in sandy land.

Elizabeth's Diary

Next morning after Adam had spent two hrs. on his business mission, we had breakfast & went to see the Porcelain collection. We had hoped to go to Meissen to see the china works, but it took a half day, was expensive & I was afraid rather too fatiguing, so I gave it up & we went to see the Porcelain exhibit instead. This was something we had never seen before. A whole wing of the flat etape of the museum was given up to Chinese porcelain. They were in many fine varieties in size & design but blue in various patterns & size predominated. They are great on large, very large, vases, both covered & uncovered, & bowls &c..

The Japanese [porcelain] came next & seemed to have been borrowed in most ways from the Chinese designs. A fanciful epergne[16] had a semblance in brass wire of a bird cage around the base in which were birds of china or porcelain. The Japanese had something like this too. Among all the blues I did not see any like ours, but the open work pattern as a rim around spiral plates was not infrequent.

Then came the Meissen ware. The most interesting stage to me in the display was early in 1700, about 1715 & 25. They had really lovely china both in all sorts of pieces & in design & shape & quality. This somehow rather impressed me. The interior of places like that old castle at Salzberg [sic] do not suggest dainty, very expensive or fragile ornaments or utensils, but some had them beyond a doubt. It is wonderful how far back the Chinese had wares of this kind. Their tea cups were in many cases as small as the doll cups I had when a child. I wonder if they drank often & used the cups instead of fans for something to toy with?

After this sight we went out to find the exhibit of jewels & articles of vertu[17] in the Royal Palace.[18] We had some difficulty in locating it as it opens from an inner court. We ran into a change of guards & the band playing wh. delayed us for some time. (we tried to see several of the fine church interiors, but they were always fastened.

I went in to see this display [of jewels &c..] & Adam went to see the quays &c.. This was one of the most wonderful collections of priceless things in one room I think I've ever seen. Only one room was given up entirely to jewels: jewels in necklaces, in decorations, brooches, bands, crowns, swords & innumerable combinations. One section of this was divided [into] diamonds, sapphires, emeralds, &c. the jewels being classified in this way.

One very magnificent thing in here may have been a gift from some Indian Prince. It was laid out in detail of men & horses & camels & elephants & men & native slaves & princes & one central figure on a gold throne. It was so ornamented with gold & jewels that the value was inconceivable. It may have been a gift from the Sultan of Turkey but it was Eastern because of the black slaves & the elephant & camel as being ridden by men or women. The sultan or whoever sat on the throne & on the broad steps leading up to him on either side was a guard of men. The whole space was filled with jeweled people & trappings almost & was worth seeing all by itself.

There was a side of this room with gilded doors that was a cabinet, one door was open & a set of crown, sceptre and jewels exposed to view. In the other rooms were other jeweled things, notably caskets, caskets of beautiful & varied design & value & ornamentation with different jewels. There were very beautiful bronzes too, those of figures of slaves ornamented with jeweled hands & necklaces &c.. There were at least half a dozen most beautiful large inlaid tables & so very & many beautiful things in the way of clocks, cabinets, figures &c. &c.. There was a room of bronzes too, which was well worth seeing. Among other carved wares there was a chain of the finest ivory carving I ever saw. It was almost like lace; it was so very fine.

After this we had dinner & then went back to the gallery & saw the "modern" pictures, pictures of modern artists. There were not half a dozen I saw that I would want except as curiosities of what might be done by fanatics. How anyone can find any satisfaction in the semi or wholly impressionist school[19] amazes me. Whatever it is, it is not what I want in a picture & it would have been inconceivable to any of the old masters that such paint madness should ever be called art.

Then we had to get off to the station. Adam went to the hotel & paid & had the porter bring over our bags & I met him there. We were only 2½ hours coming to Berlin. The country is very flat & uninteresting & we did not spend much eyesight on it. One thing did interest me & that was the reforestation on the sandy places.

We had been recommended to the Hapsberger Hotel by the German whom Adam met in Ottawa & again as we were leaving Montreal. It is just near the station we came in at & we find it clean & comfortable. We struck a new phase of the feather quilt here & in Dresden. Up till Dresden we had a sheet & blanket & the feather bed quilt on top which we certainly did not need in this weather. In Dresden hotel (Carleton) there was no sheet & no blanket, but what might be a thick comforter done up in a bag like two sheets sewed together & nicely buttoned at one end. One either had to sweat under the warmth & wgt. of one of these or go without any. I tried it the first way & couldn't endure it, then the 2nd way & couldn't so I put on my stockings & dressing gown & finally my coat & put in the night. Wed. night it happened to be cool enough, I wore the bed top. Here in this fine new hotel it is the same. I sweat a heap under the edge of it last night, but I think I'll take the table cover & my dressing gown tonight!

It is a sanitary arrangement because no one has to sleep with anyone else's blanket under their nose, but it isn't comfortable & must add very much to the washing & ironing. There is a piece of mattress so which is placed under the under sheet & then there are 2 pillows & the thin feather tick quilt & the smaller sq. feather quilt. Yes indeed, it is not merely the bigger & thinner feather or other bed quilt that you have to contend with alone, but there is the fancy square one, much thicker & with trimmed cover, with insertion showing the red through from the interior. So that with two feather beds & two large fluffy pillows, one is nearly lost when in bed.

Saturday, 26 August

Adam's Diary
Berlin fine modern city but not so attractive as some of older ones. Called at British Embassy. They had tried to arrange for me but had no definite reply. Seemed very suspicious. Hoped to make arrangements. Went to P.O. and saw various shops. Spent afternoon at Picture gallery.

Elizabeth's Diary
Sat. morning Adam went to see Ambassador Goshen[20] but could not get on any farther—the German end of it seemed to have lost connection some-how. In the afternoon we went to the Austelling [*sic*][21] & it is huge. We were here in the midst of modern painting & sculpture. There were not many, outside of portraits, that I was very much in love with. There were three very large sea pieces that were great. One of the surge on the rocky shore just in the copper fading light of day was very good, indeed, & the others were fine too.

We saw here a lot of impressionist & semi-impressionist [paintings] and I pass them by in a hurry. I cannot use my eyes all the time without care, so I go round a room & just wait to look at those that are especially interesting to me. Adam takes a closer inspection & I sit down often & take a rest while looking at some special corner. Sightseeing is fatiguing to anyone & I am thankful I have been able to do so much—even under my limitations. I am thankful indeed that I have been so much stronger & more able than last summer.

As soon as it became too dark to see well, they turned on the electric light (from 7 to 8 when it closes). When we felt we were not seeing well enough [inside] we went out, intending to go to the Zoological Gartens [German: *gardens*] to an outdoor concert, but on coming out & consult-ing our guidebook we found there was to be a good one just adjacent to the Kurist Austullung [*sic*], so we went to it. It certainly was a sight. The place was spread out mostly in tables around the square (a fountain & trees & gardens being in the middle) with a vast no. of electric lights. The fountain had red & yellow & bluish purple globes of light in the basin, at least through which the water came, which colored the water in the fountain to a blending of these colors which had a pretty effect at night.

One side of the sq. was sort of terraced & we went there under a nice tree & had a table to ourselves where we had our evg. meal & listened to the music. It was more classical than those we have heard before & had selections from Mozart and Verdi and Wagner &c.. It certainly was a sight to see the great number of people there & the open air & the terraces & the trees & flowers & fountain & music. Below us below the next terrace was a distributing centre & a collecting centre for food & utensils & it was interesting to see forks & spoons & knives handled by the half bushel & carried to & fro, not to mention plates & platters & beer glasses by the 1000.

Sunday, 27 August

Adam's Diary
Forenoon at Zoological garden.[22] Very good, many rare animals. Afternoon, took drive to Charlottesburg[23] on coach. Saw tombs of Kings &c. Very fine drive to see parks, public buildings &c. Had a busy and tiring day.

Elizabeth's Diary
We started out about ten to the Zoological Gardens & found a direct [street] car route. We wandered about from one den to another & saw the tigers & bears & lions & wolves & Emus & Yaks & Zebras, rhinocerus [sic] & elephant & seal & Giraffe & monkeys & birds & deer &c.. &c.. It is situated something like the English zoo in a very fine large Park.

It was very interesting. I was much taken with the large collections of Zebras & particularly with the mixed productions of Zebra & Shetland pony. It was a bay with dark stripes, not so defined or distinct as in the Zebra, for it is cream color with black stripes. There is quite a variety of markings from fine very regular ones, to broad & less frequent stripes. The most perfect in the small stripes had them round each leg & then round the belly & very evenly marked in the face. They are stout built & the Shetland bay Zebra was quite well set & plump & shiney & bigger than any ordinary pony.

The bears were good: brown & black & grey & white. A brown one displayed the meaning of the saying "being as cross as a bear." For being irritated by flies it cupped its own ears & then being cross because of this &

also that he was not being fed what he thought to be his share of the tid bits of the visitors, he just let out a snappy yelp & just walloped both ears with his front paws (he was on his hind feet at the front of the cage). We looked & looked at the Giraffe—it is so very peculiar, so tall & so stolid & so incapable looking. I felt like the man who said after looking at it for some time: "Ye can't fool me; there ain't no such animal." I wonder it isn't extinct before this.

And the stag with the horns too. What a fearful handicap in a forest to have a branched tree at the top of its head. We saw more than one who [sic] having "moulted" its horns was growing new ones, sometimes very unevenly & they look something like the cactus that has small hairs only of course under the stag's hairy or downy look is a sort of living, pink. There was a beautiful collection of birds but the great number of parrots kept up a fearful screeching & clatter.

We did not try to go very far afield in the park, for after we had dinner there in the open with hundreds & hundreds of others, we went in the elevated [train] around to the station nearest Unter de[n] Linden where we were to get the coach at three for a three hours drive of seeing Berlin. I was interested at the 2:00 [p.m. departure gate] to see such a very great number of fathers & mothers with the children & I was struck with the number of good looking, & very well dressed children. I also saw quite a number of nice looking well dressed young women & men but it was the exception to see fine looking people past middle life or even many shapely ones.

The coach did not start promptly on time which gave a chance if one wanted to sit & to partake of more drink. So Adam & I took lemonade which with tip came to more than beer. The coach had four good horses a top hatted driver & a guard who called out the items of chief interest as we went along. Unter de[n] Linden is not so fine an avenue as I expected, but it is very wide & a great [source of] pride & resort for walking & driving & of course it has many fine buildings on or near it & is called Berlin's "*Via triumphalis*" [Latin: *street of triumphs*]. It must be rather irritating to the French to see so many things that are in a sense commemorating their dismay & defeat, but of course they are the pride of the victorious. Even at the start off in this drive the Brandenburg gate crowned by the chariot of victory which is considered fine & of course much more than gate implies is mentioned as having been carried off by the French [in] 1807 & brought back to Berlin [in] 1814.

As soon as we emerge from this gateway & the Paris Plaza where are several monuments of royalties we are at the first corner of the Tiergarten or Park of 650 acres.[24] It is a most beautiful Park of natural wood which has innumerable drives & walks & ponds & seats &c. &c. not to mention such a great number of monuments along & in the margins, especially the side on which Berlin's "400" [i.e., the city's elite] have their residences & on which they look. Through what is called the Avenue of Victory before we reach these residences, there are some 32 marble monuments to ancestors of the Brandenberg Prussian Royal House. Certainly Berlin does it proud in the way of monuments to members of the Royal House & to men renowned in war. Bismarck has more than one fine monument & von Moltke also one, but after all it is Frederick's[25] and William's[26] that do abound. On this margin of the Tiergarten there are among other monuments a very fine one to Wagner, of recent time 1903.

Before reaching Charlottenburg Platz we see the fine Emperor William Memorial Church & it is fine too (1895).[27] We reach Charlottenburg Palace which is not very imposing & the party unloads (by means of the ladder &c.). Headed by the guard or guide, we dip through the gate & court of the castle & out into the private Park past a row of royal monuments, down & up & across by path (cement) & away into the wood—to the mausoleum a sort of Greek parthenon, with entry part & main part.

On entering the bluish lighted hall, one sees a large monumental angel guarding the tombs. Passing around this we enter the mausoleum proper where are four tombs & four floor tablets. On marble couches lie the marble effigies of Queen Louise[28] & Emper. Frederick William iii[29] & then of Empress Augusta[30] & Emp. William 1st. They are of course reclining full figure marble effigies & are in the bluish light & in quiet beauty very impressive. The blue light is produced by blue glass in that part of the room which would be the "cave" or part between the wall & the ceiling & the outside light comes through this & no other window.

After looking as long as we like we troop back to where we left the coach, but it is a long block or two farther down by a "Restauration." I would not partake of any more, so I sat on the coach till the others (Adam was by the coach & so was the driver) had their fill & then we came back another way on what is called the Zelten. I forget the street but even for Germany, there is an unusual procession of gartens [German: *gardens*]. I counted four or five in succession all crammed with people eating or drinking. I suppose thousands would drink & eat on that one block alone this afternoon. They have music to their food. I might almost say instead of potatoes & bread for we do not see much evidence of these with their meals.

We pass a great number of very fine monuments of bronze & of marble, some of hunting scenes, & often of groups. There are a great number of very fine buildings among which figure schools of artillery, Armorys [*sic*], Academies & there is the National Museum & several others & the very handsome new (1905) cathedral[31] on the square where the Imperial Palace stands. It is a very handsome square. This cathedral has a number of bronze figures in groups of two at the sides of the main portal & on each side a very handsome bronze relief in which Luther is the prominent figure. I thought these were very fine.

The palace has monuments of people in ones & twos on the top & a great gilded dome &c.. It was begun in 14 century & has been added to. Just near it is the residence of the military head & around the corner from it the palace of the crown Prince. When a purple flag flies from the palace the Emperor is in town. Of course a great deal more was pointed out & we arrived back soon after six. After sitting awhile in Unter de[n] Linden till Adam consulted the map, we wandered about & then went back to our hotel & had something to eat & I went to bed while Adam read the paper.

Monday, 28 August

Adam's Diary

Again at Embassy but no results from German officials. Saw numerous fine shops and got copy of picture of battle of Queenston Heights. Saw pictures in afternoon and much taken with general work. Round by public buildings and monuments.

Elizabeth's Diary

Adam went to see Ambassador Goshen & I wrote all the morning. In the afternoon A. went with me to see Alice Salomon out at Neue Ansbacher-strasse &, owing to it taking him an hour to go to the Bank & another hour to find Miss Salomon, we had no afternoon for sightseeing. They number the streets here down one side & up another. Then when they want to lengthen the street they have to call it something—like new or other tho. it is the same st..

Dr. Salomon[32] was very busy getting ready to go on Friday to Stockholm to the International Council [of Women] meeting of the Executive. Her Sec., Miss Braskell, who was Sec. to Mrs. Ogilvy Gordon,[33] who preceded Dr. S. [as the Council's corresponding secretary] was there. She is English & that must help Dr. S. much tho. she speaks English very well herself.

She tells me there is no great stir about woman suffrage her[e] tho. recently women (the educated workers) have been taking a part in politics, something as the Primrose league[34] &c. has for a long time done in Eng.. The Social Democratic party is the one that favors women having equal rights with men. She tells me they have trade unions all right both of women with men's unions & women's alone. It will be a number of years here before there is much "doing" about women voting. In small districts where women happen to be the land or other magnate she has legally a right to vote & does by having a man deposit it for her, but this was not intended for women. It is because of the right of property which was not expected however to be controlled by a woman. I think that right existed in Eng. nearly a hundred years ago but fell into disuse or became annulled.

She tells me that vice is licensed here. They are not segregated—the harlots—but have to go twice a wk. or something to Drs. to be inspected as to disease & are licensed if free [of it]. I don't know what happens if they are not. She tells me there are 400,000 [sic] illegitimate children born in Germany in a year. That so far as she knows the houses of prostitution are mostly filled by girls from Roumania &c.., I suppose all more ignorant &c..

After we left there we took train & then elevated to the Bourse station & Ad. went to the post office & I inspected the outside of the Cathedral & National Art Gallery & Museum, all of which are splendid. We could not get into any of these as it was so late. As we were standing there, a Zeppelin air ship[35] came over the Royal Palace straight over our heads & low down, so we had an excellent chance to see it & how it worked. It had a beautiful calm time for its experience. I should never want to go up in one of those. Even if tired of life there would be other easier deaths than falling with one of those.

We then went out to inspect the wonderful monument & collonade [sic] in front of the Royal Palace. It is something in this shape: two open temples at each end of the open colonade [sic] (which opens on the rear, on the canal & a small garden) & in the curve of the collonade this magnificent monument in front of the Royal Palace. The dominating figure at the top is a splendid bronze horse on which is a fine bronze full figure of King William[36] with a full figure on foot at his bridle rein of victory awarding him the palm of victory. There are four immense groups at the base of this of Lions stretched on the implements of war & figures carrying laurels & then two intermediate ones of scabs. empty & helmets & sword & cloak & crown in a heap.

It is large in conception & I think they said it cost 2,000,000 marks. It is dated 1870 or 71, I suppose the commemoration of their French victory.[37] Certainly here they seem to magnify war & the men who succeed in war or glorify war. The people must have a reverence or fear or something of royalty for the number of monuments of them is remarkable. Of course Berlin is not an old city like Vienna, but it is gorgeous in its admiration of war & war gods & royalties. One monument of great historic interest is that of Frederick the Great[38] in front of the Parliament Blds..

After this we returned & had our evg. meal by the fountain in the court yard of our hotel (which fountain is of 3 women holding an iron net & under which urchins blow up water & water also ascends through the iron net in a jet of falls with pleasant sound into the basin). When starting out in the coach drive we had our picture taken, the coach & its load of people, & on returning were presented with the photo, for which of course we were asked a mark. It was quickly done & not bad for being in a glaring sun.

Tuesday, 29 August

Adam's Diary

Went out and hunted up books and reports on German Civil Service. Got some good ones, but heard nothing more from officials whom I was to meet through foreign office. Visited upper end of Interden [*sic*] Linden. Saw a Zepp[e]lin airship pass over city.[39] Not much popular excitement over Morocco question.[40]

Elizabeth's Diary

Our last day in Berlin was not much of a success. Adam went out on Civil Service business & as the Germans could not get themselves to be of any use nor could Ambassador Goshen do anything to get them into working shape [through] communication [or] conversation Adam had to hunt the facts up for himself in their books & literature. I wrote all the forenoon hard, so hard that I was nervous.

We did not get lunch till 2 indeed it was 2:30 before we got upstairs to pack & after that was done we went back to the great Austelling[41] &c.—collections of modern pictures & statuary & stayed till it closed at 7 o'clock. We then went back to the hotel & had our evg. meal & then waited till it was time to go to our train & Adam had run the gamut of tips. We tried a sleeper this time. They cost about the same as in Canada & are quite different. For instance ours was like a steamer cabin—small. We had a compartment with the upper & lower berth & fixings & a wash [basin] & other conveniences in the cabin. That [wash basin] is folded up against the wall & which [*sic*] is let down for washing. *Waschge fassi* [German: *washing barrel*]—it is comically called. We covered that long stretch between Berlin & Ampesdorf.

Wednesday, 30 August

Adam's Diary
Came to Amsterdam during night. Difficult to locate hotel. In afternoon went to Tiergarten[42] which is very good and interesting. Concert in evening. Amsterdam very interesting and quaint but hotels expensive. People not so stout as Germans, and more like English.

Elizabeth's Diary
Before we were up in the morning, about 7 the customs man knocked & came in & gave a perfunctory look & questions & departed. As soon as we were dressed we had a look at the country: flat & wet & verdant where there was not water. In the meadows were more cows (they looked like "Alderneys")[43] to the square acre than I ever saw in my life. They dotted the meadows nearly as thickly as the weary willets do [in] Green & Hyde parks in London at night.

It is a new sight to see the land ditched so frequently & to know because of its flatness that there is machinery at the shore for exhausting the canals. It it [*sic*] is so of Amsterdam & I hear it is for the country [in general]. Amsterdam huge & old & quaint is built on piles because the sand & wet of the soil would not otherwise hold up large buildings. There seems to be a wealth of vegetables & fruit & cream & milk & butter & cheese. The market is a great display of these & of other wares: dishes even hardware, being exposed for sale. There is a great fish market as one could imagine.

We went by somebody's advice to Hotel Amstel, a huge one on what might be called the Grand Canal, but on arrival found it full. So Adam went in search of quarters & the next, Hotel Bellevue was full. However, he found this lovely one, Brach's Doelen Hotel, which means The Hunters' Club Hotel, it being famous as such in the days when Rembrandt was one of its frequenters there. It is quite near the centre of things, near Sophia Plein & the mint[44] & next to a very magnificent one, Hotel d'Europe. We have a very comfortable room with the usual great amount of furniture & looking over one of the big canals. It is a beautiful scene here in the twilight or evg.. We have the open square & 3 sections of canal with the streets opposite each & the lights & the canal craft going to & fro.

We have only seen wooden shoes twice but I have in each country seen queer headgear. The most exaggerated of all was that of some babies' nurses in Berlin: great frames like a trellis under the white starched waving screen on top of their heads. We started out after we got settled & began w a bookstore where Adam looked at prints for a long time but fortunately did not [buy] any, then a bookstore for a guide book & then we drove for a delightful hour & saw the palace & the big churches & post office & Botanical Garden & Zoological [Garden] & Parks & Aquarium & Guildhall & the great harbor with its American & East Indian liners lying amidst hundreds of other steamers & craft. It was a fine sight of one of the world's biggest harbors.

We saw a number of the streets & ended at the big Museum.[45] We stayed here till lunch time looking at the porcelains of which they have a fine selection but not so extensive of Chinese & Japanese as that in Dresden. After lunch at the hotel we went to the Zoo & the Aquarium.[46] The Aquarium closed at five & then we spent the rest of the time till seven in the Zoo. We saw some animals we had not before, notably the wombat,[47] which is like a fat, smallish pig without a tail. There is a very fine display of brilliant Parrots mostly from S. America. They were sitting on high (about 4½ ft.) perches along each side of the entrance avenue & around a plot as well. After hearing & seeing the lions roar & roar & the other wonders, such as the flamingo, we had our evg. meal at the restaurant there & stayed for the Wed. evg. band concert which was very good. We did not stay till the finish but I came away with the Torreador swig in my ears. The Aquarium was very interesting but not as large as I inst. [*sic*] it would be. I do not think it nearly as extensive as New York's.

The language is queer, as queer as Bohemian almost. Some words are spelled the same or nearly the same as English, for instance "school," but not pronounced the same. Shoen is shoe &c. & then most words are quite unguessable, zrep being soap & Canemberin, cream cheese, &c.. In the Hotel Amstel were mostly Americans & Eng., I think, & manager, Porter & waiters spoke it [English]. Here [at the Brach Doelen Hotel] the manager does & the waiters a little, so we get on.

We are now using Guelden [*sic*][48] & cents, but 100 of their cents make a guelden which is somewhere in the region of 39 or 40 [Canadian] cents. Their 10 cent pieces are very wee, quite a bit smaller than our five [cent coin]. I like these people. I suppose my ancestor Armeke Laus Bogardis, came from here & there is something familiar in my blood to it.

Thursday, 31 August

Adam's Diary
The Queen's birthday[49] and holiday crowds everywhere. Quaintly costumed people arrive by boat from fishing towns. Watched processions and street

scenes. In afternoon at Art Gallery[50] which is very fine, especially the Rembrandts and the Modern School.[51] Other Art objects interesting also.

Elizabeth's Diary
It is in very fact the last of Aug. 1911 & now we enter on the autumn. Here in Amsterdam (or Amstel—the river which gave [the city] the name) we just seem going on in a strange, new kind of life, as if Adam & I were on a voyage to the moon. We do sometimes hear people speak English but we have not come across a person we know since we left England & here the language is quite a piece of guesswork. However they have so many Eng. people come over that most of them (in shops & hotels & cafes) know what you want & know a few words of English.

Today is the Queen of Holland's birthday & the people are making merry in great crowds. In some places there is [*sic*] just swarms & swarms. I do not know what is the great attraction, but there is much going to & fro.

Adam could not get into the Archives & there was no market to speak of. We could neither get into the palace nor the Dam cathedral[52] nearby & so we went on to the Rijksmuseum which is the great one of Dutch painters, more especially Rembrandt. His great "Nightwatch" is in a room by itself & is splendidly placed for light. It is a great picture & has as many faces in it almost as he has single faces in his other pictures. In the next room were a number of other of his pictures, the "Syndic," being another group of men of his particular style of men & painting.

We have seen such a splendid collection of Dutch Masters today. Teniers[53] & Gerard Dou,[54] Jan Steen,[55] [illegible], Van de Velde,[56] Van Dyck (his Princess Mary & Prince William is here) has quite a large number here & several of Rubens. Ruysdaels [*sic*][57] & Van de Velde are two of the best landscape ones of that school to my mind. Paul Potter[58] is much in evidence & I of course like his animals. I do like the genre pictures of Teniers, Van Ostade[59] & Jan Steen very much. We spent the afternoon there & must go back tomorrow.

Just now it is about six & I am in the hotel before the open window, looking over one of the canals & music nearby is drifting in delightfully. The organs of the street are large & quite good & are much ornamental on the front by what looks to be colored pictures in porcelain. As I look out, I see across the bridge in a sidestreet a whole mass dancing in rings & pairs to the music of one of these. It being a holiday there is not much traffic except st. cars & this side street being paved is as good as any outdoor place of dancing.

There are quite a few odd costumes from outside but not such a great many. I have not seen any evidence of firecrackers yet. But there was the usual display later of rockets &c. at a little distance & the *Festa*[60] [German: *celebration*] went on till midnight (the *Zimmer nadchen* [sic] [German: *chambermaid*] said till 2 o'clock). The costumes peculiar to districts are seen to best advantage in their districts, Gelderland[61] being one of the most interesting districts. Occasionally, like a holiday of this kind, some come in to Amsterdam & are seen here, but girls coming in to service assume the blue check dress & the usual cap. The fishing people are the most exaggerated perhaps, the men wearing pants so wide & full that they put the divided skirt in the shade. The cap in variations is the most marked feature among the women.

One thing is said of the Dutch women: that they make cleanliness a sort of fetish—dirt is their abhorrence. Anyway as daily evidence you see servants beating & brushing the family rugs on the sidewalks in the midst of the throng of passerbys, there being no yards. I suppose it must be the roof or the street.

The houses & buildings of Amsterdam are built on piles. It is said there are more than 1300 under the "Queen's palace," the soil being of sand & so wet, it is of course necessary. It is said that Amsterdam people are curious & when out, always have time to see what's doing. Rotterdam[62] is quite too business like for this & the Hague[63] to[o] dignified. Anyway, I like the Dutch.

One thing tho.' seems changed. There seem to be almost no fat men & women compared to Germany, & as one expects from pictures of older times. The women of middle age & past are fine looking women intelligent & active. There seems to be very little beer drinking compared to Germany & almost no outdoor restaurants tho' there seems to be here, as in Germany & Austria, any number of mendicants & half beggars who persue [sic] you to buy something you don't want: a boutinère, bootlaces, post cards &c. &c..

Friday, 1 September

Adam's Diary

Another half day at Gallery, drive round the city, docks, old churches and other places of interest. Saw some interesting old prints of Quebec &c about 1784 but price much too high. Got some souvenirs and left for Flushing in evening to take boat for London.

Elizabeth's Diary

We set out after breakfast and looked in a number of shops and bought a few trifles. One has a constant need of restraint to keep from buying things quaint & beautiful in each place. After a visit prolonged to an old bookshop, we arrived at the Municipal Museum[64] & had a fine time among modern Dutch Artists & they are fine. I began to be doleful about modern painters after the Austelling [*sic*][65] in Berlin i.e. as compared with the Old Masters. Here however one is gladdened by excellent [modern] pictures & work.

Israels[66] (who has so recently died that his chief works relating to himself or Jewish [subjects] were draped), Mesdeg [*sic*],[67] Mauve,[68] Maris,[69] Klinkenberg,[70] Broack [*sic*],[71] Theyer [*sic*],[72] Sadee (seapieces I liked), Springer[73] (fine), Poggenbeck [*sic*][74] & many many other good ones. I am so glad I had a chance to really see Israels' pictures. Most of them are quite large & very fine. One the *de Sturin* is the wife of the fisherman sitting in fear & anxiety in the doorway (the storm being just over), the mother standing, a figure of resignation, leaning against the wall & a small boy with overclouded face dallying with his spoon & supper. It appealed to me much: the look the differences took in the faces of [the] three & w[ith] clearing sky & the cottage interior.

[There are] other big fine ones—*Passing the Mother's Grave*: a fisherman carrying a young child & leading a small boy, passing a simple wooden cross near the sea shore on his way home. A very large one is David praying before Saul. There are a large number. There were a number of sea pictures which I liked by Maris, Mesdag, Calame[75] & Sadee & others & there were most often groups of people within or without their especial kind of surroundings that reminded one of Teniers,[76] Van Ostade,[77] Jan Steen[78] & others of earlier times. We saw a number of Paul Potters:[79] fine views in wh. occur his fine cows &c., two or more of Alma Tedemas [*sic*][80] Ary Shaffers [*sic*],[81] a Corot,[82] a Messioner, a number of Van Dykes & others.

There were many excellent portraits of men or of women, particularly of men & I was glad to notice not so many nude women as in Germany, but still there were too many. That is one of the things I object to. I fancy if the women I know were directors of any Academy of Art there would be none of these unnatural pictures. They are absolutely unnatural because women are never nude doing up their hair or sleeping &c.. & it is only to appeal to men's passions that these pictures are made & hung or because of ———. I am not a prude & I think a woman's body very beautiful when normal, but I do not think nor see blindly & I have been about quite a bit & men's amatory passions are too much cultivated without the public corruption of boys & young men who go to galleries because of art & are shown what they never should see.

After we had spent all the time we could we went to get a bit of lunch & then back to the Rijks or big museum. We found more of the modern pictures here & we stayed as long as we could & then Adam went to see engravings & I went to see more pictures & sculpture, tombs, statues &c.. We have to leave Museums at 5, so I went home & Adam went looking after old books & maps &c.. We had a very fine dinner & then took train for Flushing after the usual gamut of tips: maid, elevator boy, other boy porter at hotel, porter at train from hotel, tip to general factotum, then tip to porter to put in the valises, then again to take them out at Flushing & put them on boat, then to another to put them in cabin, then another to put them on the London train in the morning & another to take them out.

We passed through Utrecht[83] & Rotterdam & Dordrecht[84] &c.. Rotterdam harbor seemed very fine & it had big canals too. They say the sea level is a foot higher than the land at Leyden & all along the sea coast—it is the Dykes & the Sand dunes that keep the water back. It is a great farming country & also great for vegetables & fruit & bulbs. I do not see myself why people don't suffer in health from so much semi-stagnant water. There is exhausting machinery at the sea coast which as it were sucks it out at Amsterdam & this creates an ebb & flow, but I saw green scum lying over the surface of water in many of the canals & I was sure I smelt that sort of malarial oder [sic] of stagnant water[85] in the very early morning.

An amusing thing in the Municipal M. [Museum] was a sort of pharmaceutical display of [the] old time a lying-in room:[86] woman in bed smiling up at a stuffed smiling husband, nurse & friend & baby & all the accoutrements. Next room a cell for lunatics: leather chair with straps for arms, body & legs, padded cell, padded sleeping cot which locked. Then, old laboratory. It was quaint. There was a display of uniforms too of diff. ranks in diff. parts of the Dutch Dominions.

The Dutch love their Queen Wilhemina [sic] & her two year old daughter & they are good to look at. I believe they [the Dutch] are about 3/5 protestants & the other 2/5 is divided mainly by Jews & Roman Catholics. The big R.C. church is called Moses & Aron [sic] which I think that [sic] is the 1st Mose [sic] & Aaron church I ever saw. We could not get into the churches, being at wrong times I suppose.

The boat we came over on [from Flushing to England] was better than the one in which we crossed the North Sea last time & I did sleep most of four hours in the badly ventilated place. We found [in London] Mrs. Rose could take us in but had not rec. my letter sent from Vienna (so she said) & that she had sent some of our letters to Dr. Doughty, not knowing where to send them, which shows she did not put down any address & we made a mistake not to write it down ourselves. But some have gone astray in Vienna, anyway.

Notes

1 Georg Brandes, cited in David Clay Large, *Berlin* (New York: Perseus Books, 2000), 20.

2 Sheryl Stotts McLaren, *Becoming Indispensable: A Biography of Elizabeth Smith Shortt 1859–1949* (Ph.D. diss., York University, 2001), 324.

3 Cecilia Morgan, *"A Happy Holiday": English Canadians and Transatlantic Tourism, 1870–1930* (Toronto: University of Toronto Press, 2008), 279–81.

4 Richard J. Evans, "Prostitution, State and Society in Imperial Germany," *Past and Present*, 70 (February 1976): 113, 115.

5 The quotations in this paragraph are drawn from Richard J. Evans, whose clear and prompt email on these points was greatly appreciated; Richard J. Evans, personal email message, 17 May 2007. Edward Bristow has further indicated that in this period many prostitutes from other countries passed through German cities like Berlin and Hamburg on their way to more distant locales like South Africa and South America, but these women did not remain in German centres for any length of time; Edward J. Bristow, *Prostitution and Prejudice: The Jewish Fight Against White Slavery 1870–1939* (New York: Schocken Books, 1983), 52, 127.

6 University of Waterloo, Elizabeth Smith Shortt Papers (hereafter cited as ESSP), WA10, file 1772, Smith Short Diary, 23 August 1911.

7 In 1911, Kassa was the main political, economic, and cultural metropolis within southeastern Slovakia in the Austrian-Hungarian Empire.

8 Dresden's Semper Gallery, built in 1846, contained several significant Renaissance and Baroque paintings, such as Raphael's *Sistine Madonna*.

9 David Teniers the Younger (1610–90) was a Flemish painter of the Baroque era celebrated for his portrayals of peasant life. He later became a prime mover behind the creation of the Brussels Academy of Fine Arts (1663) and the Academy in Antwerp (1665).

10 Saloman van Ruysdael (1600–70), a prominent Baroque landscape artist of the Netherlands, was famous for his depictions of Haarlem and its surrounding area, where he lived his entire life.

11 Jan Steen (1626–79) was another genre painter who delighted in illustrating scenes of everyday life, particularly in taverns, in which both he and his father had worked.

12 Paulus Potter (1625–54) was a minor figure among the Dutch masters of the seventeenth century, but his representations of animals in his paintings and etchings have drawn considerable praise.

13 The European pear, formally known as *Pyrus communis*, is the most popular variety in Canada.

14 The Grosse Garten (Great Garden) in Dresden was opened in 1676, and boasts noteworthy botanical and zoological gardens, as well as a pleasing landscape.

15 Dresden's famed Zwinger Museum, built between 1711 and 1732, contains pewter, porcelain, and scientific collections.

16 An *epergne* is a centrepiece for a dinner table, often consisting of bowls for fruit, decorations, etc.

17 Articles of "vertu" are objects having a rare or stunning appearance.

18 The royal palace, which traditionally housed the electors and kings of Saxony, was constructed between 1530 and 1535, and held many priceless treasures.

19 Impressionist painters like Claude Monet, Pierre-Auguste Renoir, and Edgar Degas thrived between 1867 and 1886, and placed a new emphasis on the manipulation of colour, tone, and texture to create more accurate "impressions" of objects as their appearance varied with time and place.

20 The Rt. Hon. Sir William Edward Goshen was appointed the British ambassador to Germany in 1908, after a distinguished diplomatic career throughout the world, beginning in 1869, *Who's Who, 1915* (London: A. & C. Black, 1915), 860.

21 Note the incorrect spelling in Elizabeth's diary of the German term *Ausstellung* (exhibition). The same word is also misspelled on three further occasions in this chapter.

22 The Berlin Zoological Garden and Aquarium was founded in 1841, when King Frederick William IV of Prussia presented his pheasantry and royal animals to the general public. It was soon noteworthy for its rare collection of unusual breeds, like the cross between the zebra and Shetland pony, which fascinated Elizabeth Shortt.

23 Schloss Charlottenburg (note the incorrect spelling in the transcription of Adam's diary) was the Berlin summer residence of the German emperor. It became increasingly elaborate, as the Hohenzollerns, the Prussian ruling family, extended their power throughout Germany.

24 The Tiergarten, or "Animal Garden" (zoo), was originally a royal hunting preserve before its conversion into Berlin's largest and most popular park.

25 Frederick II (1712–86), the third king of Prussia, called the Great, ruled from 1746 to 1786 and made Prussia a major power, nearly doubling its size through war and diplomacy. In his later years, he sought to implement his vision of enlightened despotism within this augmented realm.

26 William I (1797–1888) was King of Prussia from 1861 and German Emperor from 1871 until his death in 1888. He mainly relied on key advisers, such as Otto von Bismarck and Helmuth von Moltke, to extend the Hohenzollerns' territories and power.

27 This neo-Romanesque church was constructed by Franz Schwechten between 1891 and 1895 as a memorial to the recently deceased Emperor William I.

28 Queen Louise was the daughter of Prince Charles of Mecklenburg-Strelitz, and in 1793 she married the crown prince of Prussia, Frederick William. During his reign, which began in 1797, Queen Louise buttressed the King's often weak resolve. Her early death in July 1810 was regarded as a great tragedy by the Prussian people.

29 Frederick William III (1770–1840) was King of Prussia from 1797 to 1840, but never an "Emperor," as Elizabeth asserts here. He was most noteworthy for his submissiveness to foreign powers, but nevertheless was generally liked by his subjects, who admired his simplicity, good intentions, and dignity in the midst of several personal misfortunes, including the loss of his wife, the beloved Queen Louise, at a young age.

30 Empress Augusta was a sharp-witted, temperamental princess from Saxe-Weimer-Eisenach. She married Crown Prince William in 1829. She encouraged William to distrust constitutionalism, both before and after his assumption of power in 1861.

31 The Berliner Dom was the German capital's Lutheran cathedral, built in 1905 by Emperor William II as a monument to the Hohenzollern dynasty. It houses the remains of more than ninety Hohenzollerns in its lower vaults.

32 Alice Salomon was a German feminist who in 1908 had acquired a Ph.D. in economics from Berlin's Friedrich Wilhelm University. That same year she founded the Social School for Women in the German capital, which eventually developed into the contemporary Alice Salomon University of Applied Sciences. In 1909, Salomon became the corresponding secretary of the International Council of Women, which promoted feminist values on a cosmopolitan level; Andrew Lees, ed., *Character Is Destiny: The Autobiography of Alice Salomon* (Ann Arbor: University of Michigan Press, 2004), 3–4.

33 Mrs. Maria M. Ogilvie Gordon was a British scientist and the first woman to receive a Ph.D. from Munich University in 1900, following studies in geology and paleontology. She went on to become a worldwide expert in these fields, while pursuing a successful marriage and raising three children; *Who's Who, 1915*, 1622.

34 The Primrose League was a Conservative club in Great Britain with a large number of female members. It was formed in 1883 to propagate the ideals of Tory democracy as enunciated by Benjamin Disraeli, later the Earl of Beaconsfield.

35 The Zeppelin was a large dirigible created by Count Ferdinand von Zeppelin. By 1910, Germany had acquired supremacy in this field of aircraft development, based upon commercial flights linking a number of European cities.

36 See ch. 6, n. 26.

37 In the Franco-Prussian War of 1870–71, Prussia crushed France decisively. As a result, the formerly independent states of southern Germany recognized Prussian hegemony in a new German Empire presided over by the king of Prussia, who became the perpetual German emperor or kaiser in a ceremony at Versailles, France.

38 See ch. 6, n. 25.

39 Adam seems to be confusing this scene with an event noted by Elizabeth on the previous day; see ch. 6, n. 35.

40 The Second Moroccan Crisis arose in 1911, when France established a protectorate over Morocco without consulting Germany, which retaliated by sending a gunboat to the Moroccan port of Agadir. A war among the major European powers, including Great Britain, threatened, until the crisis was defused in November by the cession of 100,000 square miles of territory in the French Congo to Germany in return for Berlin's recognition of Paris' control over Morocco; John Merriman, *A History of Modern Europe*, 2nd ed. (New York: W. W. Norton, 2004), 961–62.

41 See ch. 6, n. 21.

42 There is no "Tiergarten" in Amsterdam, but this term is also used to identify the largest public park that Adam had recently visited in Berlin, see ch. 6, n. 25. Probably Adam is actually referring here to Amsterdam's Zoological Gardens; see ch. 6, n. 46.

43 In 1911, "Alderneys" were various breeds of cattle, originally found in Great Britain's Channel Islands, which by then were common in many other countries such as the Netherlands.

44 The picturesque mint tower in the Sophiaplein public square was a prominent landmark in Amsterdam during the early twentieth century.

45 The Wilet Holtkuysen, created in 1895, was noteworthy by 1911 for its displays of porcelain and furniture.

46 Amsterdam's Zoological Gardens, founded in 1838 by G. F. Westerman, house both animals and fish.

47 The wombat is a nocturnal Australian marsupial resembling a small bear.

48 The basic monetary unit of the Netherlands is the guilder, or Gulden in Dutch, but not "Guelden," as Elizabeth asserts here.

49 31 August 1911 was the popular Dutch Queen Wilhelmina's thirty-first birthday. She, like the Shortts, was renowned for her strong religious sentiments.

50 The Rijksmuseum (State Museum) in Amsterdam hosts one of the largest and best collections of Dutch art, as well as selected works by foreign painters and other artistic objects, including sculptures, applied arts, and prints.

51 In art, the "modern school" refers generally to art from the late eighteenth century onward. The term implies a self-conscious awareness of history—i.e., a continuation or rejection of past forms and conventions; Fred S. Kleiner and Christin J. Mamiya, *Gardner's Art Through the Ages*, 12th ed. (Toronto: Nelson Thompson Learning, 2005), 805.

52 The Nieuwe Kirk was built in the fourteenth century to accommodate Amsterdam's growing population. It is located in a corner of the city's famous Dam Square; hence Elizabeth's reference to the "Dam cathedral." Since 1814, all of Holland's monarchs had been crowned there.

53 See ch. 6, n. 9.

54 Gerard Dou (1613–75) was a prominent Dutch painter belonging to the School of Leiden, who became famous for his personal portraits and genre depictions of home life.

55 See ch. 6, n. 11.

56 There were two well-known Dutch painters who bore the van de Velde surname: Esaias (1590/91–1630), who was one of the first Dutch realist landscape artists of the early seventeenth century; and Adrian (1636–72), who specialized in portraying animal-populated landscapes that often revealed Italian influences.

57 See ch. 6, n. 10.

58 See ch. 6, n. 12.

59 Two van Ostade brothers emerged as prominent painters in seventeenth-century Holland. Adriaen (1610–85) was noteworthy for his genre representations of Dutch peasant life. His younger brother, Isack (1621–49), attained considerable distinction for his winter landscapes and scenes of figures resting outside inns and cottages with horses and vehicles.

60 *Fest* (pl. *Feste*) is the German word for "party" or "celebration"—but with an "e," not an "a." Why Elizabeth used a German term to describe a Dutch scene is unclear.

61 Gelderland is a Dutch province, bordering Germany, of rich agricultural lands and some of Holland's finest recreational areas.

62 By 1911, Rotterdam was mainly a commercial and port city, as well as the centre of the Netherlands' extensive shipping operations.

63 The Hague is the political centre of the Netherlands, and as such accommodates the national government and parliament, and the diplomatic representatives of foreign countries. The Hague also serves as the capital of the province of Zuid Holland.

64 The Stedelijk Museum is Amsterdam's art gallery, which presents art from around 1850 to the present. It was opened in 1895 after the municipality

constructed a new building to display works by recent painters and on modern themes that could not be quartered in the Rijksmuseum because of space limitations.

65 See ch. 6, n. 21.

66 Jozef Israels (1824–1911) was a painter and etcher from the Hague and the doyen of the peasant genre school, which flourished in that city. Later he devoted much of his work to themes drawn from his Jewish background.

67 Note the incorrect spelling in Elizabeth's diary, which should read "Mesdag." Hendrik Mesdag (1831–1913) was a protége of Jozef Israels. Mesdag principally devoted himself to seafaring subjects, which earned him the prestigious gold medal at the Paris Salon in 1872.

68 Anton Mauve (1838–88) was a landscape artist who largely dealt with life in Holland's countryside, as well as Dutch fishing villages, work which won him considerable acclaim.

69 Jacob Maris (1837–99), along with his brothers Matthijs and Willem, created the Hague School of painters in the late nineteenth century. Jacob specialized in landscapes where the chief physical object is overshadowed by the scene's environmental aspects.

70 J. C. K. Klinkenberg (1852–1924) was another genre painter residing in the Hague whose most famous piece illustrated the city's Spui Canal in winter.

71 Note the incorrect spelling in Elizabeth's diary, which should read "Broeck." Henrik van den Broeck (c. 1530–97) was born in the Netherlands into a family of artists, but spent much of his life in Rome, where he focused on religious topics.

72 Note the incorrect spelling in Elizabeth's diary, which should read "Thayer." Abbott Handerson Thayer (1849–1921) was an American painter whose portraits of women, children, and animals were highly prized in both the United States and Europe.

73 Cornelis Springer (1817–91) was a Dutch painter and printmaker who concentrated on townscapes, such as his *Townhall and Vegetable Market at Veere* (1861), which was purchased by the Rijksmuseum in Amsterdam.

74 Note the incorrect spelling in Elizabeth's diary, which should read "Poggenbeek." G. J. H. Poggenbeek (1853–1903) also fixed his attention on genre paintings dealing with urban subjects, such as *The New Market at Amsterdam*.

75 Alexandre Calame (1810–64) was a Swiss landscape painter who spent most summers in the mountains of Switzerland illustrating the awesome nature of the terrain, which this fervent Calvinist saw as an expression of divine power.

76 See ch. 6, n. 9.

77 See ch. 6, n. 59.

78 See ch. 6, n. 11.

79 See ch. 6, n. 12.

80 Sir Lawrence Alma-Tadema (1836–1912) was a Dutch painter who after 1863 concentrated on subjects drawn from ancient Greece, Rome, and Egypt, which he portrayed in a precise, realistic fashion. Alma-Tadema moved to England in 1873, and became a British citizen. In 1899, he received a knighthood from Queen Victoria.

81 Note the incorrect spelling in Elizabeth's diary, which should read "Ary Scheffer." Ary Scheffer (1795–1858) was a French artist of Dutch lineage who devoted himself to portraits, religious themes, and topics drawn from Goethe's *Faust*, though many of these works were sharply criticized by certain critics both during his life and after his death.

82 Jean-Baptiste Corot (1796–1875) was a popular French landscape painter who also composed portraits, household panels, and church frescoes, which brought him prosperity and fame during his own lifetime and a favourable reputation after his demise.

83 Utrecht is the capital of the province of Utrecht, and is well known for its old canals and buildings. It hosts the Netherlands' largest university and several major museums.

84 Dordrecht is a Dutch city at the junction of the Oude Maas and Beneden Merwede rivers. Its busy waterfront provides an important link between Antwerp, in Belgium, and Rotterdam.

85 Dr. Elizabeth Shortt was well acquainted with malarial odors and their origins, since her father, Sylvester Smith, contracted malaria from partially burned trees on his farm and never entirely recovered from the ravages of this disease; *Silas Smith, U.E.L., and His Descendants*, compiled by R. Janet Powell from history collected by Miss Gertrude Smith and other descendants (n.p., n.d.), 16.

86 "Lying-in" means "of or pertaining to childbirth"; *Funk and Wagnalls Canadian College Dictionary* (Toronto: Fitzhenry and Whiteside, 1989), 808.

Chapter 7

"Back in London" and Glancing Forward

Their return to England necessitated that the Shortts deal with a number of loose ends in Europe, or, as Adam put it, he "got details wound up" (6 September). At the same time, they prepared for the resumption of their daily lifestyles in Ottawa. Hence, Adam devoted a good part of 4 September to visiting the headquarters of the British post office, where officials provided useful information and the promise of a still-more-thorough report on patronage operations within the royal postal service. The next day, he had one last talk with his personal friend, Sir Hartmann Just, at the Colonial Office (5 September). The commissioner of Canada's civil service returned to the Dominion assured that he had fulfilled his principal responsibility of securing helpful data for a subsequent reform of the national bureaucracy.

However, in 1911, Adam was a highly active scholar as well as a leading civil servant. Indeed, two years later, he and his close associate, A. G. Doughty, began releasing the encyclopaedic Canada and Its Provinces series, which eventually ran to twenty-three volumnes.[1] It is not surprising, then, that Shortt found time to visit the distinguished Macmillan's publishing house to comment on its approaching printing of the Grey-Elgin letters, which had a formative influence on central Canada's political development in the pre-Confederation era (5 September). Adam had been acknowledged as a worthy consultant by a major book producer in London, which was, "for the aspiring Anglophone Canadian writer ... a cultural capital of overwhelming significance."[2]

Meanwhile, his wife was eager to conclude her own work in the Old World as a social feminist. On 5 September, she entertained Mrs. Malden, the literature convenor of the British Mothers' Union. This led to Elizabeth's purchase of several pamphlets, which might prove useful in her struggle for the advancement of women and children back in Canada. As Mrs. Shortt contemplated the immediate future, she also continued her practical efforts to secure servants for Christina Smith and herself. Beth's attempt to find such domestics through the Imperial Institute merely resulted in a vague promise that "she [Miss Lefroy of the Imperial Institute] would try to send a few others to Ottawa in October" (5 September). Dissatisfied with this problematical response, Elizabeth sought to recruit Miss Milly Wale, a third-class passenger on the *Royal George* with favourable credentials, as a servant for the Shortt household. However, Beth was hopeful rather than certain that this initiative would lead to the employment of Miss Wale at 5 Marlborough Avenue (10 and 12 September). Mrs. Shortt's overriding commitment to domestic responsibilities was further revealed when she contemplated a return to Canada. Toward the end of September, Muriel wanted to host a ball and her mother cautioned her not to finalize the details until she could discuss them with her eldest daughter (12 September). She also hoped that George would be able to make his "debut" on this social occasion (2 September). Afterward, Elizabeth would help George prepare for his first year at the family's beloved Queen's University (11 and 14 September). Mrs. Shortt did not exaggerate when she declared on 2 September: "Oh I have things to do in plenty."

Poor weather led to a return of the seasickness that had initially plagued the Shortts on their journey to England (9–13 September). Writing on 11 September, Elizabeth was disturbed by the rain, winds, and chilly temperatures: "We had rather a slow passage as there were two heavy days when a great many of us were very miserable. Adam caught a cold too which did not make him feel any better. I have appeared at table each time but have been on my back most of the time till yesterday." Inclement conditions also meant that Beth could seldom go out on deck and enjoy the seascapes (13 September). To make matters worse, her need to recuperate from the eye operation in London meant that she could not read throughout the long jaunt home (12–13 September). A good book was, for Mrs. Shortt, "the best way of passing time" (11 September).

However, Elizabeth did find other ways to improve the return voyage to Canada. On 10 September, she attended an Anglican service on the *Royal George*, which revived her spirits. Mrs. Shortt frequently employed "a good sing" from a Church of England hymnal to improve her disposition. The next day, she began playing cards, which supplied the principal entertainment for Mrs. Shortt during the remaining days of the excursion (12–14 September). Even on the final train ride from Montreal to the Dominion capital, Elizabeth cheerfully reported, "Mrs. Ewart & I played half whist patience & we put in a very good time till we reached Ottawa" (14 September).

Two days before, Adam made a more ominous comment when he observed in his final diary entry that the *Royal George* came near an iceberg and almost halted until a heavy fog had "cleared somewhat" (12 September). A little more than seven months later, in the same vicinity, the captain of the *Titanic*, E. J. Smith, did not display the same caution. "He had confidence in his new ship, and steered it blindly towards the ice that he knew lay ahead."[3]

Such dire thoughts were absent from the euphoric family reunion that awaited Adam and Elizabeth when they arrived at their residence on 14 September. The latter ended her revealing diary on the happy note that, "next night we unpacked the trunks & it was as much delight as a big Christmas." The Shortts' travels in the Old World had been generally pleasant and rewarding, but they were overjoyed to be back in their native land and their own home.

Saturday, 2 September

Adam's Diary[4]

Back in London, much detail to look after. Go to Bank, High Commissioners and long talk with Griffith.[5] Getting boxes out of store and looking up Can. Northern offices. Not much effect of recent strike visible.[6]

Elizabeth's Diary[7]

I went out after breakfast to Covent Garden to see it & to go to the Bank with Adam. He went on to Can. Com. for mail & I came home, too tired to do anything. We received a batch of letters from the children & Maud & Gertie & Mrs. Leslie & Mrs. Desborough. It is good to hear that George— my poor dear boy—had passed his matriculation with two supplementals: Geometry & German composition. He would have passed in Geometry if he had been well & I think will get them off in Sept.. That gives me something to think of: my boy thinking of College this year & Muriel wanting a ball. Oh I have things to do in plenty.

That evg. of Sat., being restless to achieve something, [I] washed my gloves, brush & hair & being tired went to bed before my hair was quite dry & in consequence had a very bad cold.

A Letter from Elizabeth to Muriel[8]

I did not get this started, having left off on George's letter, for my ink ran out & sight too to a certain extent. We left Amsterdam yesterday evening around 8 in the evg. & went on board the *Julianna* about midnight & (you see we had to go down to Flushing to get the steamer) & we reached Folkstone about 5:30 [a.m.] & [after] a lot of customs officers & fuss we got off for London & reached here before time. Although I got your father off to the Canadian [high commissioner's] office as soon as I could, we did not get back till after twelve & by the time I had read all the letters it was too late to get them at the Imperial Inst.[9] office, so I don't know whether they sent a servant, yet I will try to find out on Mon. & send you word—a card anyway.

If they have not been able to, you had better go to that agency on Albert St., & get them started to find one as well as Miss Mitchell. You will tell them we want a good general [servant], & if a good one, we will pay [$]15.00 [per month], but I will expect her to iron & wash the small things for I see we have come to the place where we must either have a wash woman come in or send out the sheets, tableclothes &c.. I expect we will have an awful pinch of money, but I really must have more servants even if we do without some other things.

I would like to talk to you about the dresses & other things. I think we will have the party. I think, as you know that that is only fair and reasonable, of which more again after I talk with Papa. I think the terms you write of are quite reasonable. About the dresses my dear. I only thought you would really need one new one and that that would be one to supply the place of the old green one, a dress you could wear short (& low necked evgs.) & wear afternoon occasions. I will read your letters over again, but, if I get a tunic one, I think I will not get any other. If you come over next year you will be able to get some when you are here. I have spent so much & Papa & I are both getting so many clothes to last awhile, & you had a turn last winter you know, with the idea that I was to have my turn this year. Well then you see if George goes to Coll., it's going to be [a] heavy [expense] & the party will be a goodish bit and then if you really want a muff, I'm afraid you will have to manage with one wholly new one [dress] unless we get a great bargain.

If I get a tunic, I think that other dressmaker can make the slip dress for underneath & it would not cost quite so much. They charged me [$]12.00 at one of the big places in the centre of London & supplied the satin & chiffon &c. & I supplied the tunic, so I don't think we should pay [$]12 for the simple making of a slip. I meant, of course, a gold (dull) silk slip with black ninon over it, but, if you would rather have a tunic I will look. I found it difficult to find things to suit me & being here & [*sic*] I am afraid to risk buying anything quite made up—lest it did not fit you well.

I've seen a number of simple things that might have done if you liked them & they fitted you. I was inclined to buy the strawberry one of Mrs. D. [Desborough], for I think she would have gladly sold it, but your father did not like it for some reason. It was a great bargain; I mean without the slip. I think it looked very well indeed when made up, & if a dress is not too expensive [and] is nice one gets much more out of it.

The reason I did not tell you about my dresses was partly because Miss Gibson was there, & you will see them very soon, but I am afraid they will be much crushed. Another bother in bringing any silk remade is the trouble about duty. We have a good bit of luggage & I've about as much as I can account for. How I do wish I had left the white dress & the strawberry one at home.

You speak of the letter next after the one you wrote from Edith Cory's[10]—well, it went astray. Today where you take up the story on the 16th of Aug. there is gap in your allusions. So why it did not reach us either in Vienna or Berlin I don't know nor did the two you forwarded with it [come] so far as we can remember. Yes, we are satisfied about Mrs. Laird & you are the dear, capable girl to get this settled as well as many of the other things. I think George must sort of make his debut at your party, just before he goes to Queen's. He will be 18 on 28th Sept.. I don't know what day that is, but it might happen to be a good one [for Muriel's party], but we can speak of it later. Papa brought a new evg. dress suit & his other one can be made to suit G. & he can wear it. You may be sure one waited anxiously to hear of nature [*sic*].

P.S. I see I am off in my dates on re-reading your letters. You see we will not get home before [Sept.] 14th or 15th. It would be so very sudden for me to have the party on the 22nd. Could the boys not wait till 26th! If they cannot, why we could strain a point, but 26th would be a soon enough [date], if the boys could wait. See if they can't.

Tell George I shall be so sorry he is not at home when I get there but I see on re-reading that he has to be in K. [Kingston] at that time. It is your letter written on 10th of Aug. that has gone astray. You speak of having written on Friday. I have a good deal to do on Mon. & Tues., but I'll look at tunics. My mauve hat is done up: I can't wear it home as it is.

I suppose George will return as soon as he can after writing on German Comp.. I hope you were able to help him a little & that he took time & energy for studying, whether he did any archives work or not. I have a good

FIG. 8   George Shortt. Courtesy of University of Waterloo Library, Special Collections & Archives, Elizabeth Smith Shortt fonds (WA10, file 2307, George Shortt).

many things ahead. It seems queer to imag[in]e George at College. I did not write him about your party & the evg. clothes but you can. If they don't fit we can get a tailor to fit them. That suit that he tried on we will pass on to someone else for he might as well have these better ones.

Will write Mon., I think.

Sunday, 3 September

Adam's Diary[11]
Tried to go to Temple church[12] but still closed as also The Abbey. Went out to south side of London on electric car, spent most of day going and getting back by another route but saw much of that side of city. Rather uninteresting.

Elizabeth's Diary

We started out in the morning for 10:30 service in the Temple church in Chancery Lane where there is such good choir music, having confidence that it was "just up there" & knowing that Temple Bar & the Law Courts were not so very far away. We walked & we walked. I find that Adam's usual way is to find out where a thing is by hunting for it while my plan is to ask in order to save energy. So going on Adam's plan we walked & walked up Chancery Lane, but no church, so I asked a man & he said it was away back near the Strand at the end of Chancery Lane, across the st.. Following his direction we found the church by going under an archway (as the man said opposite the end of Chancery Lane) but it was closed for what is called the Long Vacation i.e. during August [and early September]. Just over the arched entrance to this passage to the church &c. are four windows from which the sketches by Boz[13] were taken, four small screened windows.

Coming back to the Strand, we had a look at what commemorates the historic Temple Bar,[14] the Bar or Gate which gave entrance to London from Westminster in the days when London proper was walled or gated: how a handsome pillar in the centre of the Strand where it once stood tells & illustrates what was there of yore. Then we went toward home but turned off down another quiet lane & down some steps to the beginning of the Embankment Gardens.[15] After looking at some of the monuments & sitting down a bit, Adam proposed a st. car trip so we took the upper deck of a st. car & went across Westminster Bridge out beyond the other side thro. St. George's Sq., past Spurgeon's tabernacle, past a fine Park of flowers & seats & trees & people, [past] Streatham Common & later Kennington Park out to Norwood and changed cars & went on to Perley [*sic*][16] where we had tea & bread & butter & jam.

Then when we had returned to Norwood we went toward Sutton but changed back & went [on] a long road through Mitcham Common which was not very nice, having scrub of hemlock or something in many places. Then we changed cars at Tooting Junction[17] & while we waited there we saw another exhibition of London drinkers: a small frame structure divided by label outside into Public Bar [and] Private Bar. Before the first men drank in public & set their glasses on a shelf outside or went inside. The other a slightly better groomed looking lot of youngish men went in to & came out wiping their lips. Once a woman came out with a pitcher of beer & scuttled away.

When we reached home we still had time to have something more to eat & have a rest before we set out for Capt. Desborough's for supper at seven.

We began supper, just the four of us, in good spirits & before we were through Mr. & Mr. (Uncle & Nephew) Woollcomb came in & the uncle was *very* interesting. He wanted Adam's opinion for one thing: whether it was desirable for men to be emigrated without their wives. I discouraged this very much & Adam voted against it. Earl Grey & Lady Evelyn[18] had both been trying to make him think it would be a good plan, so the man could have a home ready for them. I think probably Lady Evelyn's sad impression came from families emigrated in the Fall. I told Mr. W. that we had so much desertion to contend with, that it was undesirable to help it on. Adam said if a man had to be assisted out, he would not give that man the chance to desert. I also told Mr. Woollcomb what Col. Sherwood[19] had said about the many appeals to him on that head from England.

After these gentlemen had left we subsided into more & more talk & came away before eleven saying friendly goodbyes & hoping to see each other again. Mrs. Desborough had a woman Drusilla Clutterbuck who wanted to go out [to Canada] as a servant because her husband & boy were going & they all had to work. So next evg. the woman came to see me & then next evg. the husband & woman but the husband is the drawback & I don't think there will [be] anything come of it.

Monday, 4 September

Adam's Diary
Spent most of day with Sir Alex King[20] and Mr. —— his assistant at the Post Office headquarters. Very interesting discussions. They have promised to compile report on working of British P.O. system. To Desborough's for evening[21] and usual good chat on many things.

Elizabeth's Diary
I wakened so ill with the cold in the head & body I could not go anywhere that morning & yet I did. We went up to Oxford St.[22] to get Adam's dress suit underway & bought George a dressing gown & then Adam went seeing men & I went [for] more shopping but gave it up at 12 & went home. We had a late lunch at Cecil Cafe[23] & then home & Adam went after more men. I had to rest most of that afternoon but later put a few things to rights.

Mon. before I left London—4th Sept.—I went to see Dr. Percy Flem[m] ing 70 Harley St. again & he was not very encouraging about my left eye & said to put a drop in every night [during the] crossing & to keep [a patch] on every second night till I had it operated on. That is another reason I don't want to read [during] this trip of any account. It is a dread to have this over me. Dr. Flem[m]ing is very kind & nice & I had quite pleasant chats [with him]. He may travel out to Can. some of these days.

Tuesday, 5 September

Adam's Diary
Did shopping most of forenoon. Saw Macmillans[24] re Grey-Elgin letters[25] &c. Spent afternoon at S. Kensington Museum,[26] especially in picture section. Interested in the engravings. Saw Sir H. Jost [*sic*][27] of Colonial Office in morning.

Elizabeth's Diary
I was still so miserable that I stayed in & did a few little things till noon. Then Adam & I went out to Kensington Museum & had our lunch & after I spent a little time there & found my eyes were not good for that sort of thing I went over to see Miss Lefroy at the Imperial Institute[28] about servants & emigration. She is a quaint, amiable looking Miss of many summers but has kindness written all over her. She told me that Ontario Provincial Govt. assisted domestics to £4 to come out, but those so assisted through them had to go to Miss Fitzgibbon in Toronto as she had to see after their return of [this] loan but she would try & send a few others to Ottawa in Oct..

After a very interesting conversation I came out & did some shopping on Brompton Road,[29] getting veil, gloves, blouse & blk. tights all in one place. Then when I reached home I found Mrs. Malden Literature Convenor of the Mothers Union waiting for me. We had a very nice talk about these things. I found her very nice & like most other nice women who do outside things, she was busy at home with husband & family & house, tho. now the family was getting quite grown up: one daughter studying to be a doctor & one at home helping her. She thought our library scheme a good one & offered to send me a list for Mrs. Woolround & her committee which she did next morning with pamphlets for which I paid 15 & 6D. & have not yet looked at.

Wednesday, 6 September

Adam's Diary
Got details wound up. Packed and got off to Bristol where we took the Royal George in evening, having a very comfortable stateroom adjoining the

Library. Much confusion in getting luggage and table seats. Mr. and Mrs. J. S. Ewart[30] on [board].

Elizabeth's Diary

After packing up the most of the remaining things, we went to Army & Navy store [illegible] along Victoria St.. It was a sight & I was glad I went. I know now what Christina McNab meant when she said in the mornings they always went or talked about going to the "staves." This Army & Navy store contains everything from a needle to an anchor & is indeed continued in another building across the street. Adam got his C.M.G. decoration[31] & a few things & I wanted to look at what Lady Hanbury Williams[32] told me about—the cane that unfolded as a seat. They had them in many varieties but they were not just as small & unnoticeable as I fancied they would be & did not feel yet that they would be of service.

We went home again after calling at the Canadian High Commissioner's & getting letters from Muriel & Minnie & Violet[33] & a bunch of papers. I read the letters while A. got water ready for Horlicks & then we finished up and Rogers (the handy able manager down stairs) secured a bus for us which took all our luggage & us to the train. It took about an hour. Arrived at Paddington [Station, where] there was quite a hurly burly of people getting off by the special to Bristol.

One of the guards' devices for gaining a lot of tips is to paste a label, "Retained" on the window of each coach & then you come hurrying along, passing each of these "Retained" looking for a coach. He steps up & says "how many seats, Sir? Two, oh this way" & he takes us back a little way & pops us in. Watching I saw him do the same to two young ladies who as well as Adam gave him tips. But no person else came to the coach, so who "retained" it? When one of these young ladies was talking to a young man before the door I heard him say "Dr. & Mrs. Shortt are going over by this boat." It was Charlie McLaren [*sic*],[34] but I don't know the young lady & yet I think I ought to.

When we went down by train we went a good part of the same route as to Oxford. The country still showed the effect of the drought. We caught a glimpse of Windsor Castle, & passed by Reading, saw the Thames a number of times &c. &c.. Arrived at Avonmouth (which you never hear of, but is the place one really sails from & not Bristol) we found the 3rd class passengers all on & we had a great plenty of time for there was such an awful lot of baggage. They did not get away till seven in the evg. & we went to dinner soon after.

While we were in the harbor two or three steamers with large excursion parties were sailing about. I think I never saw such a crowded steamer as these: they were on everything but the Two [illegible] it seemed. The scenery is lovely all along from Avonmouth: the wooded & settled land & the slope & the water was [sic] lovely & the moon rising.

Adam soon engaged chairs & got our places at table arranged for the Purser's table. The Ewarts & Mr. & Mrs. Moss[35] are on this boat & Charlie McLaren [sic] & Jack Sifton, tho. I have not seen the last two to talk to yet. There do not seem to be many, if any of the old waiters but there are some of the same Stewards. We have a very nice room: 127. It is on the deck on which the Library or writing room is & we are next to the writing room. Our cabin is wide & has a sofa wardrobe & usual bureau which holds all articles.

There are a great many passengers on: 200 first & a big crowd of others. A lot of the 2nd class are of 1st class kind. A Mr. & Mrs. Deacon (she is a daughter of the bad Hon. Emmerson)[36] have three fine looking little children & there are several children on board. There are a few of the passengers who went over with us, but not many. We have a stout person at our table, but not Mr. Johnson.

I must not forget that when we were going out on our st. car excursion in London we saw a big balloon sailing along with people in it. I do not know where it was heading for, but I see that mail is [to] be taken from London to Windsor by air ship. I don't know of what kind. We have had the papers which we got at Can. [high commissioner's] Office to read since we came on: *Globes* & [Ottawa] *Journals*. I have glanced over the last & feel I know something of what's on. I sit next Mr. Ewart at table. He is an odd mixture. Last night Mrs. Ewart & a few others dressed for dinner but I haven't got to feel like that yet. Perhaps I will later.

A Letter from Elizabeth to Muriel[37]

We leave in a few hours for Bristol & to sail. I could not write Mon. because tho. I found Mrs. Lefroy had not sent any servant, I was in pursuit of one I hoped to bring with me, but that is at least postponed. Miss Lefroy can send me one in early Oct.. We will, please God, be home soon after this letter. I hope you are not suffering much for the lack of servants but we will have a busy time.

I bought a tunic [for you], but not the least like Mrs. Doughty's nor what you spoke of, as I couldn't see one of bronze & green but I think you will like it. Love to each of my dear ones, but I suppose one of them is in K. [Kingston] when this reaches you. With so much love.

Thursday, 7 September

Adam's Diary[38]
Off Ireland in morning, very fine day but not going fast as machinery heating. Not very interesting passenger list. Judge Iddington[39] on. Officers of Can. contingent including C. H. McLaren.[40] Quite a number of Jews and some interesting young Englishmen going out on Engineering work.

Friday, 8 September

Adam's Diary
Another fine day and every one on deck. A number of young fellows going out as clerks for Can. Bank of Commerce. A Mr. and Mrs. Deacon of Toronto, broker, wife daughter of Hon. Mr. Emmerson.

Saturday, 9 September

Adam's Diary
Cold and disagreeable with sleet and fog. Not much pleasure on deck, fewer at meals. Read papers brought from England, and some things loaned by Ewart. Talks with Ewart, Iddington, and Deacon.

Sunday, 10 September

Adam's Diary
Some disagreeable weather.

Elizabeth's Diary
Yes this is Sunday on board the *Royal George* and the day is passing much like other days, mostly in taking three meals & two sups for those who can breakfast till 10 o'clock, then bouillon or beef tea at 11 luncheon at one & tea & bread & butter at 4 & then dinner at seven. I made up my mind to skip the tea & generally the beef tea & eat but little at each meal & no tea or coffee unless early in the day & no [illegible] &c. to fill my stomach with fluids & I am the better of [sic] this regime, the only thing my stomach actually rejected being a dose of Eno which I was foolish enough to try. I think too the port wine of which we take part of a glass at luncheon & dinner helps to keep us up & to sleep.

I do dread the night because of the confined sleeping quarters of the berth. Yet when I began to think of one or two fat people on board & how they could manage I thought I could live somehow. Theoretically the majestic motion of the boat over the big waves is all right but it has a trick of rolling human stomachs or nerves with it. It is odd how some people escape: Mr. & Mrs. & Miss Ewart are on board & they are not affected at all. Mrs. Ewart's nerves are well protected & you would judge it would take a lot to upset them.

I sent word to the matron in charge of the steerage to come & see me so I could find if there was a possibility of getting a servant. She is a Miss Price of good family & quite a varied experience in philantrophies [*sic*], emigrants &c.. Her description of the way the women & men in the steerage go on is truly schocking [*sic*] & this occurs on all the boats & yet we wonder at girls coming to grief. Girls & men lying on the deck with their arms around one another who two days before had never seen each other: married men & young men & these silly girls feel as if no rules or codes held them on board ship. There must be something done to protect them by giving more definite authority to the woman in charge. I felt sorry for Miss Price. She said she was a straw on the stream & they resented her advice as an interference &c..

Judge Idington [*sic*] is on board & is a genial big fellow & I am afraid I have been unjust to him through report but maybe he is a stern father anyway. It is not always safe to take hearsay as fact. Today being Sunday, we had Service which is always Anglican. If several Anglican parsons are on board they are all asked to take part but the service is the Morning Prayer: chants & hymns & lessons & Psalms. It only lasts about an hour. I had a good sing & enjoyed it & have felt better since. It is quite cold in our cabin which is on the north side & is quite cold on deck. There is a fire in the grate in the music room, but only a few can cover that [*sic*].

Monday, 11 September

A Letter from Elizabeth to Mother and Gertrude[41]

We are nearing Canada & expect to be in the [Cabot] Strait by midnight & so on the way up to Montreal, but we will not likely be in Montreal before Wed. night. This will I hope go off at Quebec [City] & will tell you that we are so far toward home in safety. I have had such very strange experience[s] since I left home & have travelled so far that I feel as if I have been away six months or a year. Time is truly measured in one's mind by events & so it is no wonder if it seems long since I lived at home in Ottawa.

I received a letter from you when I reached London & was very glad to hear you had both stood the summer's heat so well. It has been a summer to remember for heat & drought. Just think that we could be in England a month & not get rained on & only one cloudy day & no fog. I did not see a foggy wet day in England. And the same everywhere: so bright, so hot, so dry. I wore the thinnest most young womanish clothes & tho. I oozed a lot by perspiration, I rather enjoyed it, feeling by much drinking, perspiring & bathing that I would thus acquire better health, and I think I have. I think I look a lot better "fed" in the face and surely I can walk, or could walk, a lot more than when I went over.

I had the best of training you see. I had Adam's arm to hold to & we often did the unexpected & this put a trial on my muscles which at first upset my heart once or twice, but which in the end must have strengthened it too, for I've done too much once or twice more recently & have not had any effect on my heart so far as I know. I never expected to walk so much again each day, but, as I say, I had Adam's arm or in any case an umbrella for a cane.

I never ventured out without the umbrella for a cane, but, in any case I was able to do much & see much, tho. often so tired I was done up till I had a rest & a cold bath. Being hot & not always confident of their water we drank a *heap* of weak tea. We would have a "pot of tea" & a pitcher of hot water & in that way we would slake our thirst most frequently. I never had but one cup of good tea while on the continent & no where even in England do they think of giving one cream in the tea unless you ask for it or pay for it specially. Anyway, they don't seem to know how to make tea. They can make coffee all right. I suppose it is only "mad English people" who want water or tea to drink. As far as Switzerland there was consciously [*sic*] the "mad American or Eng." in the "tea room" but Austria & Germany are so given over to beers & wines that I saw no special tea rooms. But still we could get what they called tea when we asked for it & it served as drink, but I am longing for a real cup of tea as Canadians know how to make it.

The post offices in Austria & Germany do not seem to get things done with any despatch. We did receive some letters in Vienna, but some have gone astray. No doubt they are in Vienna or Berlin. It is rather difficult to guess whose letters they were that Muriel forwarded. She may be able to throw light on it when we get home. I think the German people are too much given to beer & thinking beer, for it seemed as if 9 women out of ten past middle life were all gone to fat & looked out of shape & unlovely or unintelligent in the higher sense, in the face.

We liked Amsterdam & the people. I seemed in going about the streets to feel I was akin & wondered which of its old streets my early parental ancestors frequented. I did not see any allusions to Anneke Laus, but there were frequent "Jansens." Adam went to see the archives but could not get in (it being Queen Wilhelmina's birthday). I wanted to go, but, as any documents would be in their own language it would not have profitted me much I suppose.

Our ideas of the Dutch as fat will have to undergo some change surely, for after Germany I did not think there were many fat [people in the Netherlands]. The women looked well kept & intelligent & active even when grey haired. There is an air of good living & thrift but no beer gardens as such. We found the streets of Amsterdam very interesting & could have enjoyed a longer stay than we had. As we went through Holland I was astonished by the number of cattle to the acre. I never saw so many cattle in a day as we passed by train getting to Amsterdam. I should not want to live there tho.. It is so very very low & wet & there is to me a sort of stagnant water smell, tho. they say there are engineering devices at the coast to suck the water out of the canals in Amsterdam so as to prevent malaria.[42] Much fruit is grown in some parts of Holland, & with plenty of cheese & milk & cream & fruit & beef &c.., they have every chance of [a] good living & a good market near them in England.

We sailed across to Folkstone in the night & to London by train which we reached on Sat., 2nd Sept.. We were thus too late to make our visit with Prof. & Mrs. Glover[43] in Cambridge, for we only had time to finish up & get away on Wed., 6th. We have had rather a slow passage as there were two heavy days when a great many of us were very miserable. Adam caught a cold too which did not make him feel any better. I have appeared at table each time but have been on my back most of the time till yesterday. I was anxious about my left eye, to have had drops in it each night, but so far it is all right.

There is a big passenger list: 200 & more first class about 300 2nd & something over 500 third. The time seems long for I do not dare to read & that is the best way of passing time. I have lots to do when I get home, if George is going to College & Muriel is set on a dance before he goes. With much much love to each.

Tuesday, 12 September

Adam's Diary[44]
Passed close to iceberg and slowed down almost to stop till fog cleared somewhat.

Elizabeth's Diary
We are in the Gulf of St. Lawrence & it is now raining & a high wind. I thank heaven it did not occur 24 hours earlier or our stomachs would all have been rolling about within us. It is thundering too & some lightening. I am so glad to be nearing home, tho. we are still quite a way from Quebec [City]. It is such a comfort on the ocean when one gets into Marconi [radio] connection & then later gets it with the shore as well as with some of the [other] liners. There are white caps & quite rough for the Gulf, but as we get farther up we will feel it less. This is just after luncheon & I have risked taking coffee.

Last Evg. we had a "whist drive" in progressive whist & we had a very good time. Adam & the purser invited the people to take part. There were 9 or 10 or more tables. There was a concert in the 2nd Cabin & an auction of food. So people were much engaged. Only a few have dressed for dinner evgs., but tho. I was willing to, I was always too cold. However, Adam & I both did last evg.. I wore my beetle green tunic & blk. satin [dress].

Today there have been sports on deck: pillow fights, threading the needle, potato [bag] race, cock fight, tug of war but the afternoon part has to be postponed on account of the rain. Yesterday afternoon Mrs. Ewart & I played double dummy at Bridge & competitive patience for quite a time & that put in some hours. I cannot read & I've written seven letters so cards form a good amusement. There are quite a few interesting people on board but being too under the weather at the start, I've not made so many acquaintances as perhaps I [normally] would.

I had another talk with Miss Price. She has found a girl Milly Wale who is going to Ottawa to her parents & also promises to come to me as general servant & is to report on Monday. She has the recommendation of having been in her [former] places 3 & 5 years & that seems good. I hope she turns up.

I suppose George is writing on his geometry today & is in Kingston. It will not be as I pictured it, to get home & no George there. People [on board] are interesting & various, quite various & yet common. I sit next—Mr. Ewart at dinner & he is interesting. He is a clever lawyer & writes too. They were most[ly in] Sweden & Moscow. Acquaintance improves Mrs. Ewart very much. She does very kind things. One should not judge people without knowing [them well].

A Letter from Elizabeth to Muriel[45]

Well dear heart we are in the Gulf of St. Lawrence & so tomorrow morning or possibly late tonight we may be able to send off mail & receive it at Quebec [City]. I hope I will receive a letter from you for we did not get any at Bristol. We received a letter from you in London before the post card. I received your card in London the day we left, so I asked both the post office Steward & Capt. Harrison, but no letter was forth coming. Capt. Harrison says he will forward it when it turns up. You did not say there was "Royal George" on it, but even if it were just Bristol care of Capt. Harrison, he said [it] would reach him & possibly might be sent on to Montreal to him. Well, we hope to reach Montreal Thursday & so if possible get on to Ottawa & be with you once again please God.

We are in the Gulf & it is quite cold. The sports are going on today but it is so cold I have not gone on deck for that reason & another in which you have more interest & that is engaging a servant. When the woman I thought was coming [on] this voyage failed to come I began to think of what might be on board this ship. I found that all of those who received [provincial] government help in their passage had to go to their destination [in Toronto].

However there is a Miss Price acting as matron to the 3rd class passengers & I applied to her & she has sorted one out of the hundreds who is going to Ottawa to her parents on Cobourg St.—I think 72 or somewhere near there. Her name is Milly Wale & she is 23, but she is no great cook. Her sister is being married on Sat. & she does not want to come to work for a week or ten days. She promised to come & see me on Mon. next to report. She has she says been 3 yrs. in one place & five in another. Of course you may have someone now, but I did not want to lose any chance. Don't do anything final about the dance till I can talk it over, as to date & people &c..

Papa has a cold, but we will not be seasick anymore now I think. I was all right yesterday & last evg. we had a progressive whist your father & the purser got up! We had a very pleasant evg. & your father seemed to enjoy it very well. Most of the ladies wore evg. dress & so did I, tho. it is the first time I've been warm enough to do it on board. Mrs. Ewart dresses for dinner every night but none of them are seasick a bit.

Well, goodbye for a couple of days & then we will have a lot to talk about. I think you will think I am looking better than when I went away. I am sending a letter to Geo. too to Kingston. I shall be sorry not to see him when we get home. I wish sups. had been held in Ottawa. With love & more love.

Wednesday, 13 September

Elizabeth's Diary[46]

Sept. 14th.[47] It was a case of crowing too soon for the wind or gale increased & in a short time made about half the passengers sick. I felt sick too & tho. I did not give up but played cards all evg. still it was the first meal I felt I would not take & did not. We were playing with Mr. & Mrs. Ewart & he had some sandwiches & lemonade brought up late in the evg..

Tues. [12 September] went as most days. They had sports in the morning which on account of rain did not get finished but were run off yesterday [13 September]. Last evg. the prizes were presented. Mrs. Deacon got two: one for a race, a souvenir pin of Royal George & for putting the eye on the pig, a box of candy. Yesterday afternoon Mrs. Deacon (neé Emmerson), Mrs. Butler (Col. Butler & wife are travelling to Canada on a tour—English) & a Mrs. Breckinridge & I had a nice game of bridge. It has been too cold to stay out, sit out, on deck & yesterday it rained. Going over I played but little [cards], but as I'm not suppose to read & too cold to sit out, I've played a good deal. Last evg. we had some very good music: a Mrs. Froelich from Berlin who now lives in Montreal. Her husband is with her & we call him the mosquito. It is funny that small resemblance to some animal that some have.

It was very lovely all day yesterday—I mean the scenery, not the weather, & the sunset behind the hills & the shadow which falls on the near shore when sunshine is still on the opposite hills. We had music in the early evg., & then the prize-giving & then Mr. & Mrs. Deacon [and] Miss Dodds (a very fine Eng. girl who is going to Winnipeg as governess to Mrs. Colin Campbell)[48] who is on board [*sic*]. We arrived at Quebec [City] about 11:15 [p.m.] & it was quite unsettling to come into contact with every day life on shore. The quarantine officer & other officials & mails & telegrams came on board, but the steerage passengers were not put off till early morning.

Thursday, 14 September

Elizabeth's Diary

This was a lovely morning & the River & banks are beautiful. I have been out on deck walking & standing for a long time but was driven in by the cold. They are bringing the baggage up from the hold to be in readiness for the landing at Montreal which we hope to do this evg. between five & six. We were not so fortunate, as to receive any letter at either Bristol or Quebec [City], tho. I quite expected one from the children. I am getting anxious for it is now weeks since the date of their last letters. There's a lot of packing going on this forenoon, but it will not take us long to do ours.

Now the stewards & waiters & all sorts are beginning to be excessively solicitous about one. The only time I've rung for the Stewardess she did not come & I've had no books from the library & I've not patronized the tea room, so I am not personally feeling under many obligations. Those who exact a lot have the deck steward, the café or tea room steward, the bedroom steward, bath steward/stewardess, boots [cleaner], table steward & head dining room steward & librarian to tip & the[y] most of them want from a dollar up, except the boots [cleaner] & librarian perhaps.

We have a whole lot to do before we land at home in the townships. There are quite a lot of Americans on board & a "colony" almost of Jews from Montreal & [the United] States & quite a few coming to see the country & pay visits as well as returning Canadians & those who like Miss Dodds & the young Bank clerks who are coming out to the Bank of Commerce & the young engineers for C. Northern & the men & officers of Can. artillery returning with their trophies won across the water. A *very* few got up at 5 [a.m.] & had a drive around Quebec [City] before the boat went on its way around 8 o'clock. The heat was on last evg. & we were warm enough again.

A perfectly lovely day but cold. I went up for a good walk up & down & up and down the deck, looking at the beautiful scenery along the great St. Lawrence River. It is fine: the sloping banks & the villages & farms & churches, the big churches & spires & monasterys [*sic*] or convents, make one feel that Quebec is as much dominated by R. Catholics as Austria.

Every one was more or less on the *qui vive*.[49] Some watched the trunks being taken up by pulley hoist from the hold to be put on the deck ready to [be] put off. Others watched the cleaning up of the rear deck where the usual crowd was missing, having been put off at Quebec early that morning. I stayed up on deck as long as I could stand the cold & then went down to the music room & joined a card table for one game [with] Mrs. Baugh of Hamilton & two others.

After lunch we packed & then went on deck for another walk. It was so lovely I wanted to stay out, but it was too cold. Later Mrs. Ewart, Mrs. Deacon of Toronto & Mrs. Butler (of Bristol, Col. Butler & wife being on a tour of Canada) & I had two good rubbers of bridge up in the café where we could see the shore from either side. Later when Mrs. Ewart had to go, Mr. & Mrs. Butler & Adam & I had tea & a talk. The C. [café] served what the[y] called high tea at 5 o'clock as we were supposed to get in at six. It was a dinner without vegetables as near as I remember. We had a very good meal, for we knew we would not have time for any later. We soon became much interested in the outside world & the time we would be docked. We had another chat with Captain Harrison about his two sons out west & his adored military-inclined younger son before we reached M. [Montreal].

It seemed a long time before we were able to get ashore at seven, for we knew our train went at 8 & we would have a hard time to catch it. We found that all the arrangements were very good. The great [baggage] shed is lettered & all baggage under S. is in one place & M. in another & so on. As it is carted ashore it is put in these respective lettered goals. Ours all got into place very soon except the small trunks of papers & we waited & waited for that—finally Adam thought of looking in the 2nd Class S. [shed] for it & found it. The custom office was obliging & the G.T.R. men too & we paid the cabman a dollar & he tore across the city to the station & we were in time all right.

It seemed impossible that we were really on the train for home. Mr. & Mrs. Ewart were also on & Judge Iddington & we steamed on. Mrs. Ewart & I played half whist patience & we put in a very good time till we reached Ottawa. We got out in the confusion around the building station & for the first time in our travels there were no porters available & we had to carry our own bags. We were not able to bring our trunks, but they came on next day all right.

When we got to our corner we saw the lights were on & I knew they were expecting us & sure enough all three were there. George found he could write on sups here & had already written on his geometry. It was good to see them again & see them so well. Lorraine had grown so much; she is up to my shoulders now. Everything was in fine shape & all were well. Lorraine going to school & taking her music [lessons]. They were all so delighted with their presents & felt very rich over it. It was such a pleasure to buy them presents & to see their pleasure in their own & mine & everything. We only had a few things [on hand] that night, but next night we unpacked the trunks & it was as much delight as a big Christmas. Next day was putting away day & now we are nearly settled into grooves & must turn to the day's work each day. Muriel wants a dance next week & then in ten days George hopes to go to the University & begin his course there.

Notes

1 Carl Berger, *The Writing of Canadian History: Aspects of English-Canadian Historical Writing, 1900–1970* (Toronto: Oxford University Press, 1976), 28.

2 Morgan, *"A Happy Holiday": English Canadians and Transatlantic Tourism, 1870–1930* (Toronto: University of Toronto Press, 2008), 365.

3 Alan Hustak, *Titanic: The Canadian Story* (Montreal: Véhicule Press, 1998), 77.

4 Queen's University Archives, Adam Shortt Papers (hereafter cited as ASP), box 11, Adam Shortt Diary, 2 September 1911.

5 Beginning in 1903, William Lenny Griffith was the permanent secretary at the Canadian High Commissioner's Office in London. Previously this Welsh immigrant had established himself as one of the first major exporters of wheat from western Canada to Great Britain; *Canadian Who's Who, 1910* (London: Times Publishing Company, 1910), 97.

6 There were two strikes in August, 1911 which deeply affected everyday life in London: a dockers' walk-out and a national railway stoppage, which together left the nation "in danger of collapse"; Juliet Nicolson, *The Perfect Summer: Dancing into Shadow in 1911* (Toronto: McArthur, 2007), 187; see also John Merriman, *A History of Modern Europe*, 2nd ed. (New York: W. W. Norton, 2004), 769.

7 University of Waterloo, Elizabeth Smith Shortt Papers (hereafter cited as ESSP), WA10, file 1772, Smith Short Diary, September 2, 1911.

8 ESSP, WA10, file 493, Smith Shortt to Muriel Clarke, n.d. [2 September 1911].

9 See ch. 3, n. 24.

10 See ch. 5, n. 30.

11 ASP, box 11, Adam Shortt Diary, 3 September 1911.

12 See ch. 2, n. 74.

13 "Boz" was a pen name occasionally employed by Charles Dickins.

14 This gate originally marked the western limits of the city and has at various times served as a ceremonial entrance for the British monarch, a site for displaying the remains of executed traitors, and a pillory where criminals were humiliated.

15 There were in 1911 three embankment gardens along the Thames riverside, but here Elizabeth appears to be referring to the Victoria Embankment Gardens which contain famous monuments dedicated to the Scottish poet Robert Burns and to Robert Raikes, who initiated Sunday schools in Great Britain.

16 Despite her misspelling of the name, Elizabeth is apparently referring to the London suburb of Purley, which from 1900 onward had become renowned for its impressive homes and gardens.

17 Tooting Junction was a transportation hub in the Tooting district, another London suburb which accommodated London's rich and famous such as the

celebrated British music-hall performer Sir Harry Lauder, who resided there from 1903 to 1911.

18 See ch. 3, n. 36.

19 Lieutenant-Colonel Arthur Percy Sherwood was the commissioner of Dominion police for Canada since 1882 after an illustrious military and law enforcement career. Like Adam, he lived in Ottawa and belonged to the Rideau Club; *Canadian Who's Who, 1910,* 207.

20 Sir Alexander F. King was in 1911 the general secretary of the General Post Office in Great Britain, an institution he had ably served since 1901; *Who's Who, 1915* (London: A. & C. Black, 1915), 1201–2.

21 Adam is apparently confusing events that had occurred the previous evening with those taking place the night of 4 September.

22 See ch. 2, n. 19.

23 The Cecil Café was a dining room in the Cecil Hotel on the Strand, which became the largest hotel in Europe when it opened its six hundred rooms in 1886.

24 The Macmillan & Co. firm began publishing in 1843, and by 1911 had become one of the most significant publishing houses in the world. Its chairman, Frederick Macmillan, received a knighthood in 1909.

25 The Grey-Elgin letters constituted the correspondence between Lord Elgin, governor general of Canada from 1847 to 1854, and Earl Grey, the British secretary of state for war and the colonies from 1846 to 1852, as they worked to implement responsible government and other reforms within central Canada.

26 The South Kensington Museum was originally founded in 1852 by Prince Albert, Queen Victoria's consort, to display one of the finest collections of applied art on earth. It is now known as the Victoria and Albert Museum.

27 See ch. 1, n. 80.

28 See ch. 2, n. 39.

29 Brompton Road was originally an ancient path from old London to the village of Brompton. It became a major shopping district with the creation of Harrod's department store in 1905.

30 See "Frequently Mentioned Names" on p. xxi.

31 Earlier in 1911 Adam had been made a companion of the Order of St. Michael and St. George by the British monarch; *Silas Smith, U.E.L., and His Descendants,* compiled by R. Janet Powell from history collected by Miss Gertrude Smith and other descendants (n.p., n.d.), 44.

32 Lady Anne Hanbury-Williams was the wife of Brigadier-General Sir John Hanbury-Williams, who was in 1911 in charge of the administration of Scotland. He had previously enjoyed a long career in the British military, which included

service as the governor general's military secretary in Ottawa from 1904 to 1909; *Who's Who, 1915,* 945.

33 See "Frequently Mentioned Names" on pages xxi–xx, and ch. 1, n. 66.

34 Although Mrs. Shortt misspells his surname, Charles Henry MacLaren was the son of the prominent Canadian banker and investor David MacLaren. He had been called to the Ontario bar after receiving a B.A. from Queen's in 1902 and an LL.B. from the University of Toronto three years later; *Canadian Who's Who, 1936–1937* (Toronto: Murray Publishing, 1936), 685. See ch. 7, n. 40.

35 The Hon. Sir Charles Moss was the chief justice of the Ontario Court of Appeals, a position he assumed in 1902, and he had married Emily Sullivan, the second daughter of the Hon. Robert B. Sullivan, a justice of the Court of Queen's Bench for Upper Canada. The couple had five children, three sons and two daughters; *Canadian Who's Who, 1910,* 168.

36 The Hon. Henry Robert Emmerson was an industrialist and politician who had served in both the New Brunswick (1888–1900) and Canadian (1900–1907) legislatures, including stints as premier of New Brunswick (1897–1900) and federal minister of railways (1904–7). In the latter year, he retired from politics to head two coal companies in North America, while maintaining residences in both New Brunswick and Ottawa, where, like Adam Shortt, he belonged to the Rideau Club; *Canadian Who's Who, 1910,* 73–74.

37 ESSP, WA10, file 494, Smith Shortt to Muriel Clarke, 6 September 1911.

38 ASP, box 11, Adam Shortt Diary, 7 September 1911.

39 The Hon. John Iddington was a judge on the Supreme Court of Canada, having been appointed to that esteemed position following a distinguished career as a lawyer and judge in Ontario. Like Adam and the Hon. H. R. Emmerson, Judge Iddington was a member of the Rideau Club; *Canadian Who's Who 1910,* 113.

40 Charlie MacLaren had served in the Canadian militia since 1900. He would play an important role in the Canadian forces dispatched to Europe in World War I, during which MacLaren rose to the rank of a brigadier general; *Canadian Who's Who, 1936–1937,* 685. See ch. 7, n. 34.

41 ESSP, WA10, file 1035, Smith Shortt to Damaris I. McGee Smith, 11 September 1911.

42 See ch. 6, n. 85.

43 See ch. 2, n. 71.

44 ASP, box 11, Adam Shortt Diary, 12 September 1911.

45 ESSP, WA10, file 494, Smith Shortt to Muriel Clarke, 12 September 1911.

46 ESSP, WA10, file 1772, Smith Short Diary, [13 September 1911]. See next note for explanation of appropriate date.

47 While this entry in Elizabeth's diary is dated 14 September, the events clearly occurred on the previous day.

48 Mrs. Minnie Campbell was the wife of the Hon. Colin Campbell, the attorney general of Manitoba. They had one son and one daughter; *Canadian Who's Who, 1910*, 34.

49 This French phrase literally means "who lives." To be "on the *qui vive*" connotes "to be on the lookout ... or wide-awake"; *Funk and Wagnalls Canadian College Dictionary* (Toronto: Fitzhenry and Whiteside, 1989), 1107.

Conclusion

In this final part of the book, I seek to connect the diaries and letters presented within to other questions of identity not discussed elsewhere. How, for example, did these 1911 writings relate to the Shortts' concepts of gender and class? What do they tell us about Adam Shortt's ongoing relationship with Queen's University at this time? What terms did the Shortts use to define the mother country's national identity? How did Elizabeth Shortt assess the visual art she confronted in Austria, Germany, and Amsterdam? Once again, the material furnished in the previous pages draws us into identity issues.

The introduction showed how the Shortts defined their gender relationships before and after their marriage in 1886. In accordance with contemporary values, Adam became the primary breadwinner in the family through his professorial position at Queen's University and his subsequent appointment in 1908 as one of two civil service commissioners in Ottawa. Looking after the home and children was Elizabeth's main priority, though in the early years her earnings as a teacher and medical doctor contributed vitally to family solvency. Once Mr. Shortt attained an adequate wage to support both his wife and children, Mrs. Shortt left the work force to concentrate on her growing familial responsibilities. As McLaren puts it, "home and children were almost entirely her responsibility as they were for other middle-class women of the times."[1]

For numerous Canadian women, these tasks provided a full and rewarding lifestyle during the late nineteenth and early twentieth centuries. However, Elizabeth remained interested in promoting women's rights, and she pursued this concern for many years to come. When she visited England in 1911, Shortt defined this commitment while favourably describing

Mrs. Malden, the literature convenor of the British Mothers' Union: "I found her very nice & like most other nice women who do outside things, she was busy at home with husband & family & house" (5 September). Married women looking after husbands and children in the home should also strive to advance women's rights within the outside world. For Beth, this meant improving social, economic, political, cultural, and educational opportunities for females through organizations like the NCWC and the Mothers' Union in Canada, as outlined in the introduction. This, then, was the heart of her social feminist creed. Meeting with like-minded women in Great Britain and Germany during her 1911 tour strengthened Shortt's determination to foster their common ideals.

However, the early writings in this volume further indicate that a devotion to multiple activities could create serious difficulties for Elizabeth. More specifically, the letters leading up to her decision to join her husband on the European trip disclose that by 1911, heavy family, social, and activist obligations had driven Beth to despair and depression. The impending trip abroad had become a virtual necessity for Mrs. Shortt on both a physical and a psychological level. "I am firmly convinced of this—that I must get away from every care & responsibility for awhile.... I feel I cannot go on doing & thinking as I have been or I will not live very long. I have never felt the broken feeling, the prostration I have the last time of being down" (12 June). The high cost of being a good wife, mother, and feminist was made evident in this correspondence before Elizabeth's departure for Europe.

Some historians have suggested that Mrs. Shortt suffered a more devastating blow during the years following her marriage to Adam. Bowden, for example, writes that "their common ground was sufficient for them to build a lasting marriage but their differing viewpoints resulted in a partial inward withdrawal by them both."[2] More recently, McLaren has contended that for Beth, in the period between 1886 and 1918, "her marriage was far less blissful than either she or Adam had hoped. Adam's frequent absences and the financial problems resulting from their failure to live within their means would continue to strain their relationship in the years to come."[3]

These views of a deteriorating bond between the Shortts may or may not be true. However, the couple's correspondence and diaries during their 1911 European visit fail to support this conclusion. On the contrary, the interaction of the Shortts in the Old World generally presents an image of mutual support and caring love.

Only one subject on the long journey caused Elizabeth to seriously criticize Adam's behaviour. On 30 July, in a desperate tone, Mrs. Shortt informed her daughter, Muriel: "Your father runs off occasionally to old book stores & we will have to buy another trunk or case to ship them all home. It fills me with despair to see so many more going into the house" (30 July). A little more than two weeks later, while in Berne, she lamented that "Adam was taken with the morbid desire to spend an hour or more in a 2nd hand book store looking for things he did not have" (15 August). More will be said of Mr. Shortt's obsession with buying and collecting historical volumes and artifacts when we discuss his class identity. Here it suffices to note that it was only natural for a conscientious housekeeper like Elizabeth to deplore sharing any further space in their Ottawa home with an ever-growing number of printed materials, which were prone to collect more and more dust.

However, this single annoyance was more than counterbalanced by Adam's numerous displays of a deep affection for his wife during their travels in the Old World. Elizabeth noted that Adam was "busy all the time" during the early days in London (26 July), as he met many British officials to discuss civil service issues. Nevertheless, he always found time to visit his wife at Miss Lancaster's hospital while she recuperated from her eye operation. And for Beth, "Adam's daily visit" constituted "the best hour of each day" (9–16 July). Mr. Shortt also assumed her responsibility for corresponding with their children, as well as his wife's mother and sister in Hamilton (8, 9, 10, 14, and 18 July).

This last activity could be viewed as an emergency measure necessitated by Mrs. Shortt's temporary hospital stay. However, even after she returned from Miss Lancaster's establishment, Adam played a vital role in the shopping pursuits that were so important to his spouse during her visit to England. In fact, Mr. Shortt accompanied his wife on three separate excursions to clothing stores (21, 24, and 31 July) and at least once spent an entire "forenoon" there (24 July). Moreover, Adam sometimes assumed a major role in the decisions that were made at these outlets. For example, on 21 July, Mrs. Shortt purchased a tunic and then reported: "I had no intention of buying a tunic but Adam liked it and it was such a reduced price I did take it."

In at least one instance, Mr. Shortt even exercised a veto over a likely acquisition by his wife. On 2 September, Beth informed Muriel: "I was inclined to buy the strawberry one [dress] of Mrs. D. [Desborough], for I think she would have gladly sold it, but your father did not like it for some reason." Adam's objection to this purchase for Elizabeth's wardrobe was enough to prevent the move. Mr. Shortt was a useful consultant in Mrs. Shortt's final decisions about what should be acquired in London's vast, but also perplexing, clothes market.

Beth could also be a supportive force in Adam's personal pursuits. Bowden reveals that she "and her daughters always were proud of his intelligence and his accomplishments."[4] This assertion is evidenced by the Shortts' involvement in a dinner at Oxford on July 28. Writing to Muriel two days later Elizabeth proudly outlined her husband's dominance at this gathering of academics: "we spent the evening listening to your father talk & it was talk worthwhile too. Adam kept asking him [an Oxford professor] questions whenever he came to a stop which meant that the others of us only occasionally did anything more than listen. The men ate & smoked & drank coffee & smoked again & then again & then had lemon & soda & then smoked again, so it was beautifully arranged—your father not smoking did all the talking while the others did as above mentioned." McLaren has pointed out that throughout her life, "Elizabeth clearly loved being the centre of attention."[5] But by 1911, she was willing to let her adept husband embrace that position where it seemed fitting, as it had in Oxford.

Occasionally the Shortts exhibited a united front on prominent issues, which made their comments all the more formidable. This was the case at a soirée presented by the Desboroughs, where one of their uncles wanted to know whether the Canadian guests thought it was appropriate for the British government to encourage financially the relocation of male emigrants, but not initially their wives, to the empire's colonies throughout the world. Once the men had established themselves in colonial settings like Canada, it was assumed that they would finance the emigration of their wives so that the families could be reunited on more prosperous terms. Both Elizabeth and Adam decisively rejected the proposal. The former denounced the project because it was liable to foster the already high rate of desertion in her homeland. Her husband was even more blunt: "if a man had to be assisted out, he would not give that man the chance to desert" (3 September). Nothing is known about the uncle's response, but at least he could not find fault with the clarity of the Shortts' replies.

There were times when the Shortts went their own ways, and their relationship was flexible enough to accommodate such diversity. For example, in Switzerland the athletic Mr. Shortt could not resist a temptation to join two Germans in a mountain climb near Spiez. This decision reflected gender assumptions in a period when such an activity was considered a "masculine pursuit."[6] Meanwhile, Elizabeth spent an enjoyable day writing up her diary, which had been neglected after the onset of her eye problems

(12 August). A few days later, when Adam was visiting the Swiss state department to talk about civil service operations, it was Mrs. Shortt's turn to go "on a toot of my own" in Berne. Here she witnessed a marketplace site, which was unique and interesting (15 August). Beth, still recovering from her eye operation, proudly informed her children, "I did a big stunt all by myself" (16 August).

On occasion, an independent Mrs. Shortt could dominate a situation just as Adam had done at the Oxford dinner. For example, she was expected to get the Doughtys, as well as Mr. Shortt, going while they all resided at the Savoy Mansions. As her diary made clear, the task was not an easy one: "It was the difficult thing to get anyone to start mornings. I think they must have got into bad ways while I was at hospital. Adam was able to get underway long before the Doughtys & she [Mrs. Doughty] was the most indulged & often miserable" (4 August). Elizabeth could be an effective leader whenever she was asked to undertake the role. The diaries and letters appearing in this volume divulge a complicated gender relationship between the Shortts. However, it further demonstrates love, understanding, and reciprocal help. These qualities may have declined in the future, but during the couple's 1911 visit to Europe they remained vibrant and impressive.

The introduction, further, revealed how the Shortts defined their class attitudes. They generally moved in circles belonging to the upper middle class. However, when the opportunity arose, they ardently pursued contacts with the upper class, which in turn caused several problems for Adam and Elizabeth. First, it encouraged a social snobbery, which historians like Bowden, Ferguson, Allen, and McLaren have detected. Second, it led to overspending and chronic financial difficulties for the Shortt household, as "Elizabeth and Adam succeeded in convincing the well-to-do and powerful members of society that they belonged to their group."[7] The Shortts' diaries and letters during their 1911 travels further document these conclusions.

As we saw in the introduction, shortly after his arrival in Ottawa, Adam Shortt and Arthur Doughty, the Dominion archivist, became academic collaborators. Soon they were intimate friends, as well. Thus, it was only natural that the newly remarried Doughty and his bride, Kathleen, decided to travel with the Shortts on their sojourn to the Old World. More surprising was the Doughtys' offer to share their accommodations at the Savoy Mansions with the Shortts in London. By then, Elizabeth was suffering the full effects of glaucoma and the distressed couple had made no prior reservations. Nonetheless, the Doughtys were in Europe to honeymoon, a situation in which a premium is usually placed upon privacy. The Doughtys were indeed good friends, and a fine example of the sort of successful middle-class professionals with whom the Shortts generally associated.

Not long afterward, Adam supplied to his two oldest children a list of other Canadians whom he had met at Lord Strathcona's reception for colonials at Debden Hall, his country estate. These were all persons whom Muriel and George "would know," and by inference the kind of people that Adam hoped they would know even better in the future: "Mr. & Mrs. Ewart, Senator & Mrs. Power, Senator Watson, Hon. Geo. E. Foster, Lt. Gov. Gibson of Ont., Mr. O'Halloran, Wilfrid Campbell, Mrs. Fielding ..." (18 July). John Ewart was a distinguished constitutional lawyer residing in the federal capital, who often travelled to London to present briefs on behalf of the Canadian government to the British authorities. Gibson was the lieutenant governor of Ontario, who had been appointed by the Tory Whitney government after distinguished political service in Liberal provincial administrations. All the others belonged either to Ottawa's political or bureaucratic elites.

Mrs. Shortt's need to convalesce from her recent eye operation prevented her from attending this lavish open house, supplied by a self-made Canadian millionaire who represented his native land as her high commissioner in London. However, Elizabeth obviously regretted this circumstance, because, as she stated, "it was the place I most wanted to go" (21 July). Whenever possible, she and her husband were also eager to mingle with the upper class.

This inclination became readily apparent on their crossing to England during June and July. In the process, they revealed a snobbery that often characterized their social life. On board the *Royal George*, the Shortts and the Doughtys formed an exclusive quintet with Lord Percy, the heir to the Duke of Northumberland's title (28 June). He was returning home to wed a daughter of the Duke of Richmond following a stint as aide-de-camp to Earl Grey, who had recently stepped down as Canada's governor general. Two days later, Adam reported that Percy "mixes with none beyond our party" (30 June). On the next day, Mr. Shortt expressed "little interest in [other] passengers," including those in the first-class section, whom he had previously dismissed as "very ordinary people" (29 June). Adam was content to enjoy our "good chats at our alcove table" in the dinner room (2 July) and other activities, such as a tour of the ship (4 July) and card games (5 July) within the select circle he had organized among the Doughtys, Lord Percy, and his wife.

Beth was also enthusiastic about establishing "a table by ourselves" (28 June). In a similar fashion, she did not show much more regard than her husband for the other first-class travellers on the *Royal George*. As Mrs. Shortt wrote, "I do not fancy they are very interesting, tho no doubt some of them would be if talked to" (2 July). However, she did little to initiate conversations—which would have tested this theory—except for two teas with Jessie Ewart (29 June and 4 July), the wife of John Ewart. As we noted in Adam's comments a few paragraphs ago, this couple was numbered among the Shortts' close friends in Ottawa. Nevertheless, on the journey to Britain, Mrs. Ewart was reduced to a minor role, as Elizabeth and Adam seemed intent on pursuing their primary relationship with Lord Percy and the Doughtys.

A desire to mingle with the upper class was further evident during the visit to England. As we saw in chapter 3, Beth was thrilled by the visit of Lady Chichester, the head of the British Mothers' Union, on 31 July. Adam was equally intent on spending time with another aristocrat, Philip Kerr, who was destined to become the eleventh Marquess of Lothian. Kerr had already called on Shortt in Ottawa, where they had developed a close rapport. Mrs. Shortt noted that her husband, "had been dined & wined & suppered & tead by quite a few men" in England, but Kerr stood out as the one "he likes ... well" (19 July). When Kerr and Shortt got together for a private dinner on August 3, the latter provided some rare details of the conversation in his typically brief diary accounts: "Talked Irish Home Rule, Imperialism, Immigration & c. till midnight. Very interesting evening." It was one of the few occasions on the trip where Adam had described an encounter as "very interesting." As Elizabeth noted, her husband "had a very long tete a tete with Kerr" (3 August).

However, the person who most profoundly affected Mrs. Shortt on her European excursion was a Canadian, Maude Grant. Mrs. Grant had wed her husband, William Larson Grant, on 1 June 1911, and she was for Beth "a type after my own heart, about as near a complete woman I know of.... I think W. L. was indeed lucky" (28 July and 3 August). Two days later, she further described Mrs. Grant as "delightful ... up to date & cosmopolitan" (30 July). After a final meeting on 4 August, Elizabeth hoped that she would see the Grants soon after they had all returned to Canada. Mrs. Grant had favourably impressed the older Mrs. Shortt to the point of achieving almost ideal dimensions. Thus, an examination of Maude's class origins and orientation reveals a good deal about Elizabeth's own perceptions on this subject.

Maude was a daughter of George Parkin, and he soon recognized her as the most intelligent child in the family.[8] Like the Shortts, Parkin became deeply immersed in education. For example, appointed in 1895, he served as the headmaster of Upper Canada College for seven years, converting "a moribund institution" into "the premier private school in Canada."[9] In 1902, he left this comfortable position to become the first secretary in charge of the Rhodes Scholarship program. Constantly travelling throughout the empire and the United States until his retirement in 1920, he made these grants into one of the most highly esteemed awards within the English-speaking academic community. While on these journeys, Parkin never lost an opportunity to promote imperial unity and British interests on the world stage.[10] His aggressive views on these subjects often alienated many anti-imperialists within the empire during the early twentieth century, including Adam Shortt.

Parkin's daughter, Maude, was more supportive, and she emerged as "his confidante," because he "could talk to her as to no one else in the family." Like Elizabeth, Maude distinguished herself on the university level. Miss Parkin won a scholarship to McGill, where she became one of the first women to graduate from that institution. Five years later, Maude emerged as the assistant dean of women at Ashburn College within the University of Manchester. Whenever possible, she worked with her father to complete his biography of Sir John A. Macdonald for the Makers of Canada series, where Adam Shortt had achieved considerable success after publishing his account of Lord Sydenham's life. Soon Maude's busy schedule in Manchester limited her ability to assist her father in this task. Thus, George Parkin prevailed upon William Lawson Grant, who had previously taught at Upper Canada College when the former was principal, to help both him and his daughter with their literary enterprise.[11]

Willie Grant had recently been appointed a lecturer on colonial history at Oxford University. While there, he often visited the Parkins in their home at Goring-on-Thames. Moreover, he welcomed this opportunity to facilitate a sorely needed volume on Canada's first prime minister. His intellectual cooperation with Maude on the Macdonald book eventually developed into a deep mutual love. Shortly afterward, William "wrote a sweet but somewhat priggish letter asking her to marry him so that, together, they could do great things for Canada." Maude accepted the proposal, and the couple were wed in Goring's Anglican church on 1 June 1911.[12]

The marriage united two of the most prominent families in Canada's intellectual elite. George Parkin's place in the Dominion's educational circles was firmly established by 1911. William Grant was the son of George Munro Grant, the former principal of Queen's University who had such a profound influence on both Adam and Elizabeth and many other Canadians, including Parkin. The latter recognized the historic significance of the union when he congratulated Maude and Willie on their naming of a son, born on 13 November 1918: "It is good of you and William to wish for the combination of names which will carry onward the two family traditions. I hope he will prove a worthy descendant of the really great grandfather [George Munro Grant] as well as my humbler self."[13] George Parkin Grant ably fulfilled this expectation by dedicating himself to a highly successful teaching and publishing career at the university level. Moreover, in pursuing this vocation, H. D. Forbes notes that George P. Grant "belonged to an educational and political elite identified with loyalty to the British empire and belief in its civilizing mission."[14]

The Shortts liked the company of academics and intellectuals as well as government men and their wives, and especially those who had distinguished themselves in either or both fields. Maude Grant's ties to Canada's academic elite by birth, career, and marriage made her attractive to Elizabeth, whose letters divulge an abiding interest in socializing with university personnel, even after the move to Ottawa. For example, Beth's letter to her mother on 12 June 1911 revealed that during the past few days, the Shortts had entertained several academics, such as Prof. Mathieson and "Prof. Andersen Tearasen from California." Even more impressive were visits by two heads of the relatively small number of Canadian universities operating in this period: President Walter Charles Murray of the University of Saskatchewan and Principal David Miner Gordon of Queen's. Finally, the next evening had been reserved for "a Queen's dinner" in Ottawa, where Mrs. Shortt was scheduled "to speak ... to the women graduates." It was obvious that the Shortts had retained numerous academic contacts, even after their move to the nation's capital and Adam's assumption of a leadership role in the federal civil service.

The subsequent trip to Europe further indicated that Mr. Shortt's connection with Queen's as a trustee gave him considerable clout in determining that university's future development. On 28 July, Mrs. Shortt's diary observed that "Adam saw the Principal [Gordon of Queen's] often these days about new men" for the university's faculty. In fact, Gordon and Shortt had been commissioned by Queen's to hire full-time teaching staff for the institution in England without any further consultation with the existing faculty or administration back home. It was an extraordinary responsibility, especially since the two were making decisions for departments in which neither had extensive training, such as English and classics (18–20 July). There was no doubt that Adam remained a major player in influencing the evolution of Queen's.

Nevertheless, the Shortts' social interaction with academics, politicians, and senior civil servants in Ottawa was not entirely a positive experience. The frequent dinners, teas, and other forms of entertainment proved costly, and often led Adam and Elizabeth into debt. McLaren, for example, included the 1911 excursion to Europe among the "trips they could not afford": "They sailed first class on the S.S. Royal George and stayed at the 'fancy Savoy Mansions' in the wealthier section of London. They also bought a considerable amount of clothing when they were away, though Elizabeth complained constantly about having nothing to wear. The costs of that trip increased dramatically when she underwent surgery for glaucoma while away."[15]

Some of these criticisms appear unfair. The Shortts could not have anticipated the unexpected medical expenses arising from Elizabeth's sudden encounter with glaucoma. The onset of this serious disease also meant that the distressed couple had to obtain suitable accommodation almost immediately after their arrival in London. However, McLaren's comment about the Shortts' purchase of a considerable amount of clothing seems very relevant, particularly with regard to Elizabeth's activities in the imperial centre.

Elizabeth's own list of such acquisitions, which is appended to the Shortts' other writings in this volume, attest to Beth's extravagance when shopping for clothes. In all, some nineteen items were bought. On 2 August, about halfway through the journey, she confessed to Muriel: "I've bought all I intended to and more and have paid a bit more than I intended." Nonetheless, a number of further articles were procured. As Mrs. Shortt prepared to return to Canada on 2 September, she informed her eldest daughter that the two dresses the latter had expected would be reduced to one new outfit, because "I have spent so much on clothes." Elizabeth readily admitted the overindulgence during her eight visits to London's alluring clothiers.

On only one occasion did Adam record a personal visit to an establishment where he "did shopping and ordered clothes &c." (8 July). However, his prodigal habits became evident during numerous trips to bookstores and shops that marketed historical artifacts. Shortt simply could not resist entering these outlets to hunt for rare materials, especially those relating to Canada's history. Across Europe, he sought such objects on no less than fifteen separate occasions (18, 22, 23, 24, 26, 27, and 31 July; 2, 4, 15, 25, 28, and 30 August; and 1 and 2 September). Shortt did not identify the books he purchased, though he displayed an interest in "1st editions of Dickens" (23 July). However, he was more specific about some of the artifacts he secured. In England, Adam bought a "portrait of Lord Durham" (11 July), "old Queen Ann Candlesticks" (22 July), and "prints of people connected with Canada" (27 July). On the continent, he resumed the search, and in Berne "got an old map of America, Munster's 1596" (15 August), and while in Berlin, a "picture of battle of Queenston Heights" (28 August).

These were interesting and valuable acquisitions, but the prices were no doubt high. Moreover, as we have already seen, Adam's bibliomania deeply offended his wife, who dismissed the trait as a "morbid desire" (15 August). Most importantly, it revealed that both Shortts had serious problems creating a realistic budget, even after Adam's entry into the federal civil service considerably enhanced their income. As McLaren states, "they became more interested in upholding social pretensions than living within their means."[16]

The Shortts spent much more time in England than any other country during their 1911 excursion, and their writings on the mother country extend over four chapters of this book. Thus, their examination of the British identity deserves special and thorough attention. Like most English Canadian visitors to the mother country, Elizabeth and Adam viewed London "as the centrepiece of a transatlantic world."[17] There was a great deal that they admired about the British people and the traditions and institutions they upheld. At the same time, the Shortts joined a number of anglophone Canadians in criticizing various aspects of the British way of life.[18] In the end, they presented a well-balanced analysis of the English identity.

Some of the principal attractions for the Shortts in England have already been discussed within this volume, such as Elizabeth's interest in British clothes shops and the appeal of London's bookstores for Adam. However, the Canadian couple also enjoyed many more features of the British culture, which have yet to be mentioned. For instance, Mr. Shortt was moved by the "beautiful singing" of the boys choir at St. George's Chapel in Windsor (9 July). His wife was even more delighted with her visit to this site at a later date: "It was the best boys singing I suppose there is & it was most satisfying" (30 July).

Lord Percy had secured tickets for the Shortts to watch the British parliament debate constitutional issues raised by the refusal of the House of Lords to pass the Asquith government's national insurance bill. Mrs. Shortt came away from this lively exchange with the confidence that both houses of parliament "have such an appearance of richness & stability that one is quite satisfied with it as the home of English History" (2 August). For the Shortts, the essential solidity of the British parliament provided the foundation for Canada's own political soundness.

The Shortts were especially interested in historic sites, and Elizabeth was pleased to discover that their London guides, the Desboroughs, lived in such a setting at 20 Cheyne Court. "Everything is Cheyne around there, named after Lady & other Cheynes hundreds of years ago, but made famous by Carlyle's residence on Cheyne Row nearby & which we saw" (2 August). Mrs. Shortt also praised the practical efficacy of many English organizations, such as London's water supply and sanitation system. Her activist campaigns in Ottawa focussed around similar interventions by local governments, and she regarded the imperial centre's more advanced reforms as progressive improvements. Later that same day, Elizabeth lauded an initiative of the British national government: a retirement home for old soldiers in the Chelsea barracks. Nearby was a school for children of contemporary service men. She viewed both institutions as a "credit to one civilization that must have its soldiers" (7 August).

However, Adam and Elizabeth also reacted negatively to various aspects of the English lifestyle. Mrs. Shortt was, for example, shocked at the poor working milieu, which even first-rate physicians like Dr. Flemming had to endure in London. She sounded like a twenty-first-century environmentalist when she proudly wrote: "In Canada all the expenses are less ... we live, we have a chance to have ground enough to have something green & our view is not confined to bare stone or brick in walls & pavements" (31 July). As we will soon see, this was not the only, or even most noteworthy, criticism that Shortt levelled against the British medical system.

Elizabeth believed that the English people were poorly informed about the actual circumstances in Canada, an attitude Beth shared with many other English-Canadian travellers to the mother country. As Morgan states, "imperial stereotypes and ignorance of Canada might linger and, at the very least be a source of irritation."[19] Elizabeth was convinced the British perspective on Canada was mainly drawn from unreliable immigration agents in the Dominion who presented false impressions of conditions there (31 July). Here she was reiterating an evaluation presented by her husband in 1895: "the immigration literature circulated with regard to Alberta and other parts of the North-West is grossly deceptive ... the advantages are greatly over rated ... the disadvantages and hardships which are faced are almost ignored."[20] Mr. and Mrs. Shortt were again displaying a unity of thought that shaped many of their responses.

Elizabeth became further disturbed with the English handling of another emigration question: the movement of potential servants from the mother country to Canada. British servants were generally considered "superior" among most middle-class Canadian housewives, because recruits from the mother country were deemed "both capable & respectful, characteristics often lacking in native-born women."[21] Thus Beth avidly sought potential employees for her sister-in-law and for herself at London's Imperial Institute. This organization was dedicated, among other things, to relocating prospective servants from the mother country throughout the British Empire's self-governing colonies. Mrs. Shortt admired this objective, but she was disappointed with the organization's inability to deliver on the noble purpose.

For Elizabeth, the Institute's well-meaning employees were hopelessly mired in "red tape." They were simply "doing things in a perfunctory, mechanical sort of way" (3 August). In this instance, a negative result was readily apparent. Mrs. Shortt left Great Britain without any firm promises for aspiring servants to help either Christina Smith or herself.

Sometimes Adam and Elizabeth responded both positively and negatively to the same event. For example, after attending a Sunday service at the renowned St. Paul's Cathedral in London, Mr. Shortt noted the "good music" but also the "wretched sermon" (23 July). His wife displayed the same ambivalent perspective when she described the speakers at Hyde Park as "freaks and faddists" who indulged in "crank talk." At the same time, these quarrelsome figures carried on the vital tradition of freedom of speech, which was such a significant aspect of the Anglo-Saxon legacy in Canada. Moreover, as Elizabeth observed, this cherished trait was much needed in Great Britain at this fateful moment in the country's history: "Now in the crisis & altercation about the powers of the Lords & the lively state of English politics there is room for a lot of talk certainly" (30 July).

As was indicated in the introductions to chapters 2 and 3, the Shortts were delighted with their trips to Oxford and the Festival of Empire in Sydenham. However, in the midst of both these satisfying events, the Canadian couple found negative elements to criticize. In Oxford, Elizabeth complained about the lack of modern conveniences: "It is odd to think that in the 20 or 21 Colleges at Oxford that they still have no baths. Their daily bath or whatever must be carried there & carried off again & the bath is taken in what we would call a baby's bath tub! It is only three years since All

Souls got electric light & they have no telephone at all in Oxford & a horse car system that is not very frequent or expert" (29 July). When he visited the Festival of Empire, Adam was disturbed by the vendors of bogus services while his wife lamented the constant need to pay for questionable benefits (1 August).

The Shortts also agreed that the Canadian presentation at this exhibition was, in Mr. Shortt's words, "very good." However, this led Beth to reflect again on Great Britain's persistent failure to comprehend Canada's multiple achievements: "the English seem to take no interest in Canadian affairs unless it be cabinet changes—or the north west harvest—which is entirely a money interest" (1 August). She was repeating a theme developed by many previous anglophone Canadian visitors to the mother country, especially those arriving in the late-Victorian and Edwardian periods.[22]

Thus, the Shortts' evaluation of the British identity included both positive and negative elements, an approach that also characterizes another topic, which Elizabeth covers in great detail within her diary. During her long stay at Miss Lancaster's private hospital in London in early July, Dr. Shortt presented an astonishing, yet balanced, critique of the medicine practised there. More specifically, the physician from Canada delivered a revealing analysis of the differences between the medical therapy in England and her native Ontario, which merits a thorough account in this conclusion.

Throughout the ordeal, Elizabeth lauded the surgeon who treated her glaucoma, which could easily have led to partial or even complete blindness. As she put it in a letter to her mother and sister after the successful procedure had been completed, "I think truly the Lord led me across devious ways & all wonderful to get to this surgeon to save my sight.... It is a wonderful operation & I was fortunate to have one of London's best men to do it" (22 July).

Dr. Percy Flemming emerged as an "interesting friend" for Mrs. Shortt (2 August). Nevertheless, her admiration for the doctor did not deter Beth from grumbling about the high cost of his fees and the other expenses incurred at Mrs. Lancaster's private hospital, which seriously depleted the couple's resources (22 July). Dr. Shortt's criticism of Dr. Flemming's charges do not seem entirely justified. As we have seen, Elizabeth acknowledged that he was one of "London's best men." This placed him in the city's medical elite, where the monetary rewards were exceptional. If the sick employed members of "the London 'great' as they were called.... Patients were expected to know their place," while paying their bills promptly and without complaint.[23]

However, the steep prices at Miss Lancaster's enterprise were another matter. The prominent British medical historian, Brian Abel-Smith, has pointed out that "exorbitant charges were demanded by many of these private operations which in early twentieth-century England were called 'nursing homes.'"[24] During this era, Sir Henry C. Burdett, a contemporary expert on hospital administration in England, suggested that a rate of four guineas per week would leave a nursing home with a fair profit.[25] Dr. Shortt was nonetheless paying around fourteen guineas per week for the various services at 29 Wimpole Street (17 and 22 July). Miss Lancaster's invoice appeared immoderate in terms of the medical costs existing in early-twentieth-century London.

Abel-Smith further asserted that the services in these expensive nursing homes were often "unsatisfactory,"[26] an accusation Elizabeth documented in her diary. She complained about the anaesthetist who committed two errors even before the operation had begun. "I should have had a liver cathartic at once, when Dr. F. said I had to be operated on & then I should have had strychnine sometime before the chloroform" (7 July). Nothing else was said about these oversights, but greater attention was directed at various failings of the nurses who attended Elizabeth. Herein lay the main sources of her grievances against Miss Lancaster's nursing home.

From Beth's perspective, the nurses at 29 Wimpole Street failed to fulfill "the many personal service tasks of bedside care, feeding patients, assisting them with ablutions, and maintaining the cleanliness of bed and patient alike," which were considered essential responsibilities by contemporary nurses in Canada.[27] Shortt's diaries furnished several examples of the British nurses' shortcomings in this regard. One attendant refused to facilitate a bowel movement for some six hours, because the procedure was not scheduled within this temporal framework. She relented only after Shortt's refusal to eat finally caused the nurses to acquiesce on this matter. Another nurse neglected to bring her tea before a meal so that she could regain a proper heartbeat. Moreover, Shortt described a night nurse looking after her as a "modern Sarah Gamp"[28] who was unable to arrange the pillows in a comfortable fashion. Later she also failed to turn Beth's head properly before she retired. Finally, the same attendant advised her patient to take aspirin if she had trouble sleeping. Once more, Dr. Shortt simply ignored the nurses' injunction (9–16 July).

Shortt believed the main cause of these flaws originated in the "more or less perfunctory" attitude of the English nurses (8 July), a failing she later associated with the ineffective employees at the Imperial Institute

(3 August). This, in turn, could be traced to a pervasive stress on routine in their training and job performance. Maggs describes the tutelage of British nurses during this era in the following terms: "The probationer who survived the trial period and the training itself was likely to be the woman who had enough 'commonsense to learn from fellow-nurses the routine of the ward and (to) quickly fall in line.' She was in consequence the woman who despite being 'niggled' by the etiquette which pervaded all activities, "liked the way in which 'everything went by clockwork.' Life for her might have been hard but 'the strict routine gave a certain security.'"[29]

Elizabeth believed that whatever benefits this approach contained were cancelled out by the British nurse's frequent submission to a thoughtless procedure. For example, Beth expected immediate help for a bowel movement when the need arose. However, in Great Britain, "most hospitals had 'fixed hours appointed for this work,' which had to be adhered to for the sake of 'general order and convenience [sic] of all.'"[30] Dr. Shortt preferred the Canadian method of dealing with such pressing matters. As she put it: "I think Canadian nurses have quite a bit more individuality & we do know something they do not in England" (9–16 July). Individual initiative was more frequently exercised in the Dominion, where the nurses would often improvise to make patients more comfortable.[31] The Canadian physician obviously preferred the more individualistic option in her native country, and she made this clear in her revealing critique.

Elizabeth presented a mixed review of English medical practices. The surgeon was excellent and the operation was an overall success. However, the costs were excessive, while the anaesthetists and nurses neglected the more modern and individualistic procedures available in Canada. In developing this elaborate perspective, Dr. Shortt displayed her considerable courage, persistence, and insight which made her a formidable analyst.

For the Shortts, Great Britain held a unique and special place in the world community, a view which they shared with most other anglophone Canadian visitors to the mother country. As Morgan points out: "Despite its foibles and failings, the vast majority of these Canadian tourists understood Britain to be the epitome of a 'real' nation and, in contrast they found countries such as France, Germany and Italy—no matter how pleasing many of their aspects—lacking."[32] Elizabeth and Adam were, for example, alienated by the militarism they encountered in Berlin, as well as the cultural and religious stagnation in Austria. The couple thought more highly of Switzerland and the Netherlands, but their stay in the latter country was very brief and their interaction with Swiss culture was very limited. Great Britain

provided for the Shortts a mother country that could at times be annoy-
ing and backward, but whose culture and protection seemed so essential to
Canada's well-being in the present and the foreseeable future.

As the Shortts travelled through Europe, they visited several art galleries.
Their comments on the works viewed at these venues present telling critiques that were shared by many other English Canadians around 1911. Their
general perspective, which was mainly articulated in Elizabeth's writings,
began with two negations: a total dismissal of nudity in art and a repudiation
of Impressionism as a valid option for contemporary painters. While Mrs.
Shortt was recovering from her eye operation, her husband visited the Royal
Academy of Art in London and declared that he found "some very fine pictures" at this site, which happily contained "few extremes" (14 July). For the
Shortts, nude and Impressionist works presented undesirable "extremes."

Elizabeth made this clear in Vienna when she associated nudity in art
with the excessive drinking that was accelerating Austria's current decline
(23 August). The relationship between nudity in art and overindulgence in
spirits was never spelled out. However, Beth made her personal objections
to nude paintings much more explicit on September 1: "I fancy if the women
I know were directors of any Academy of Art there would be none of these
unnatural pictures. They are absolutely unnatural because women are never
nude doing up their hair or sleeping &c. & it is only to appeal to men's passions that these pictures are made & hung or because of ———. I am not a
prude & I think a woman's body very beautiful when normal, but I do not
think nor see blindly & I have been about quite a bit & men's amatory passions
are too much cultivated without the public corruption of boys & young men
who go to galleries because of art & are shown what they never should see."

Despite her contrary assertion, Mrs. Shortt expressed what one Canadian expert has called a "depressingly prudish attitude to art." The same
author traces this prudishness to the late-Victorian era, when Beth and
her husband adopted a moral code "based on the maintenance of an
appearance of respectability."[33] Such values were not compatible with the
"unnatural" and "amatory" productions that Elizabeth associated with
depictions of the nude in art.

Nevertheless, within English Canada these attitudes were quite prevalent
during a good part of the twentieth century. As late as 1972, Morris, assess-
ing the work of the Canadian painter, Le Moine Fitzgerald, revealed, "I
know of several of his best paintings of the nude which may not be shown
because of their owner's Victorian sense of propriety."[34] The straitlaced
morality of the Victorian age had a long shelf life in English Canada.

The Shortts were also adamantly opposed to the Impressionist techniques that emerged in Europe, especially France, during the late nineteenth century. S. E. D. Shortt tells us that Adam considered this new orientation "a denigration of true art."[35] Once again, his wife further elaborated this position while visiting the Dresden Art gallery: "There were not half a dozen I saw that I would want except as curiosities of what might be done by fanatics. How anyone can find any satisfaction in the semi or wholly impressionist school amazes me. Whatever it is, it is not what I want in a picture & it would be inconceivable to any of the old masters that such paint madness should ever be called art" (25 August). The following day in Berlin, Beth resumed her assault on Impressionist work: "We saw here a lot of impressionist and semi-impressionist paintings and I pass them by in a hurry" (26 August).

Once again, the Shortts were expressing not only their own opinions but those of most Canadians. Some Impressionist works obtained critical acclaim in Montreal, but few collectors in the Dominion's principal art centre were willing to purchase them. Only one gallery displayed Impressionist paintings in the city, and even at this venue the supply was unpredictable.[36] In 1912, A. Y. Jackson returned to his native Montreal, proudly carrying Impressionist canvases that he had created during an extended visit to Europe. However, not a single painting was sold at this exhibition.[37] As another art historian puts it, Impressionism had gained "a foothold" in Montreal, but nothing more. Even this tenuous acceptance was lacking in Canada's other major focal point for art, the city of Toronto.[38] Here few people were even acquainted with the term "Impressionism." As Denis Reid states, "unlike in Montreal at the time there is no sense in exhibition reviews or articles on art in Toronto of an awareness of Impressionism."[39] The Shortts' lack of interest in Impressionism was shared with many other Canadians, including those belonging to the fine-arts community in Ontario's capital.

Although French Impressionist works were the rage in the United States from 1886 to 1914,[40] Canadian critics and collectors in the same era were mainly preoccupied with another group of painters, the Hague School in the Netherlands. Hurdalek tells us, "Never before or since have Canadian collectors focussed their attention upon a single European school as they did from the last decades of the nineteenth century until the First World War."[41] The French Impressionists, like Pierre-Auguste Renoir, bitterly resented traditional values and earlier art forms.[42] In contrast, the contemporary works of the Hague School emanated from the established practices of the past and especially the art of the Dutch masters of the seventeenth century. Marta Hurdalek reveals that the modern school of Dutch artists, as the painters in the Hague were often named, saw their variations as an extension rather than a rejection of the artists who had preceded them. "Motivated to some extent by nationalistic feelings, the Hague School search for artistic innovation led them initially to their own seventeenth-century traditions. They strove to understand the art of their illustrious predecessors by copying their paintings and closely studying their subject matter, composition and techniques ... [in] significant works by Jacob van Ruisdael, Jan Vermeer, Paulus Potter, Meindert Hobbema, Emanuel de Witte and, above all, Rembrandt." This evolutionary approach to art appealed to the Shortts and provided them with a foundation for a positive definition of art. Having repudiated nudity in art and the Impressionist vision, Elizabeth and Adam endorsed as alternatives the oeuvre of the great painters of the past, as well as their admirers within the more recent Hague School. Today a comparison of the two groups may appear doubtful. Nevertheless, Hurdalek notes that in the late nineteenth and early twentieth centuries, the paintings of the Hague School were considered on a similar level to those of their forefathers of the seventeenth century.[43]

The Shortts' love of well-established artists of a distant past was evident during their visit to the Dresden Art Gallery. For Adam, the works presented there were "very good," while his more expressive wife asserted that, "We spent the afternoon looking mostly at old masters and it was well worth seeing." Even more explicitly, Elizabeth placed Rubens, Van Dyck, Rembrandt, Teniers, Ruysdael, Jan Steen, Potter, Holbein, and Raphael in her select circle of "old masters" (24 August). Her husband seconded the nomination of Rembrandt when the couple visited the Rijksmuseum in Amsterdam (31 August). Here Mrs. Shortt added some more names to their list of historic artists, with particular references to Gerard Dou, Van de Velde,[44] and Van Ostade.[45]

After defining their concept of exceptional art from former times, the couple endorsed what Adam called "the Modern School" of Dutch painting, which was well represented at Amsterdam's Municipal Museum (31 August). Beth could barely contain her joy when she encountered the works of the Hague School there: "We arrived at the Municipal Museum & had a fine time among modern Dutch Artists & they are fine. I began to be doleful about modern painters after the Austellung [sic] in Berlin i.e. as compared with the Old Masters. Here however one is gladdened by excellent modern pictures" (1 September).

Elizabeth was particularly drawn to the oeuvre of Jozef Israels where this social feminist found many important themes being articulated. As we saw in the introduction, during 1910 she was busy promoting the creation of daycare centres in Ottawa, which sought to help both working mothers and their young children within the federal capital. Later she would become active in the administration, as well as the legislation of a Mother's Allowance system for single mothers throughout Ontario.[46] Israels often depicted the suffering within families exposed to dire circumstances. It was only natural that such scenes would appeal to the sensitive Mrs. Shortt. Thus she was fascinated by Israels' painting *de Sturin*, which portrayed an anxious mother, wife, and boy awaiting word of a fisherman's fate following a severe storm. A similar theme permeated Israels' *Passing the Mother's Grave*, wherein a downcast father "carrying a young child and leading a small boy" sadly passed a burial site on his way home. For Mrs. Shortt, the loss of a father or mother constituted a calamity that ought to be avoided at all costs. Beth also appreciated the same painter's huge portrait of David seeking divine guidance in front of a vulnerable Saul (1 September). Israels personally considered this work "the crowning achievement of his career." It demonstrated his vigorous commitment to Jewish culture and religion.[47] This orientation also appealed to Mrs. Shortt, who had been well versed in both the old and new testaments since childhood. Religion continued to be a major force in defining her artistic as well as personal identity and would remain so until her death in 1948.

Elizabeth's approach to art revealed a thoughtful interplay between previously established personal values and the discovery of new insights that would modify those views. In terms of fine art, she came to Europe as a strong opponent of nudity and Impressionism within contemporary art; she was, as well, an avid supporter of the works of the great masters who belonged to a distant past. However, the Shortts' 1911 excursion to the Old World also brought Mrs. Shortt into contact with the Hague School for the first time, which furnished her with a current alternative to the Impressionist painters whom she and her husband so thoroughly disliked. They learned much from their travels in the Old World while at the same time providing revealing critiques on other topics, such as the shortcomings of England's private hospitals. In both cases, the diaries and letters of Beth and Adam supply readers with many perceptive insights, which help us understand how two notable Canadians were profoundly influenced by European travel during the early twentieth century.

Notes

1 Sheryl Stotts McLaren, *Becoming Indispensable: A Biography of Elizabeth Smith Shortt 1859–1949* (Ph.D. diss., York University, 2001), 199.

2 Bruce W. Bowden, *Adam Shortt* (Ph.D. diss., University of Toronto, 1979), 269.

3 McLaren, *Becoming Indispensable*, 261.

4 Bowden, *Adam Shortt*, 262.

5 McLaren, *Becoming Indispensable*, 67.

6 Cecilia Morgan, *"A Happy Holiday": English Canadians and Transatlantic Tourism, 1870–1930* (Toronto: University of Toronto Press, 2008), 270.

7 McLaren, *Becoming Indispensable*, 271–72.

8 William Christian, *Parkin: Canada's Most Famous Forgotten Man* (Toronto: Blue Butterfly Books, 2008), 122.

9 Terry Cook, "Sir George Robert Parkin," in *Dictionary of Canadian Biography*, vol. xv (Toronto: University of Toronto Press, 2005), 803.

10 Cook, "Sir George Robert Parkin," 805, 804.

11 Christian, *Parkin*, 209, 235, 249.

12 Christian, *Parkin*, 255–56.

13 George Parkin, cited in Christian, *Parkin*, 276.

14 "George Parkin Grant," *Dictionary of Canadian Biography Online*, www.biographi.ca/en/bio/grant_george_parkin_21E.html.

15 McLaren, *Becoming Indispensable*, 270.

16 McLaren, *Becoming Indispensable*, 440.

17 Morgan, *"A Happy Holiday,"* 161.

18 Morgan, *"A Happy Holiday,"* xxii, 85, 121, 170, 181, 227, 312.

19 Morgan, *"A Happy Holiday,"* 119.

20 Adam Shortt, "Some Observations on the Great North-West," *Queen's Quarterly* 11 (1895): 189, 195.

21 Helen Lenskji, "A 'Servant Problem' or a 'Servant-Mistress Problem'? Domestic Services in Canada, 1890–1930," in *Atlantis* 7 (1981): 5.

22 Morgan, *"A Happy Holiday,"* 184.

23 Christopher Lawrence, *Medicine in the Making of Modern Britain, 1700–1920* (London: Routledge, 1984), 69, 70, 80.

24 Brian Abel-Smith, *The Hospitals, 1880–1948: A Study in Social Administration in England and Wales* (Cambridge, MA: Harvard University Press, 1964), 190.

25 Sir Henry C. Burdett, cited in Abel-Smith, *The Hospitals*, 194.

26 Abel-Smith, *The Hospitals*, 194.

27 Kathryn McPherson, *Bedside Matters: The Transformation of Canadian Nursing, 1900–1990* (Toronto: Oxford University Press, 1996), 81.

28 See ch. 1, n. 86.

29 Christopher Maggs, *The Origins of General Nursing* (London: Croom Helm, 1983), 126.

30 Maggs, *The Origins of General Nursing*, 123.

31 McPherson, *Bedside Matters*, 100.

32 Morgan, "A Happy Holiday," 316.

33 Jerrold Morris, *The Nude in Canadian Painting* (Toronto: New Press, 1972), 4, 25.

34 Morris, *The Nude in Canadian Painting*, 11. See also Donald W. Buchanan, "Naked Ladies," *Canadian Forum* 15 (1935): 273.

35 S. E. D. Shortt, *The Search for an Ideal: Six Canadian Intellectuals and Their Convictions in an Age of Transition 1890–1930* (Toronto: University of Toronto Press, 1976), 103.

36 Laurier Lacroix, "The Surprise of Today Is the Commonplace of Tomorrow: How Impressionism Was Received in Canada," in *Visions of Light and Air: Canadian Impressionism, 1885–1920*, exhibition catalogue, cur. Carol Lowrey (New York: American Society Art Gallery, 1995), 44.

37 Joan Murray, *Impressionism in Canada 1895–1935* (Toronto: Art Gallery of Ontario, 1973), 11.

38 Carol Lowrey, "Into Line with the Progress of Art: The Impressionist Tradition in Canadian Painting, 1885–1920," in *Visions of Light and Air*, 27, 23.

39 Dennis Reid, "Impressionism in Canada," in *World Impressionism: The International Movement, 1860–1920*, ed. Norma Broude (New York: H. N. Abrams, 1990), 111.

40 William H. Gerdts, "Foreward," in *Visions of Light and Air*, 11.

41 Marta H. Hurdalek, *The Hague School: Collecting in Canada at the Turn of the Century* (Toronto: Art Gallery of Ontario, 1984), 47.

42 Peter H. Feist, *Renoir* (London: Taschen, 2004), 17.

43 Hurdalek, *The Hague School*, 9.

44 See ch. 6, n. 56.

45 See ch. 6, n. 59.

46 McLaren, *Becoming Indispensable*, 362–70.

47 Charles Dumas, "Jozef Israels," in *The Hague School Dutch Masters of the 19th Century*, ed. Ronald de Leeuw, John Sillevis and Charles Dumas (London: Royal Academy of Arts, 1983), 199, 197.

Appendix: Inventory of Purchases

Elizabeth's Inventory of clothing purchases & some souvenir items bought during the trip

A. Clothing
Miss S.E. Brown Limited – 33 Knightsbridge (Mrs. Singer [the] one I did business with & to whom Mrs. (Capt.) Desborough sent me)
1. /evg, dress ninon & satin: grey & pink with silver lace &c.. – $40.00
2. Evg. dress, beetle green tunic made by Dale & co. – $28.50 i.e. $15.00 (or 15.75) +   13.50 for slip
3. Street dress, coat & shirt: black serge with fine waist of ninon & trimming & c. – $31.50

Evans - Oxford St.
1. feather [hat] – 1.15: 9 or $8.75

Selfridge
1. white gloves – 4.11 or $3.11
2. night gown – 5. or $1.25

Marshall & Snelgrove
. short scarf & tunic – 11.9 or $2.90
. floral scarf – 8.6 or $2.10

Dale & Co.
1. white striped summer suit – 2.6 or $11.50
2. cashmere stockings – 1.11 2/4 or $1.00

Harris
  1. petticoat – 4.11, good blk., long gloves – $1.35

(I liked Harris & Williams near south Kensington [and] Brompton Road where I got)

Williams
  1. short blk. kids [gloves] – $.75
  2. black tights – $1.25
  3. white waist [coat] – $1.25
  4. scarf [and] veil – $1.25

Pemberthys [*sic*], Oxford [Street] – reliable for gloves & underwear, bought
  1. long white gloves
  2. wool underwear
  3. white underwear
  4. cotton stockings
not cheap, but gloves were especially fine

Bought my tunic of Marshall & Snelgrove's, Oxford St., which I liked & Muriel's tunic of Robinson & Cleaver

B. Souvenirs

  1. [crushed flower] – Bought at Salzberg [*sic*] on what seemed a tag day for the [local] hospital, these being used instead of ribbons or buttons

  2. [candy wrapper] – Sold on boat on the Emperor Fraz [*sic*] Joseph's birthday (81st), pretty girl selling the bonbon (chocolate in the paper) & a youth holding the money box for contributions for their navy!

  3. Orange button sold on Queen Wilhelmina's [*sic*] birthday in Amsterdam, end of August. Great crowds & dozens & dozens selling these or yellow flowers to her 'orange' subjects

Books in the Life Writing Series
Published by Wilfrid Laurier University Press

Haven't Any News: Ruby's Letters from the Fifties edited by Edna Staebler with an Afterword by Marlene Kadar • 1995 / x + 165 pp. / ISBN 0-88920-248-6

"I Want to Join Your Club": Letters from Rural Children, 1900–1920 edited by Norah L. Lewis with a Preface by Neil Sutherland • 1996 / xii + 250 pp. (30 b&w photos) / ISBN 0-88920-260-5

And Peace Never Came by Elisabeth M. Raab with Historical Notes by Marlene Kadar • 1996 / x + 196 pp. (12 b&w photos, map) / ISBN 0-88920-281-8

Dear Editor and Friends: Letters from Rural Women of the North-West, 1900–1920 edited by Norah L. Lewis • 1998 / xvi + 166 pp. (20 b&w photos) / ISBN 0-88920-287-7

The Surprise of My Life: An Autobiography by Claire Drainie Taylor with a Foreword by Marlene Kadar • 1998 / xii + 268 pp. (8 colour photos and 92 b&w photos) / ISBN 0-88920-302-4

Memoirs from Away: A New Found Land Girlhood by Helen M. Buss / Margaret Clarke • 1998 / xvi + 153 pp. / ISBN 0-88920-350-4

The Life and Letters of Annie Leake Tuttle: Working for the Best by Marilyn Färdig Whiteley • 1999 / xviii + 150 pp. / ISBN 0-88920-330-x

Marian Engel's Notebooks: "Ah, mon cahier, écoute" edited by Christl Verduyn • 1999 / viii + 576 pp. / ISBN 0-88920-333-4 cloth / ISBN 0-88920-349-0 paper

Be Good Sweet Maid: The Trials of Dorothy Joudrie by Audrey Andrews • 1999 / vi + 276 pp. / ISBN 0-88920-334-2

Working in Women's Archives: Researching Women's Private Literature and Archival Documents edited by Helen M. Buss and Marlene Kadar • 2001 / vi + 120 pp. / ISBN 0-88920-341-5

Repossessing the World: Reading Memoirs by Contemporary Women by Helen M. Buss • 2002 / xxvi + 206 pp. / ISBN 0-88920-408-x cloth / ISBN 0-88920-410-1 paper

Chasing the Comet: A Scottish-Canadian Life by Patricia Koretchuk • 2002 / xx + 244 pp. / ISBN 0-88920-407-1

The Queen of Peace Room by Magie Dominic • 2002 / xii + 115 pp. / ISBN 0-88920-417-9

China Diary: The Life of Mary Austin Endicott by Shirley Jane Endicott • 2002 / xvi + 251 pp. / ISBN 0-88920-412-8

The Curtain: Witness and Memory in Wartime Holland by Henry G. Schogt • 2003 / xii + 132 pp. / ISBN 0-88920-396-2

Teaching Places by Audrey J. Whitson • 2003 / xiii + 178 pp. / ISBN 0-88920-425-x

Through the Hitler Line by Laurence F. Wilmot, M.C. • 2003 / xvi + 152 pp. / ISBN 0-88920-448-9

Where I Come From by Vijay Agnew • 2003 / xiv + 298 pp. / ISBN 0-88920-414-4

The Water Lily Pond by Han Z. Li • 2004 / x + 254 pp. / ISBN 0-88920-431-4

The Life Writings of Mary Baker McQuesten: Victorian Matriarch edited by Mary J. Anderson • 2004 / xxii + 338 pp. / ISBN 0-88920-437-3

Seven Eggs Today: The Diaries of Mary Armstrong, 1859 and 1869 edited by Jackson W. Armstrong • 2004 / xvi + 228 pp. / ISBN 0-88920-440-3

Love and War in London: A Woman's Diary 1939–1942 by Olivia Cockett; edited by Robert W. Malcolmson • 2005 / xvi + 208 pp. / ISBN 0-88920-458-6

Incorrigible by Velma Demerson • 2004 / vi + 178 pp. / ISBN 0-88920-444-6

Auto/biography in Canada: Critical Directions edited by Julie Rak • 2005 / viii + 264 pp. / ISBN 0-88920-478-0

Tracing the Autobiographical edited by Marlene Kadar, Linda Warley, Jeanne Perreault, and Susanna Egan • 2005 / viii + 280 pp. / ISBN 0-88920-476-4

Must Write: Edna Staebler's Diaries edited by Christl Verduyn • 2005 / viii + 304 pp. / ISBN 0-88920-481-0

Pursuing Giraffe: A 1950s Adventure by Anne Innis Dagg • 2006 / xvi + 284 pp. (photos, 2 maps) / 978-0-88920-463-8

Food That Really Schmecks by Edna Staebler • 2007 / xxiv + 334 pp. / ISBN 978-0-88920-521-5

163256: A Memoir of Resistance by Michael Englishman • 2007 / xvi + 112 pp. (14 b&w photos) / ISBN 978-1-55458-009-5

The Wartime Letters of Leslie and Cecil Frost, 1915–1919 edited by R.B. Fleming • 2007 / xxxvi + 384 pp. (49 b&w photos, 5 maps) / ISBN 978-1-55458-000-2

Johanna Krause Twice Persecuted: Surviving in Nazi Germany and Communist East Germany by Carolyn Gammon and Christiane Hemker • 2007 / x + 170 pp. (58 b&w photos, 2 maps) / ISBN 978-1-55458-006-4

Watermelon Syrup: A Novel by Annie Jacobsen with Jane Finlay-Young and Di Brandt • 2007 / x + 268 pp. / ISBN 978-1-55458-005-7

Broad Is the Way: Stories from Mayerthorpe by Margaret Norquay • 2008 / x + 106 pp. (6 b&w photos) / ISBN 978-1-55458-020-0

Becoming My Mother's Daughter: A Story of Survival and Renewal by Erika Gottlieb • 2008 / x + 178 pp. (36 b&w illus., 17 colour) / ISBN 978-1-55458-030-9

Leaving Fundamentalism: Personal Stories edited by G. Elijah Dann • 2008 / xii + 234 pp. / ISBN 978-1-55458-026-2

Bearing Witness: Living with Ovarian Cancer edited by Kathryn Carter and Lauri Elit • 2009 / viii + 94 pp. / ISBN 978-1-55458-055-2

Dead Woman Pickney: A Memoir of Childhood in Jamaica by Yvonne Shorter Brown • 2010 / viii + 202 pp. / ISBN 978-1-55458-189-4

I Have a Story to Tell You by Seemah C. Berson • 2010 / xx + 288 pp. (24 b&w photos) / ISBN 978-1-55458-219-8

We All Giggled: A Bourgeois Family Memoir by Thomas O. Hueglin • 2010 / xiv + 232 pp. (20 b&w photos) / ISBN 978-1-55458-262-4

Just a Larger Family: Letters of Marie Williamson from the Canadian Home Front, 1940–1944 edited by Mary F. Williamson and Tom Sharp • 2011 / xxiv + 378 pp. (16 b&w photos) / ISBN 978-1-55458-323-2

Burdens of Proof: Faith, Doubt, and Identity in Autobiography by Susanna Egan • 2011 / x + 200 pp. / ISBN 978-1-55458-333-1

Accident of Fate: A Personal Account 1938–1945 by Imre Rochlitz with Joseph Rochlitz • 2011 / xiv + 226 pp. (50 b&w photos, 5 maps) / ISBN 978-1-55458-267-9

The Green Sofa by Natascha Würzbach, translated by Raleigh Whitinger • 2012 / xiv + 240 pp. (5 b&w photos) / ISBN 978-1-55458-334-8

Unheard Of: Memoirs of a Canadian Composer by John Beckwith • 2012 / x + 393 pp. (74 illus., 8 musical examples) / ISBN 978-1-55458-358-4

Borrowed Tongues: Life Writing, Migration, and Translation by Eva C. Karpinski • 2012 / viii + 274 pp. / ISBN 978-1-55458-357-7

Basements and Attics, Closets and Cyberspace: Explorations in Canadian Women's Archives edited by Linda M. Morra and Jessica Schagerl • 2012 / x + 338 pp. / ISBN 978-1-55458-632-5

The Memory of Water by Allen Smutylo • 2013 / x + 262 pp. (65 colour illus.) / ISBN 978-1-55458-842-8

The Unwritten Diary of Israel Unger, Revised Edition by Carolyn Gammon and Israel Unger • 2013 / ix + 230 pp. (b&w illus.) / ISBN 978-1-77112-011-1

Boom! Manufacturing Memoir for the Popular Market by Julie Rak • 2013 / viii + 249 pp. (b&w illus.) / ISBN 978-1-55458-939-5

Motherlode: A Mosaic of Dutch Wartime Experience by Carolyne Van Der Meer • 2014 / xiv + 132 pp. (b&w illus.) / ISBN 978-1-77112-005-0

Not the Whole Story: Challenging the Single Mother Narrative edited by Lea Caragata and Judit Alcalde • 2014 / x + 222 pp. / ISBN 978-1-55458-624-0